Collectivism and Charity

The Great Deception

by

Dan Wolf

If you purchased this book without a cover you should be aware that this book is stolen property. It was reported as "unsold and destroyed" to the publisher and neither the author nor the publisher has received any payment for this "stripped book."

Collectivism and Charity

Copyright © 2016 Dan Wolf. All rights reserved, including the right to reproduce this book or portions thereof, in any form. No part of this text may be reproduced, transmitted, downloaded, decompiled, reverse engineered, or stored in or introduced into any information storage and retrieval system in any form or by any means, whether electronic or mechanical without the express written permission of the author. The scanning, uploading, and distribution of this book via the Internet or via any other means is illegal and punishable by law. Please purchase only authorized electronic editions and do not participate in or encourage electronic piracy of copyrighted materials.

Cover designed by Adazing Design

Available from Amazon.com and other book stores

Other books by the author:
Do You Want To Be Free

Visit the author website:
http://www.livingrightly.net

Other articles by the author can be found at:
http://www.vachristian.org

ISBN: 978-1-311487-00-1 (eBook)
ISBN: 978-1-535108-48-5 (Paperbook)

Version: 2016.06.30

Table of Contents

Acknowledgements	i
Introduction	iii
Chapter 1: A Model of Charity	1
Chapter 2: Charity's Development	19
Chapter 3: Purpose and Collectivism	65
Chapter 4: Power	95
Chapter 5: The Need for Education	129
Chapter 6: The Utopian Dream	159
Appendix A: Timeline of Events	197
Notes	199

Collectivism and Charity

The Great Deception

Acknowledgements

I would like to thank all those who supported the efforts for both *Collectivism and Charity* and *Do You Want To Be Free?* I would especially like to thank Gayle, Ken, Felix, Cindy, and Mark for their feedback, Karen and Jeff for their editing advice, Lisa for her thoughts and support while I was trying to get started, and Sam for helping to make it happen. A very special thank you to Barb, my friend, my companion, and my wife. Her support has meant more than I can ever find words to express. Finally, I give thanks to God, for without Him, none of this would be possible.

May the Lord give you understanding in all things and make you sensible what spirit it becomes you to be of. May He dispose you to such an excellent, amiable, and benevolent life, as is answerable to such a spirit, that you may not love only "in word and tongue, but in deed and truth."

—Jonathan Edwards, 1738.

Introduction

Do we need another book about charity, when so many have already been written? Yes, for the following reasons. Our direction and actions in recent years have placed us in an untenable position, as a nation and a people. We no longer have priorities aligned with our long-term interests. Unsustainable spending, government programs that lock people into dependence, and failing to acknowledge the foreign and domestic dangers we face are just a few examples. We have lost our way, placed deliberately on a course chosen by some members of our own society for power. Self-styled elitists who view the world as a place where some are more equal than others rather than all sharing an equality of nature.

A commitment to the common good is essential to be a people, and the virtue of charity is necessary for a society to support the common good. All other virtues support charity, and virtue is an individual trait. We need to ask ourselves whether we embody virtue any longer. Do we truly understand what charity is today? Do we understand why charity matters? In looking at the challenges mentioned earlier, we would have to answer no. We have forgotten our purpose and what brought us prosperity, as this book will demonstrate.

The answer to the questions just posed will never be found within either politics or the church, nor does it lie in charity's end alone. Instead the answer is derived from both charity's ends and the means used to achieve it. If the ends alone made the difference, then the war on poverty would have been won long ago. We could not have gotten as far as we have as a people unless we at one time truly understood the

Introduction

notion of charity. And this leads to the main reason for writing this book. It is you. For I truly believe achieving your purpose as a human being will find its expression through charity, and my wish is that whatever your situation you will find fulfillment in it. But to find fulfillment, you must understand your purpose—why you are here. Understanding this not only has implications for yourself, but the society of which you are a part.

Several recent books focus on aspects of the relationship between charity and society. These works are brought up not to cast dispersions on them or their authors, but to develop the arguments presented in this book as to how we have lost our way. What would have been viewed as radical three to five hundred years ago is today accepted as commonplace. Why has this occurred? What has changed? For us to truly address the issues we face today, we must first understand both the underlying problem and how we have arrived at our present place. Some current works in this area include *Who Really Cares*[1] by Arthur C. Brooks, *When Helping Hurts*[2] by Steve Corbett & Brian Fikkert, and *When Charity Destroys Dignity*[3] by Glenn J. Schwartz. Brooks provides a wealth of information on who gives to charity (both religious and non-religious organizations), and the breakdown is instructive. His research indicates that within the U.S., roughly 33% of the population views itself as religious, another 27% as secular, and the remaining 40% somewhere in between.[4]

Further, it is the religious who give the most, regardless of whether they view themselves as conservative or liberal. The particular religion makes no significant difference as on average about 90% of those belonging to any religion contribute to charity. Not only do the third of the population who view themselves as religious give more to religious-oriented charitable organizations, but to secular ones as well. A larger percentage of people identifying themselves as religious also give to charity than do those who view themselves as secular (91% versus 66%), and they also give 3.5 times more on average. This difference between religious-oriented and secular-oriented people is not limited to monetary donations, but includes time spent volunteering. Religious people tend to both volunteer more (67% versus 44%), and volunteer more frequently (12 versus 5.8 times per year).

Moreover, there is a significant difference between the religious and secular groups depending on the political ideology they identify with. The breakdown of religious and secular individuals by political ideologies is shown in the following table. Note the figures do not add up to the totals presented earlier as not all religious or secular people view themselves as either conservative or liberal. We'll explore some of the differences between these four subgroups later.

	Religious	Secular
Conservative	19.1%	7.3%
Liberal	6.4%	10.5%

Who Really Cares describes who gives to charity and how much, but not why. As we will see later, there are some significant differences across the four groups presented above.

In *When Helping Hurts*, Corbett and Fikkert examine the role of Christian churches in alleviating poverty, specifically focusing on ways to help that do not harm others. There is much that I agree with in terms of their problem statements and proposed solutions:

> The goal is to restore people to a full expression of humanness, to being what God created us all to be, people who glorify God by living in right relationship with God, with self, with others, and with the rest of creation. One of the many manifestations of these relationships being reconciled is material poverty alleviation.[5]

This is an individualistic goal, as everyone is in a different place in terms of their abilities, resources, and needs. However, the authors make a common mistake. They advocate achieving an individualistic goal (alleviating poverty) by using collectivist means. The two are not only

Introduction

contrary, but incompatible.[6] Several examples will suffice to make the point.

First, the authors state that "while the church must care for the poor, the Bible gives Christians some freedom in deciding the extent and manner in which the local church should do this ... whenever God's people choose to minister outside of the direct oversight of the local church, they should always be seeking to partner with the local church."[7] This position ignores the individual responsibility that we have each been given to perform charity out of love for both our Creator and our fellow man. It is not only the fulfillment of His law, but it is our purpose. Christ did not tell the church that it must care for those in need; he spoke to those individuals who had come to hear him teach—indeed, the church as we know it today did not yet exist. Instead, Christ was speaking of the commands contained within the *Old Testament* to care for others in need. He also did not tell the State it was responsible for charity, even though a civil government was in place.

Second, the authors view individualistic and collectivist cultures as different ends of a continuum with "both pros and cons to each end of the continua."[8] They cite that people in individualistic cultures are taught to be "all that they can be" and that the focus is on one's personal calling. "Collectivist cultures, on the other hand, minimize individual identity and focus on the well-being of the group. Loyalty to and self-sacrifice for the sake of other group members are seen as virtuous."[9] Loyalty and self-sacrifice in this manner are virtues—virtues of individuals and not a group. This is the story of Noah: that even in communities with a collective morality, individual choices matter. Each of us individually acquiring virtues is the way in which we achieve our purpose, using the gifts we have been given by our Creator. We have been created with the ability to acquire virtues, but we are not born with them. If virtues are not found within a society, it is likely that they are simply not being taught or that the people have turned away from their Creator.

Collectivism and Charity

But the individualistic culture we see in the U.S. today is not what our Founders intended either. Corbett and Fikkert posit individualist versus collectivist culture as an either/or proposition. What is true is that cultures have a sense of individual versus collective morality. The sense of collective morality is what existed within the ancient state religion empires of Persia, Babylonia, Egypt, Greece, Rome, and many others. This changed with Christ's teachings, as *we are called to action both individually and collectively.* As individuals to care for those in need because it is the fulfillment of divine law,[10] and as a single people, specifically our Creator's people.[11] Cicero stated being a people requires two things: recognition of a common set of rights and a mutual cooperation for the common good.[12]

Our Founders selected the moral philosophy underlying Christianity as the best basis for building a society that would be successful in the long-run. They also recognized that man must be pointed to something greater than himself in order to keep from becoming lost. The moral teachings found within the *Bible* not only fulfill the need for mutual recognition of rights (and laws), but also directives to care for each other (mutual cooperation for the common good). Our culture today instead often represents the "I'm okay, you're okay" tenets of moral relativism and more recently an "I'm okay and if you disagree with me you are not" type of totalitarian thought. These are simply an evolution of man pointing to himself, or in the words of St. Augustine (Augustine), the city of man, which throughout history has always, repeat always, been accompanied by a society's failure. Indeed, based on the above definition for a people, one could reasonably argue that we are no longer a single people as we no longer appear to agree on a common set of rights, and perhaps we no longer even possess a single notion of what the common good even is. All we need to do is look at issues like entitlements, abortion, welfare, social justice, and economic justice, just to name a few.

Individualistic and collectivist cultures also have different notions of rights. The former believe in individual rights and the latter in group rights. This is one basis for many of the differences we see today, some of which were noted above. The notion of individual rights is based upon the sameness of our nature as expressed in the *Bible*, both through the manner of our creation and our descent through one man, Adam. This sameness underlies our basis for being a people. Group rights instead have their basis in the notions underlying the "isms" of communism, fascism, progressivism, and/or socialism; they are all just different forms of collectivism, and all are anti-biblical. At its core collectivism holds to the belief that some are more gifted than others, and it is the gifted group(s) that should rule. We are therefore not all equal, but rather some are more equal than others. We see this notion today in the heart of many of our society's so called "safety nets." The notion of rights and laws within this societal view therefore come from man alone and are subject to change by man. Those in power attempt to redistribute wealth, to use their power to address perceived inequalities—inequalities as those in power perceive them. As we will see, this is no different from rule within the Roman Empire.

Third, Corbett and Fikkert stress the fact that too many times when we try to help those in need we end up in reality hurting them because we are focused too much on ourselves instead of on those that we are trying to assist. I think this is too often true, but their answer is that "It is not about us, it is about them!"[13] This is followed up again a short time later with the need for "people [to] be challenged—from the pulpit and beyond—to exercise better stewardship of kingdom resources with their mission giving ... *It is not about us. It is about Him!*"[14] There is a contradiction between these two statements, because if it is about Him, then it must also be about both another and ourselves. More specifically, it must be about the relationship between our self and at least one other human being, for this goes to the very heart of what charity is: it is the love that we sometimes hear expressed as *agape*. It is a love based simply on the nature of another and a recognition that their nature is the same as ours.

The final book, *When Charity Destroys Dignity*, looks at the dependence that has been created, particularly within many of the mission churches established in Africa. Schwartz looks at the degree to which this dependency exists, the conditions which contributed to its formation, and some ideas to reduce this dependency. One condition described as contributing to dependency is the difference between church and church governance. Within this notion is the idea that we often give resources to another group, but we still retain some ownership of those resources instead of turning that ownership over to those receiving the assistance and allowing them to be responsible for their use.

Hidden within this idea is the belief that those providing resources view themselves in some way superior, and therefore they would make better stewards. This is often accompanied by a feeling of powerlessness on the part of those receiving assistance—the poor—a sort of victim mentality. When these two accompany each other in an act of charity, the action often leads to reinforcing dependence instead of creating independence. Without that independence it becomes very difficult, if not impossible, for one to achieve his or her purpose. Instead of the fatalism inherent within the superiority and victim mentalities, what is needed is the virtue of hope, the kind of hope that is created by successfully taking those steps toward becoming independent. This requires a long-term effort that provides the opportunity to care for oneself instead of a short-term focus on simply receiving stuff.

These last two books make recommendations as to how to resolve the issue of dependency, but these appear to be treating the effect and not the underlying cause. Why does this dependency exist in the first place? Why is it that all of our efforts to alleviate poverty have either had little impact or made matters worse? The answer goes not only to those receiving charity, but those providing it as well.

A final reason for this dependency is one that I have observed during church services over the last several years, and further confirms the above points. Post 2008 recession, there have been sermons/homilies given on charity and the need to give. The focus is almost always on the action of giving and that we are called to give. These are true, but incomplete. They just focus on the what. Missing from these sermons is the why we are called to give and how that giving relates to both our

Introduction

purpose as human beings and the command we've been given for stewardship. In the end, the simple action of giving, no matter how well-intentioned, is hollow and can lead to more harm to both the giver and the receiver. I am definitely not saying that one ought not give, but rather that giving must be purposeful and aimed at *assisting* another in need to *improve their own lot* in life. Giving without this additional aim robs people of both their dignity and sense of purpose —and leads to dependence.

The above all matter as over the last fifty years or so charitable contributions have increased by about 14% when adjusted for inflation, and government payments over the same period for various assistance programs have increased by over 500%.[15] Yet despite the trillions of dollars that have been spent on various charitable efforts, we find ourselves today with more people receiving assistance than before, both in terms of actual numbers and as a percentage of our population. Not only is this unsustainable, but it is contrary to our purpose as human beings and poor stewardship. We must change this trajectory in order to be successful, but we must first understand why we've arrived at this place in order to prevent repeating our previous mistakes.

The above is the economic argument, but there is also a human argument to be made. While at a conference a while back, I listened to a young Arab woman who was an Israeli citizen. She was carrying a lot of anger regarding the treatment of Israeli citizens who were Arab. She was looking for a moral answer to her questions. She was looking for justice. However, she also claimed to be an atheist. Without our Creator, you are left with only man's morality, and man alone will always fail. We have only to look at the world around us today, with its efforts to remove anything of a religious nature from the public square to see where that path leads. Indeed, shortly after this event within a one week period we saw the public dedication of a statue of Satan in Detroit in broad daylight, while monuments to the Ten Commandments (and God) were removed in the dark of night from public buildings in Oklahoma City. How upside down have things become today.

Collectivism and Charity

Clement of Alexandria lived during the Roman persecutions of the second century, and he was asked about the suffering that was occurring if our Creator was good. How can we love those who persecute us not because of what we do but simply because of what we believe? Clement wrote, "It was not that He (our Creator) wished us to be persecuted ... Accordingly, they unwillingly bear testimony to our righteousness, we being unjustly punished for righteousness' sake. But the injustice for the judge does not affect the providence of God. For the judge must be master of his own opinion—not pulled by strings, like inanimate machines, set in motion only by external causes. Accordingly he is judged in respect to his judgment, as we also, in accordance with our choice of things desirable, and our endurance."[16] Clement's argument goes to virtue being necessary for justice to exist, and the voluntary choices we must all make to fulfill our purpose. When bad things happen, it is because we live in a fallen world, and some have chosen to serve man instead of our Creator. However, the suffering this causes will be turned to good through our Creator's Providence, because this life is not the final destination. Hard for some to believe perhaps, but true nonetheless.

Some of you reading this may say, "But I do not believe. Man alone is sufficient." I say to you with love that it is okay, because even if you do not believe in Him, He believes in you. I only ask that you consider the facts and evidence before you and then make your own decisions accordingly. In the end, we are each responsible for the choices we make; no one can take that away from us.

Our purpose is to become good, but that is our free choice. Charity is the expression of our becoming good. When we are turned toward our Creator, we are more likely to act out of love. When someone else is not turned toward Him, but we are, at least we will understand why evil occurs and realize that it will still be turned to good—because we are cared for. We are loved. Whether you believe or not.

To examine the issues outlined above, this book will cover the following:

Introduction

Chapter 1 will open by creating a model of charity (pun intended). This model is based upon the differences between individualism and collectivism, and the different components which underlie individualism. These components come from Christian philosophy/theology. This model is used to also outline the relationship between the individuals within a society to that society itself. It is the implications of some of these components which are discussed in subsequent chapters.

Chapter 2 presents a brief history of charity. Inherent in this discussion is the relationship between the spheres of religious and political power, and how those have changed over time. The changes in this relationship have had great implications for society, and those societal changes have had an impact on charity. The writings of Jonathan Edwards are a primary focus. He was one of the most prolific influences during the first Great Awakening, and he also wrote a considerable number of tracts about charity. A few of the more relevant implications from his writings are discussed before concluding the chapter by reviewing the biblical basis for charity.

The contents of this chapter provide a definition of charity, for without a common understanding of what this term means, it would not be possible to have a meaningful dialogue. And we have already seen some evidence which would indicate that differences exist today between groups of individuals as to what constitutes charity.

Chapters 3 and 4 focus upon our purpose as individuals and a people from a collectivism perspective, using John Locke's writing. This is contrasted in places with individualism. Not only are these approaches incompatible with one another, but they are rooted in different parts of our being as well. The arguments around collectivism are largely emotional. They are direct and require very little thought. They are simple and largely impulsive. The arguments around individualism, however, are more complex. They are indirect, and require substantial thought. They require virtue and, while we are born with a proclivity to acquire virtues, we are not born possessing them.

This discussion is followed up with a brief look at virtue and how it is related to our purpose. Finally, no discussion of charity would be complete without the topic of stewardship, for it not only matters how we acquire wealth, but what we do with it once we have it. These topics matter from the perspective of both charity's giver *and* receiver, and serves to define the relationship which should exist between them.

Chapter 5 applies these thoughts in examining the results of our current education system. After all, we spend more money, both per child and in aggregate, than any other country in the world on education. We should know what we are getting in return, and it should be consistent with and support our purpose.

Chapter 6 expands the arguments presented in the previous chapter by looking at a couple of examples from history: the creation of the Church of England by Henry VIII and a comparison of the War for Independence and French Revolutions. Placing the Church beneath the State is a collectivism tenet, and these are periods where the State was placed above the Church. The results will be compared against the basis of charity outlined in the earlier chapters. Finally, we will take a look at how well as a country we have done with charity from a collectivism perspective by looking at the war on poverty before concluding with a few final thoughts.

As before, I will not try to tell you what to think. My goal is to present you with the facts and let you make your own decisions, for that is how

Introduction

we learn and grow—and it is consistent with your purpose. It is an act performed out of love.

Finally, there is content overlap with the previous book, *Do You Want To Be Free?* This is by design. The previous work explores the relationship between faith and governance, or the relationship between faith and state. In the end only two forms exist, what I have termed *individualism* and *collectivism*, with a few variations within the latter form. Individualism is based upon personal independence in action, whereas collectivism looks to the people as an entire body — represented by the state. This work explores the relationship between faith and purpose, or faith and church if you prefer. It is through understanding scripture, and the teaching of derived doctrines, that we are prepared for our purpose. This is not religion per se, although that is important, but rather the knowledge of morality and virtue that should be derived from religion as a society cannot long endure without them. One common body of knowledge, two applications. Just as with the book mentioned above, this one draws upon the considerable work of many writers who have already explored these topics. As before, all quotes will be exactly as they appear in the cited source.

Chapter 1: A Model of Charity

There are two rules whereby we are to walk one towards another: justice and mercy. ... This duty of mercy is exercised in the kinds: giving, lending, and forgiving.

—John Winthrop, 1630

We will see in a moment that charity requires choice. This goes to the heart of determining who is in the best position to direct a society's resources. Four governance models were identified in *Do You Want To Be Free?*[1] These models are presented below.

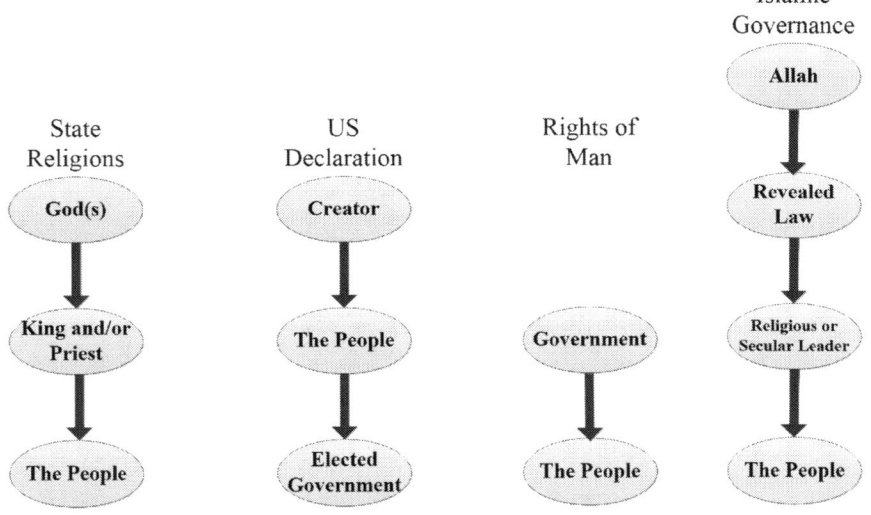

Inherent in these models, as we will see later, are the notions of political and religious power, or their structures today of Church and State. References to these power structures are denoted with a capital letter, as indicated above. References to institutions or organizations using these terms are denoted with lower case letters.

Only one of these models is based upon the notion of individual choice (individualism) and is derived from Judeo-Christian tenets. The remaining models are simply different expressions of collectivism, forms of power grounded in placing groups above the individuals within them and coming from various sources. Individualism requires a people to understand both the languages of reason and faith, while two of the three forms of collectivism focus on reason alone—they look to man. The individualism model relies on self-governance, so a people must be both virtuous and moral to be successful in the long-run. The collectivism models rely on one or more elite ruling classes, to direct the people and set the state's goals and objectives as the State is the lowest level of society that matters.

The basic question is does the State exist to serve its people, or do the people exist to serve the State? As individualism is based upon Judeo-Christian tenets, it aligns with the former. All forms of collectivism represent different corruptions of those underlying principles and therefore align with people existing to support the State.

The following words of Alexis de Tocqueville summarize some of the assumptions and problems underlying collectivism, words that would be echoed by F.A. Hayek on the same issue two hundred years later:

> The partisans of centralization in Europe are wont to maintain that the Government directs the affairs of each locality better than the citizens could do it for themselves; this may be true when the central power is enlightened, and when the local districts are ignorant; when it is as alert as they are slow; when it is accustomed to act, and they to obey. Indeed, it is evident that this double tendency must augment with the increase of

centralization, and that the readiness of the one and the incapacity of the others must become more and more prominent. But I deny that such is the case when the people is as enlightened, as awake to its interests, and as accustomed to reflect on them, as the Americans are. I am persuaded, on the contrary, that in this case the collective strength of the citizens will always conduce more efficaciously to the public welfare than the authority of the Government ... whenever a central administration affects to supersede the persons most interested, I am included to suppose that it is either misled or desirous to mislead. However enlightened and however skillful a central power may be, it cannot of itself embrace all the details of the existence of a great nation. Such vigilance exceeds the powers of man. And when it attempts to create and set in motion so many complicated springs, it must submit to a very imperfect result, or consume itself in bootless efforts.[2]

The individualism and collectivism governance models, the latter typified by the state religion and rights-of-man-based societies, can be drawn as follows.

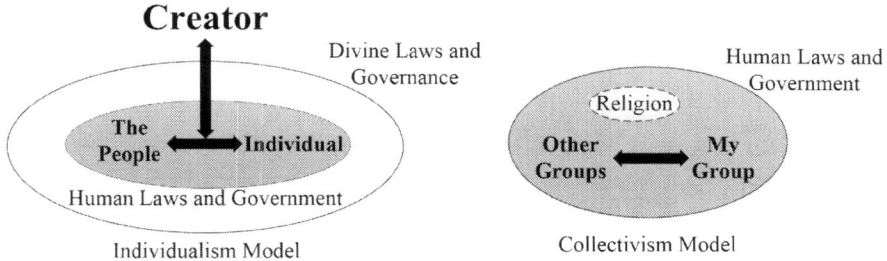

Some of the primary notions underlying the individualistic model are the following:

1. There is a Creator who is the source of everything which has been created. His divine law and governance form the basis for

man's understanding of existence, morality, and knowledge. Natural law is derived from that morality and has its basis in divine law.

2. We, as individuals and a people, have the opportunity to know our Creator. As He is the First Cause, He cannot be demonstrated, but He can be known by faith. As we are created in His image we can also know Him by reason, acquiring knowledge of Him from His word, what He has created, and understanding His image within ourselves. In the words of Clement of Alexandria, "Neither is knowledge without faith, nor faith without knowledge."[3] Both are required in developing knowledge of our Creator, and this is what we were created to do.

3. The image mentioned above is an inward image, not a physical one. We therefore all share the same nature and have also been endowed with the same rights. We are different, but no one is better, or worse, in terms of our nature.

4. The spheres of human and divine governance are distinct. The role of human governance is one of service to its people, to protect the rights of those who have been entrusted to it.

5. Human law and governance is to exist within the overarching limits set by divine law and governance. Therefore, human governance is to be submissive to divine governance, but this does not mean it is subservient to religion. The governance and religious spheres are to be separate, but both should align the human will within them with the divine will, as we will see in the next chapter. Human law and governance protect our Creator-given rights by administering the virtue of justice when one person fails to observe another's rights as described in the next section.

6. We, as individuals, were given the gift of freedom to make our own choices. This freedom is essential to the fulfillment of our

purpose, to become like our Creator to the extent we can, to become good.

7. To become good requires virtue. As the primary role of human government is to administer the virtue of justice, virtue must also exist within the people themselves in order for them to successfully self-govern.

8. Education is the means by which society perpetuates itself culturally. We are not born with what we need, but are made to acquire it; this requires education in both the languages of reason and faith. In addition, effort and practice are required on our part in order to use what we learn in developing wisdom.

9. We are also to become a people. Being a people requires at least two things: (1) a mutual recognition of rights, and (2) a mutual cooperation for the common good.

    a. These mutually recognized rights are those we have been endowed with by our Creator, and those created through human governance *which are consistent with His law, governance, and the fulfillment of our purpose.*

    b. The common good is a mutual cooperation to care for our fellow man. Loving our Creator and our fellow man is the fulfillment of divine law. This is agape, and it requires us to become good. "It is not by nature but by learning, that people become noble and good, as people also become physicians and pilots."[4]

10. Unity is obtained through obedience to our Creator. Wars and civil strife occur when individuals or a people put self-interest above the common good, when they turn away from their Creator and to themselves. This is not simply unity, but unity in conjunction with truth.

The notions underlying the collectivism models, on the other hand, include the following:

1. Creation is uncreated; it has always existed. History is generally the result of endless cycles where knowledge is acquired and then lost again by man.

2. Man is self-sufficient using reason alone. He provides the basis for his own existence, morality, and knowledge.

3. This approach is generally outcome oriented. Each man differs in his abilities, therefore we are not all equal, but rather some are more equal than others. There must therefore exist at least one elite class, and it is the elite who should rule given their superior ability.

4. The State is the lowest level within a society which matters. It determines a society's goals and objectives through its laws and governance. It is society's primary purpose to perpetuate the State.

5. The differences in man's abilities leads to an unequal distribution of society's resources. Redistribution of those resources in accordance with its needs is a primary goal and objective of the State.

6. If religion exists, it provides a moral basis for the people—one defined by the State. Morality within this approach can be an individual or collective morality. If god(s) exist, they are the creation of man. Any references to an afterlife are usually met with attempts by the State to remove them as that idea is considered dangerous to the State's authority.

7. What freedom exists is equated with economic security only for specific groups of individuals and oriented towards the State's fulfillment of its goals.[5]

8. Rights come from the State and can be changed at any time by the State based upon its goals and needs.[6]

9. We, as individuals, may make our own choices to the extent those choices do not conflict with the State's goals and objectives.

10. Education is the means by which the State perpetuates itself. It is a civic education which generally focuses on reason alone. It is secular.

11. There are many goods and many truths. These are defined by the State but can be determined by the individual where the State has not provided a definition.

12. Knowledge and virtue are for the elite, as may be citizenship. Common laborers, craftsmen, and slaves, if present, are thought incapable of acquiring or practicing virtue.

13. Unity is obtained forcefully, if need be, through coercion or by bloodshed and war. When external strife is not present, internal disruption generally arises in the form of civil unrest. The State uses division in order to retain its power.

So Why Does It Matter?

If asked, most people want the freedom to make their own choices about the things affecting their lives and family, even in non-Western cultures, but many also believe they don't live in a place where they have that type of freedom. There is often a notion that it is our leaders who are corrupt, and all we need to do is replace them with someone better. Doesn't this imply that freedom resides outside of ourselves and does not come from within? Ultimately that freedom of choice can only exist within the individualism model noted above, as freedom within that model comes from within, as we will see shortly. The collectivism approaches are generally concerned with group rights and do not recognize the equality of each man's nature; rather, they embrace an underlying notion that some men are more equal than others. Your rights are based on the group(s) to which you belong. Instead, collectivism professes to provide a different type of freedom—a freedom from want—a form of economic security granted to you in exchange for some of your liberty. A "we'll keep you safe, but this is what you'll need to relinquish" approach to governance.

So what is freedom? What are rights? We need a common frame of reference in order to have a meaningful discussion. We will use the same definition for both as before. Freedom is "the absence of coercion—to the extent that this is feasible in organized society. It means that ability of human beings to act in voluntary fashion, rather than being pushed around and forced to do things."[7] As noted above, freedom is necessary for man to fulfill his purpose. Rights "refer to specific freedoms, which are proper and derived from just or moral principles."[8] Further, virtue and morality must exist in a people in order for them to successfully self-govern, so they can both retain their rights and support the common good. Human government's primary purpose is the administration of justice, the protection of those rights that we have each been endowed with by our Creator, and any human rights we ourselves might agree to create. We will first define a couple more terms and then look at some relationships between these ideas.

What do we mean by the terms *virtue* and *charity* so that we also have a common reference point for these two notions? Virtue is simply moral uprightness. It must be grounded in morality, and the absence of virtue is vice. Morality is conforming to right standards of conduct; it involves choice. Virtue is about knowing (and being) what is right; morality is about acting upon what is right. In the individualism model, morality is defined by divine and natural law. As for charity, we will use the following definition: *the funding or aiding of those in need in a way which builds virtue in both the giver and receiver.* This definition provides the following advantages. First, it doesn't confine the form of our charity. Second, it does not specify to whom charity should be shown, or who should provide it. Third, it does not limit how charity should be provided. It states that charity is between two or more individuals; at least one person has a need they cannot fulfill on their own, and at least one other person acts to assist them in fulfilling that need, with the sole motivation being love for the person in need, simply because of their nature. "The word [charity] properly signifies *love, or that disposition or affection whereby one is dear to another*; and the original *agape* which is here translated 'charity' might better have been rendered 'love,' for that is the proper English of it."[9] Finally, the building of virtue in both the giver and receiver indicates the transformational nature of charity for *both* parties. We should be trying to become better tomorrow than we are today, and that cannot be done apart from our Creator.

Before we create a model of charity, there are two sets of relationships that we should briefly examine. The first is how reason and faith relates to virtue and morality in the support of justice. Clement wrote that both faith and reason were necessary in achieving our purpose. Individual purpose is the act of becoming good. We become good by acquiring virtue. While we have been given a nature capable of acquiring virtues, we are not born with them.[10] Therefore virtue must be learned by each and every generation, making education a key part of any society.

There is a second level of purpose, being a people. As justice is a virtue, for it to exist the individuals comprising a people must possess virtue. Justice is the virtue where each person is given his due, and it is the government's role to act only when individuals, or groups, act in an unjust manner. Notice within the individualistic society the first level of justice is between the individuals themselves, and *government only steps in when this first level fails*. The exercise of reason and faith, and the acquisition of virtue, require individual choice: freedom. Coercion by the state therefore directly conflicts with the achievement of our purpose as individuals and our ability to be a people.

When we fail to learn both the languages of reason and faith, we cease to understand freedom—what it is, why we have it, or its relationship to our purpose. Individualism requires education, and education's primary purpose is to inculcate morality within its students. It does this by teaching models and anti-models of behavior, or if you prefer, models of virtue and vice. These are absolutes and opposites. Virtue and morality are taught in two ways. First, by learning about the past through studies in history and philosophy. Second, enabling one to assess the future by acquiring the critical thinking skills necessary to evaluate situations and make good decisions through studies in areas such as math, logic, ethics, and rhetoric. The acquisition of morality and virtue lies in applying what education teaches, leading to the virtue of wisdom. The four pillars of reason, faith, virtue, and morality are necessary in order for justice to exist. Their relationship can be shown as follows:

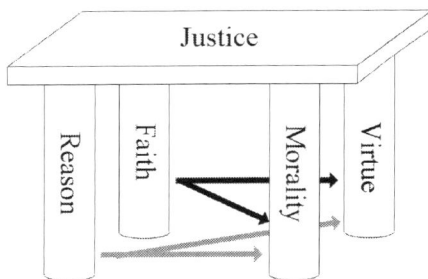

Education in the U.S. today largely comes from institutions, but morality and virtue also need to be taught and supported by example. They need exercise to grow. For most people the primary place where this takes place is the home. The parents and educational institutions should share this responsibility, but that cannot be done successfully if the institutions use reason alone. However, following what is taught and demonstrated is up the each individual and that requires individual choice: freedom.

An education in reason and faith provides an understanding of the need for virtue and morality. The four together support justice, upon which the foundation for any society rests. Some, like Machiavelli and Hobbes, argued that a people should be moral, but their leaders should either be outside of religion or the head of it, that rulers should create their own morality. Morality was necessary for a people to be ruled, but it had to be a morality which did not challenge the ruler's authority. Underlying this approach was the notion that man was a beginning and end in himself, and belief in a better life beyond the one we currently had undermined that authority, and therefore needed to be controlled by the ruler. Others, like Locke and George Mason, argued that reason alone was sufficient to produce virtue and morality. Still others like Rousseau argued that faith, and therefore religion, should be done away with altogether.

While it is possible to create a society without understanding the language of faith, I would suggest that this greatly weakens the structure, because without faith society becomes centered on man—indeed this is the end actively sought by most of the philosophers just named. History has shown this approach never works in the long-run, including Rome's fall as chronicled by Augustine in his work *The City of God*.[11] Both reason and faith must be present to prevent man from losing himself by turning to himself. Both reason and faith provide for virtue and morality's development, as shown above. It is only when all four pillars are present that justice can truly exist and endure, and serve as a lasting foundation for creating a people—and society. Coerce a people in any one of these four areas and you will eventually destroy the foundations of a society.

Now to the second set of relationships. St. Thomas Aquinas (Thomas), in his *Summa Theologicæ*, indicated that faith, hope, and charity were theological virtues as they all had our Creator as their object. He cited Augustine in defining faith as "a virtue by which things not seen are believed."[12] In regards to faith itself,

> If we look to its formal objective, it is the first truth, nothing else. The reason: faith as we mean it here assents to anything only because it is revealed by God, and so faith rests upon the divine truth itself as the medium of its assent. But if we look to the content to which faith assents, this includes not only God, but also many other matters. Even so, the assent of faith

terminates in such things only in so far as they have some reference to God.[13]

And as to charity, "charity also loves neighbor on account of God and thus, precisely speaking, its object is God."[14] Not only is God the object of faith, but "God is necessarily the cause of faith. The reason: the things of faith surpass man's understanding and so become part of his knowledge only because God reveals them."[15]

So faith and charity have our Creator as their object, and He is also the cause of faith itself. In relating hope and charity, Thomas said that "hope is operative ... granted the passing of hope in the blessed, whereby they formerly looked to their own happiness, they nonetheless continue to wish for the happiness of others; yet this is no longer in virtue of hope but now rather through the love which is charity. In a similar way, one having charity towards God loves his neighbor with the very same charity."[16] Charity is love, and it is the love for our Creator which leads to the love of our fellow man. There is a relationship here. The second love between human beings arises from the love that must first be present for our Creator.

There is also a relationship between faith and charity as "voluntary actions derive their species from the end, the object of the will ... it is clear that faith's act is pointed as to its end towards the will's object, i.e. the good. This good, the end of faith's act, is the divine good, the proper object of charity. This is why charity is called the form of faith, namely because the act of faith is completed and shaped by charity."[17] Further, as faith and charity are virtues, "It is obvious then that true virtue, without any qualification, is directed to man's principal good; as Aristotle puts it, virtue is *what disposes a thing already perfectly constituted in its nature to its maximum achievement.* And so taken, there can be no true virtue without charity."[18] Or in another form, "Now it is evident from what has been said already, that charity directs the acts of all the other virtues to our final end. Accordingly it shapes all these acts and to this extent is said to be the form of the virtues ... Hence ... Charity is likened to a foundation or a root because it supports and nourishes all the other virtues."[19] Faith and charity are both oriented toward good, particularly the good – our Creator. Virtues are voluntary actions shaped by charity, but they begin in the act of faith.

Finally, there is a difference between faith and charity in their nature. "Faith belongs to the cognitive power, whose act is of such a kind that the things known are in the knower. Charity, on the contrary, has its seat in the affective power, which reaches out to the things themselves as they exist in reality."[20] These ideas can be put into the following relationship.

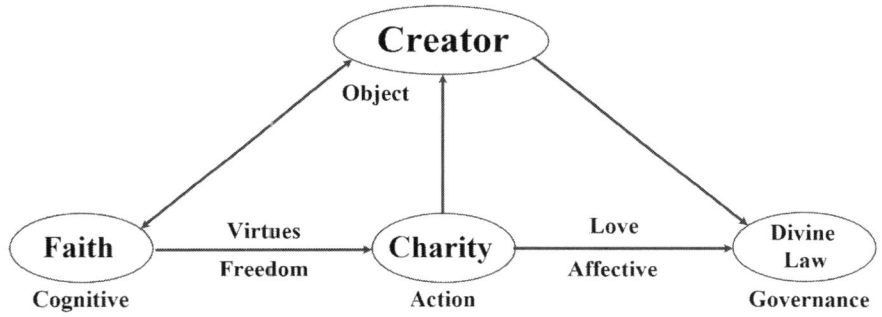

The significant concepts underlying the above diagram are the following:

1. The object of both faith and charity is our Creator as these orient man toward Him.

2. Our Creator is the cause of faith through His revelations to us, not only those written but His creation and the image of Him that we have each been given.

3. All virtues

   a. Begin in the act of faith, based upon what is internal to man—what he knows and holds in his heart.

b. Are voluntary, therefore they require freedom and the will to choose, and are grounded in moral precepts, which is why the imposition of one man's morality upon another ceases to be moral.

c. End in acts of charity, an action, performed out of love for both our Creator and our fellow man, expecting nothing in return. This is not just any love but what is called *agape*.

4. Charity itself supports and directs all virtues to their proper end. Augustine and many other early church fathers, used the terms faith, hope, and love. I have kept charity and love separate here to identify charity as an act of love, with love itself being affective, as described by Thomas. Love orients man towards his Creator as "God is love."[21]

5. As our Creator is love, He can only be experienced. The acquisition of virtue by performing acts of charity is therefore the way we become good, the way we fulfill our purpose, and allows us one way to come to know Him.

6. Divine law is His word, given to us by His revelation. We are commanded by that law to love both our Creator and our fellow man. Therefore, virtue's acquisition leading to performing charity out of love is fulfillment of His law. Performing acts of charity are complying with His governance.

Thomas indicated that the three theological virtues of faith, hope, and charity were greater than all of the others, as their object was our Creator. They oriented us toward Him. Among the moral virtues, he put justice first as "the main function of justice is to subject men to God."[22] Further, "the proper characteristic of justice, as compared with the other moral virtues, is to govern a man in his dealings towards others. It implies a certain balance of equality ... The other moral virtues, however, compose a man for activities which befit him considered in himself."[23] From these statements, the moral virtues orient man as an individual within society, the other aspect of divine law, and therefore justice ranks higher among the moral virtues as it deals with the relationships among two or more individuals. The other moral virtues deal only with an individual him or herself. Further, justice can only deal with external actions. It cannot observe man's interior feelings or his uprightness of character.[24] That is the area of divine justice alone, and rests with our Creator.

This is correct as far as it goes. However, I believe that these thoughts are incomplete. If justice is giving each man his due, aren't charity and mercy giving a man what he is not due, or rather love that he has not earned? This is where John Winthrop's quote at the beginning of this chapter comes into play. There are two related thoughts from this passage on justice and mercy. First, as we will see later, justice in this world is related to human governance and belongs to the sphere of the State; in fact, it is the primary purpose of human governance. While justice is given to individuals, the human law on which it is based is associated with us not as individuals, but as a single people. Mercy, on the other hand, is a virtue and all virtues manifest themselves as charity. As all virtues begin in faith, mercy belongs to the sphere of the Church and is given primarily at the level of the individual, regardless of the individual's membership in a larger group.

Second, justice is concerned with observable actions; it is based upon what is external. The virtue of mercy (and therefore charity) has its basis not in external actions but internal beliefs—our uprightness of character. Charity and mercy also deal with the relationships between two or more individuals. From this perspective, charity is the manifestation of the other virtues, the free giving of what another needs out of love for both the individual and our Creator, voluntary sacrifice. This leads us to another aspect of charity: charity should lead to the building of virtue in both the giver and the receiver.

Before we can finish this point, we need to have a brief discussion about grace. In Thomas' words,

> In common usage, "grace" is usually taken in three senses. Firstly, it stands for the love of someone, as we might say that this soldier has the king's grace and favour ... Secondly, it is used to refer to a gift given gratis ... Thirdly, it is used to refer to the display of gratitude for benefits given gratis ... The second of these three senses depends on the first; for out of the love with which someone regards another favourable, it comes about that he bestows something on him gratis. The third sense rises from the second, since expression of gratitude arises in response to benefits bestowed gratis.
>
> As to the two latter senses it is clear that grace sets up something in the one who receives the grace: firstly, the gift itself given gratis; secondly, the gratitude for this gift.[25]

The three senses of grace outlined above indicate both a connection and a reciprocation, and the underlying basis is love—charity. Dietrich Bonhoeffer in his book *The Cost of Discipleship* distinguishes between cheap and costly grace: "Cheap grace is the preaching of forgiveness without requiring repentance, baptism without church discipline, Communion without confession, absolution without personal confession. Cheap grace is grace without discipleship."[26] In short, cheap grace is the receiving of a gift without a corresponding change or reciprocation, without a corresponding love, a corresponding charity. It can also be the giving of a gift without that love, a mere action performed out of a soulless compliance. Costly grace, on the other hand, is costly because it "must be *sought* again and again, the gift which must be *asked* for, the door at which a man must *knock*. Such grace is *costly* because it calls us to follow."[27]

Costly grace requires an action on our part, and a reciprocation in line with that action, even though nothing is expected in return. It is the same with charity. Charity without the mutual building of virtue in both the giver and the receiver cannot be true charity, or costly charity to use

Bonhoeffer's term, as there is no virtue acquired, no love reciprocated. This is merely cheap charity, a form only without the substance which makes it a virtue. It is no different from the Pharisees who obeyed the letter of the law without obeying its spirit, although one can reasonably argue it is worse because its effects often go beyond a single individual. Are our government-imposed social programs today merely expressions of cheap charity? Can the charity we provide through many of our institutions really and truly be charity? These are difficult questions to even face, let alone answer. But if we are truly concerned about helping others achieve their independence, then they are questions we must honestly address if we want to make things better for both ourselves and others.

We've now laid out what charity is and why it should matter to us as individuals and a society. More details regarding the ideas and concepts expressed in this chapter can be found in *Do You Want To Be Free?* In the next chapter, we will take a brief look at both the history of charity and its biblical basis. Along the way we will discuss the relationship between charity and governance from the individualism model's perspective using the writings of Jonathan Edwards.

In the third and fourth chapters, we will look at the relationship between charity and governance from the collectivism perspective using the writings of John Locke. This examination will also look at his perspective on the relationship between Church and State, and the role of each in society. This content will be tied to the historical context of charity provided in the next chapter. The purposes are to show how each model supports the notions we've outlined in this chapter, and provide a sufficient understanding of charity to cover purpose, virtue, and stewardship. Finally, the chapters will provide facts and evidence for you to truly begin to evaluate the questions posed so far.

Chapter 2: Charity's Development

> *The beginning and the end—I mean faith and love— are not taught ... But knowledge ... is entrusted to those who show themselves worthy of it; and from it the worth of love beams forth from light to light ... to faith, knowledge; and to knowledge, love.*
>
> —Clement of Alexandria,
> 2nd century

This chapter covers the following subjects: a historical overview of charity, its biblical basis, and the individualism model's relationship between charity and society. The historical perspective is discussed first. It might seem odd to refer to charity as evolving over time, but that is what happened. The notion of charity has changed significantly over the last several thousand years. The state religion societies provide a baseline as this governance form existed prior to the emergence of Judeo-Christian theology/philosophy. We will next look at some of the societal changes occurring after the Roman Empire's fall through the Enlightenment at the close of the eighteenth century. This relationship from a collectivism perspective will be the subject of the next two chapters.

State Religion Societies

State religion societies include those such as Assyria, Persia, Babylonia, Egypt, Greece, and Rome in the east, as well as the Incas, Mayans and Aztecs in the west. Some of the attributes shared by these civilizations include the following:

1. Land was usually divided between three groups: (a) the temple and its priests, (b) temple lands rented to the wealthy, the elite, and (c) commoners who grew crops to meet their own needs.

2. Political and religious power were closely connected, with the palace and temple normally located in close proximity to emphasize that relationship. At times the ruler and high priest were related, and on occasion both roles were held by the same person.

3. The state was the lowest level of existence that mattered. Society's purpose was to support the welfare and perpetuation of the state.

4. People possessed different gifts, and some gifts were seen as superior. Those whose gifts were determined more valuable were therefore of greater value to society. This formed the basis for the notion that all people were not equal. Some were superior and those who were superior should be the ones who ruled. Initially rulers were often chosen by their people, but later rulers came to inherit their position, and later still often considered themselves to be gods. Consider the Roman emperors and Egyptian pharaohs.

5. As some people were superior, war was justified against those who were inferior and would not submit. Slavery was common, and slaves often formed one of the largest individual segments of a population.

6. There was a sense of collective morality, such as the belief that when someone undertook an action contrary to what the gods wanted, the entire community would be held to account for that individual's action.

7. State religions did not have congregations; instead, they had clients, and the temple priests would be requested to perform certain rites on behalf of a client.

8. Commoners had an obligation to spend a certain number of days performing work on the land held by the temple/ruler. The remainder of the time they were allowed to work land they cultivated for themselves.

The Roman Empire reflected many of these traits. Virtue was synonymous with being good; it was a reflection of one's superiority. It was thought virtue could only be practiced by those who had been freed from the drudgery of performing manual labor,[1] by those who were members of society's elite. These were the patricians, senators, and equestrians, the members of Rome's ruling classes. Full citizenship within Rome was not for everyone; it was meant only for those who were viewed as superior, those who belonged to the ruling classes. The plebeians formed the working classes, the farmers and artisans who performed many of the services necessary to support the Empire. They were free citizens, with their own elected leaders, but they were not allowed to participate in ruling the Empire. They labored to pay taxes, support their families, and often lived on the edge of subsistence. As they were a relatively large part of the Roman population, they were a force which the ruling class feared, and so found it necessary to control. Various forms of welfare were created in the Empire's later days to support the plebeian classes through difficult times. Many of the spectacles provided during Rome's latter days were meant to control the plebeian classes, keeping them fed and entertained by providing bread and circuses. Lower still was the slave class that at its height made up about half of the Empire's population. The structure of Roman society looked very much like a pyramid as shown below.

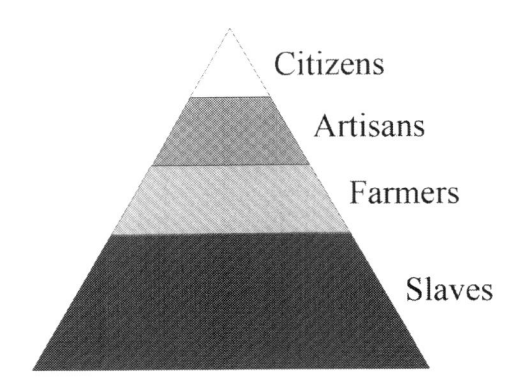

```
        Citizens
      Artisans
    Farmers
  Slaves
```
(Pyramid diagram showing social hierarchy: Citizens at top, then Artisans, Farmers, and Slaves at the base)

Charity within Roman society was considered to be a virtuous act, but it was a strictly civic form of charity that was practiced. It was normally performed by the wealthy—patrons—who chose what to give, why to give, how much to give, when to give, and to whom it should be given. It was an individual choice, based upon the giver's motives and performed primarily for the giver's benefit as a demonstration of their virtue. "At its root the Roman idea of philanthropy, like the Greek, was about civic responsibility—giving was an obligation of noble status rather than a duty of common humanity."[2]

The Roman Empire's Collapse

With Rome's collapse came several significant changes. First, political power dissipated. Large parts of the European continent were covered by mountains and dense forests. With Rome's influence gone, no other political entity was large enough or strong enough to replace it. Political power became dispersed among many smaller isolated political units. This led to relatively greater local autonomy and the need for these local rulers to better serve those they ruled as they were generally not strong enough to rule without people's consent. Second, the church still remained, although for a time it too operated in relative isolation from Rome.

Third, people no longer had to pay taxes and tribute to the Roman government. They were generally able to keep more of what they produced as they no longer had to support the lavish lifestyles of a far-off elite, pay for the building and maintenance of the many public monuments and roads, or maintain Rome's army. Fourth, slavery was already on its way out in the later days of the Roman Empire, but with its collapse came the need to find ways to replace the labor slaves had earlier provided. Slavery declined for a number of reasons including (1) slaves normally lived very short lives; (2) they created few children; (3) in its later history, Rome was no longer conquering new territory, so it was no longer adding to its slave population; and (4) the growing influence of Christianity made slavery difficult to morally justify.[3] Although slavery revived somewhat again with the Germanic tribe's conquest of much of Europe, it was out again before the end of the Early Middle Ages.

The Middle Ages

Many of today's historians will tell you that the Middle Ages was the dark period between the enlightenments of Rome and the Renaissance. In many ways, nothing could be further from the truth. The period just mentioned is contrary to the notions underlying charity that have been advanced, and as we will see a little later, the Renaissance was in many ways a return to Roman thought. But let's think of it from another perspective, a more personal one. Does the above really sound like enlightenment? To be enlightened means to increase in knowledge or understanding. Is the mark of enlightenment thinking you are better than another, or is it realizing that you are no different from another?

I would argue that the latter relates to our purpose and the notions discussed so far. The former is more likely to appeal to someone focused on themselves, on civic responsibility, and that was largely philanthropy's role in Rome. It was an expensive and inefficient use of society's resources, an exercise in poor stewardship. Rome and the Renaissance were periods of man's enlightenment created by his turning toward himself. What Rome's collapse provided was the circumstances creating the need to find better ways of doing things, the incentive for working to create them, and a relatively greater level of freedom to carry them out. They now had the opportunity and means to take advantage of the new circumstances, and the need was there as many lived in a poverty we probably cannot comprehend today. Today's poor in the U.S. are rich by these standards.

The above circumstances resulted in some fairly rapid developments, significantly impacting many areas, all of which occurred during the Middle Ages. In agriculture, the development of the heavy bladed plowshare, the development of equipment which allowed farming to switch from the use of oxen to horses, the introduction of a three-crop rotation system, and creation of fish farming are just a few. All of these served to speed-up or improve the efficiency of crop production. Transportation was improved with the invention of wagons with swivel axles, the creation of wheel brakes, and the development of paired harnesses allowing much larger teams to be used in pulling loads. Water transportation also improved with the move to less expensive shipbuilding techniques, the use of rounded hulls, the creation of a rear steering rudder, the development of complex sail designs, and the invention of the compass. These improvements in ship design not only had commercial uses, but the innovations were applied to warships, with the addition of heavy cannon to a ship's armament. Water and wind power were harnessed and made more efficient over time by moving from under-wheel to over-wheel water power and the use of posts allowing windmills to swivel with the change in wind direction. In the Netherlands, this wind power was used to create more land which could be used for agriculture.

Within commerce, the creation of better management techniques, the broader use of cash instead of barter, and the creation of credit enabled trade to be transacted in easier, more efficient ways over long distances. Other inventions which in general improved people's lives included the chimney, pane glass, eyeglasses, and an accurate mechanical clock. A much more comprehensive treatment of this subject is provided in Rodney Stark's *The Victory of Reason*.[4] To me, the Middle Ages sounds more like a period of enlightenment as we've defined it, and the periods of Rome and the Renaissance periods of relative darkness where the emphasis shifted to maintaining a particular social order. A timeline is provided in Appendix A as a visual aid for some of the relevant highlights of the periods being discussed.

Charity During the Middle Ages

So what was charity like during this period? James Brodman, in his book *Charity & Religion in Medieval Europe*,[5] characterized charity during this period as (1) expressing an altruism toward humanity, or at least for those within society who were most in need, (2) a concern for others that was motivated by a spirit of a religious character and not merely one designed to preserve a particular social order as had existed in Rome, (3) highly fragmented and inchoate as it never coalesced into a coherent or cohesive organization, and (4) only religion provided a coherence to the phenomenon expressed as charity within medieval society.[6] He further stated that there were two perspectives which must be understood in studying charity. First, that it is contrary to our nature to voluntarily give of one's property. Second, that one must examine the particular set of institutions created to transfer wealth from one group to another.[7] We'll take a quick look at the nature of these four characterizations and then the two perspectives outlined and how they changed during the Middle Ages, before continuing on to the Renaissance.

Charity's Expressions

The church's presence remained after Rome's departure. In some areas, the church was the only remaining source of authority. The central question concerning charity within the Middle Ages was *"How should love be shown for our Creator and others?"* Two approaches for expressing charity existed within this period. The first largely occurred during the Early Middle Ages and became primarily associated with the monastic movement. It was introspective and ascetic, involving self-denial, voluntary poverty, and prayer. As already noted, the largest population segment after Rome's fall were the plebeians, and many of these families lived on the edge of subsistence during and after the final days of Rome. Being extremely poor was the norm. There were simply not enough resources to satisfy everyone. But not only did the poor choose to serve using this expression of charity: many men and women from the ruling classes also chose to take voluntary vows of poverty during this time. They gave up what they had in order to become like everyone else.

Some may think those from wealthy families who served in charitable institutions during the Middle Ages did so simply because they had no other prospects. Roman law had required women to have dowries in order to enter arranged marriages, and wealth transfers at death were usually to remain within a family's male lineage. Normally the eldest son would receive the bulk of an inheritance. The remainder of the children were largely on their own in terms of providing for themselves. However, Christianity actively opposed these norms "in the sense that opportunities for conversion and teaching freed many wealthier Roman women from the oppressive constraints of arranged marriage."[8] In addition, a right to inheritance was established for women in the Early Middle Ages.[9] The wealthy who chose life within these charitable institutions largely did so out of a sense of service to others.

The second expression occurred later in the Middle Ages and became the norm during the twelfth century, the High Middle Ages. It is external, and one that is more familiar to us as it is based on actively caring for both our neighbor and the poor by performing acts of charity for them. This expression largely grew out of Augustine's writings, and many religious orders created during the latter part of the Middle Ages were founded upon the Augustinian Rule, particularly after the election of Pope Innocent III at the end of the twelfth century.

Charity's Motivations

Underlying these two approaches to charity were two very different motivations. At the heart of the first approach was the belief that we should try to improve ourselves through self-denial, as the world was not redeemable. This was represented by living a contemplative life.

The contemplative approach took the view that the individual was a learner, and the Benedictine Rule is an example of this approach. Even service was viewed as an activity to improve oneself, and often the aim of charitable acts would be to improve oneself by helping another in need, an extension of the notion of charity that existed in Roman times.

The motivation for the second approach was the belief that one should try to improve the world by taking care of others—the world was redeemable. It was living a life of action. This active approach viewed the individual as both a teacher and a learner, and the Augustinian Rule noted above was an example of this approach. Under this view, the purpose of charity was to aid another. While an act of charity might be the same using either approach, say caring for the poor, the underlying reason for the action was different. These are the same two ways of pursuing the virtue of wisdom mentioned by Augustine: "Now, the pursuit of wisdom follows two avenues—action and contemplation ... The former deals with the conduct of life ... Contemplative philosophy considers natural causality and truth as such. Socrates excelled in practical wisdom; Pythagoras favored contemplation."[10]

While one can live strictly one way or the other, Augustine suggests that one must live in a balanced way between the two approaches: "As to these three modes of life, the contemplative, the active, and the composite, although, so long as a man's faith is preserved, he may choose any of them without detriment to his eternal interests, yet he must never overlook the claims of truth and duty. No man has a right to lead such a life of contemplation as to forget in his own ease the service due to his neighbor; nor has any man a right to be so immersed in active life as to neglect the contemplation of God ... And, in active life, it is not the honors or power of this life we should covet, since all things under the sun are vanity, but we should aim at using our position and influence, if these have been honorably attained, for the welfare of those who are under us."[11] In other words, a life of service and not of being served.

Fragmentation

While Roman government collapsed with the end of its Empire, as mentioned above the church itself remained intact. But with the loss of the centralization which emanated from Rome, control within the early church was placed largely in the hands of the local bishops. Charity was local in nature and typically a response to events which overwhelmed local resources. Several types of charitable institutions developed during the Middle Ages. These included hospitals, bridge brotherhoods, hospices, and military orders.

The hospitals, however, were not the same type of institutions that we think of today. Instead, their initial aim was to offer the virtue of hospitality to travelers, often those going on or returning from a pilgrimage. The needs were short-term and the hospitals were there to assist a traveler by providing food and shelter. These needs evolved to later taking in widows, orphans and the aged, particularly those who were about to die. Their mission then extended still further to caring for those with chronic diseases, and as a result of these shifts, the focus became more long-term. Later still, they began to take in those suffering from famine, the unemployed, the insane, and those suffering from the plague.

By the time of the High Middle Ages, "every town and many villages and rural locales came to possess one or more of these institutions. The initiative for their foundation can be attributed to no single segment of medieval society, for we can count among their benefactors, bishops, cathedral chapters, monasteries and religious orders, and pious laypeople, as well as religious, professional, and municipal associations."[12]

Bridge brotherhoods also served travelers and pilgrims, and were supported by religious orders, monasteries, and lay communities. Often a hospice would come into being next to the bridge served by a brotherhood. These organizations were also local in nature. By the middle of the fourteenth century, some of the lay organizations were placed under the control of the local municipal council. While a hospice's original purpose was to serve pilgrims and travelers, they also evolved to eventually care for the poor, the disabled, and the aged. The military orders came into being as a result of the wars with Islam during the Middle Ages. Initially these orders focused on providing protection for travelers and pilgrims, but over time grew to care for the wounded, create hospitals, and serve in the negotiation and ransoming of war captives.

The Common Tie of Religion

The institutions discussed above were founded by differing groups, but as the end of the Middle Ages approached, many institutions came to be controlled by municipal councils. However, for all of the different charitable institutions which came into being during the Middle Ages, there was a common, biblically-based notion which underlay them al: "The ideology of religious charity provided the spiritual and intellectual underpinnings of the myriad of hospitals, religious orders, independent communities of religious, and confraternities and parochial organizations that sprang up in defense of the poor during the High Middle Ages ... [that] these new institutions coexisted beside older ones whose spiritual paths were more inwardly directed demonstrates the richness and pluralism of religious life and practice in the medieval era."[13]

Some Implications of Charity's Development

There are at least three implications from the changes in charity just discussed. First, the people who primarily performed and received charity changed. Acts of charity had previously been performed primarily by the wealthy. So how did this change? As noted previously, with Rome's collapse came the creation of many smaller local political units. During the Early Middle Ages, local bishops typically exerted an influence on charity, and they made some attempts to institutionalize charitable organizations thru the creation of hospitals and shelters. Members of congregations, even the poor, were generally asked to provide alms towards charity. This did two things. One, it largely shifted the burden for supporting charity from the elite onto the middle class, and therefore, in a sense, to the community at large. Two, the bishops defined the object of charity to be "only to the poor—both those in dire need and those whose previous status was threatened by economic circumstances."[14] Those in need included travelers (particularly pilgrims), widows, orphans, and those displaced from the upper classes.

A second change, as previously noted, was from a contemplative to an active form of charity. Initially, after the fall of Rome, the population of many urban areas decreased. Much of the charity performed during the Early Middle Ages stemmed from institutions that followed a contemplative approach, primarily through the efforts of local bishops and later monasteries. With the decline in urban populations during the Early Middle Ages came a loss of revenue to support charitable efforts for a population where it became increasingly difficult to determine who needed charity the most. This led many early institutions to turn to performing largely symbolic acts of charity.

By the twelfth century, this situation had changed significantly. With the technological improvements noted earlier, commercial trade was expanding and urban populations were growing once again. The complex set of social contracts which made up the feudal system were also now in place. Under this system, tenants typically worked for their local ruler for a certain number of days each year. A Gregorian reformation also began in the eleventh century and "attempted to understand and correct the relationships between society and religion. All of these changes coalesced into a new understanding of poverty that encouraged individual as well as corporate charity."[15] The results were new institutions being created based upon the more active Augustinian Rule. Finally, "church lawyers concluded that, because poverty itself was not a moral evil, individuals so afflicted should not be deprived of their legal rights."[16] With this shift, poverty in and of itself was no longer viewed as being the fault of the poor; instead, "charity and justice ... demanded that he [the poor] be assisted; society in some sense owed this to him as a form of moral restitution."[17] Charity came to be viewed as a community's responsibility, a shift from individual to collective responsibility.

Typically, within the Feudal System the local ruler did not have as much control over cities and towns as they did the surrounding rural areas. This allowed for the development of an increasing level of freedom, initially within the city-states of northern Italy, the Netherlands, and then throughout all of England in the time leading up to the High Middle Ages. The development of freedom and liberty was the third change during this period, and this change both supported and facilitated the technological changes during the Middle Ages noted above. The increase in productivity which came from these advances had several important impacts on society. These were the following:

1. Relatively greater wealth creation by individuals.

2. Businesses increasing in size, resulting in a greater need for labor and heightened competition for the best workers, leading to elevated levels of compensation for those with the needed skills.

3. More individuals providing and/or performing acts of charity.

To summarize, during the Middle Ages the following changes occurred with respect to charity:

1. The primary support for charity shifted from the wealthy to the middle class and the community at large.

2. The objects of charity were specifically defined to be the poor, including those economically displaced.

3. There was an increase in freedom and liberty, which in turn supported the many technical advances that improved their means of making a living. These technical innovations led to increases in efficiency and productivity which benefited society by (a) further increasing a community's relative wealth,

    and (b) decreasing the number who would have been poor, although these benefits were not evenly distributed throughout society.

4. The remaining poor became the increasing focus of charity, supported by development of the belief that society morally owed this support to the poor as a form of restitution.

There were also two perspectives mentioned at the beginning of this chapter. The first perspective concerned man's nature and the nature of the organizations providing charity. That it is contrary to man's nature to voluntarily give from his possessions. Is this really true? Most people lived at the edge of subsistence after Rome's fall. They generally did not have much to provide towards charity, but many provided some from what little they had through alms and other forms of charity.

Also, consider the innovations occurring during the Middle Ages that greatly improved some people's economic circumstances. If the above assertion were true, we would expect charity to decrease as relative wealth increased. However, charity increased significantly when a people's economic circumstances improved, not only in terms of the number of charitable organizations created, but also in terms of the number of individuals who devoted themselves to performing charity. What appears to be closer to the truth is that it is difficult for one to give much when they generally do not have much.

It is only contrary for man to give from his possessions when he has turned away from his Creator and towards himself, as asserted by many church fathers such as Clement of Alexandria and Augustine. When one turns toward himself, he is more likely to become prideful and less likely to care about others, to support the common good, or to become virtuous—to accomplish his purpose. *Accomplishing our purpose requires us to try to become good, we become good by building virtue, and the building of virtue is an individual process. It is more difficult to accomplish this in an environment where freedom is not present because individual choice is required. It is through building virtue and sacrificial giving—charity grounded in faith—that we find the path to happiness.* Clement agreed: "Plato the philosopher, [in] defining the end of happiness, says that it is likeness to God as far as possible."[18] For, "discipline and virtue are a necessity, if they would pursue after happiness."[19]

As to the nature of these organizations, their fragmentation should also be expected. If charity is primarily an individual act as has been asserted, then we should see the creation of many small local organizations and the participation by lay people in those organizations. This is in fact what occurred, and these organizations were staffed by both religious orders and laity. This raises a question we will discuss later. If the building of virtue is an individual process, what should be the proper role of organizations in charity?

The second perspective mentioned is that these organizations were intended to provide wealth transfers. Is this really true as well? First, wealth transfers are about outcomes and are a collectivism notion. In today's context, this would merely be akin to the government taking monies from one group and giving it to another group the government deems to need it more. However, charity is about voluntary sacrifice—a virtue—and about thankfulness, another virtue. There is no virtue in the forced redistribution of assets from one group to another, for either the giver or receiver. And if you take away enough capital from those who create it, and give it to those who consume it, you will end up reducing a society's capital—and that society will be less well off—although one could argue in that instance that everyone would be more alike. This approach is the very reverse of what occurred during the Middle Ages. Second, charity was very seldom performed by governmental units until the end of the Middle Ages, and those were instances of a political units either creating or taking control of existing charitable organizations. This is a trend which increased during the Renaissance. More about that in the next section.

Third, while there were certainly alms taken and given to help the poor, this is far from the only form of charity exhibited during this period. The primary function of many of these early organizations was to provide food, shelter, protection, and care. There is little money directly involved in these actions; instead, these actions were based upon the virtues of hospitality, humility, philanthropy, piety, and liberality. They were attempts to provide those in need with the things that they needed: the pursuit of virtues leading to acts of charity in alignment with the notion of grace expressed by Thomas earlier. Augustine summed up this notion in writing about the basic difference between the city of God and the city of man: "For it is good to have the heart lifted up, yet not to one's self, for this is proud, but to the Lord, for this is obedient, and can be the act only of the humble ... therefore it is that humility is specially recommended to the city of God as it sojourns in this world ... while the contrary vice of pride ... specially rules his adversary the devil. And certainly this is the great difference, which distinguishes the two cities [city of God and city of man] of which we speak."[20]

The Renaissance

While many individuals' economic circumstances improved during the Middle Ages, the improvements did not reach everyone, nor did everyone who saw improvement benefit equally. We'll look at Northern Italy and the Netherlands to assess the changes in charity during the Renaissance as these areas are most aligned with the changes discussed earlier and have a more direct connection to England and our own history in the U.S.

It was during the Renaissance that political units began to try and fill the gap between what private charity provided and what these political units saw as the genuine needs of the poor. By the mid-fifteenth century in Venice, the "public authorities began to view poverty as a problem of public order. Charity was then seen less in a devotional context and more of an instrument of public policy to coax ... [individuals] toward moral reformation."[21] In other words, charity became viewed by political units as a means of controlling the poor, similar to Rome's views for treating the plebian classes.

This should not be unexpected as with the Renaissance came the desire to return to the glory days of Roman rule and *Rex Regia*. At this point we see elitism increase between the haves and the have-nots. This change was certainly not reflected by everyone, but it does indicate a more general turning away from our Creator by those in power. This should not be surprising either as education had begun to shift from the teachings of Plato to those of Aristotle, both pagans, but Plato attempted to understand his Creator (First Cause) whereas Aristotle took the more traditional approach of trying to understand creation. Scholasticism attempted to reconcile Aristotle's works with theology instead of using theology as the basis for truth and accepting whatever truth existed within his pagan philosophy.

The stresses brought on by plagues and frequent famines at times outstripped the available resources of many charitable institutions. This resulted in political units attempting to reform charitable institutions to make them more efficient. The reforms in mid-sixteenth century Florence were typical. These reforms promised "greater and more reliable revenues in exchange for the surrender of institutional autonomy."[22] The reforms had the effect of binding the old and new charitable institutions together under common political control, instead of religious, for the purpose of maintaining social discipline. In Florence, this resulted in the "evolution of charity from relatively autonomous organizations that benefited from state assistance to organizations that were fully functioning departments"[23] within the local municipal government.

The changes in oversight had several effects. First, the redirection of charitable resources toward political ends—patronage—and the creation of conflicting roles as charitable institutions had to balance providing for the well-being of those in their care with determining impartially who should receive charitable support. These reforms created specific classes of the poor to be served, and regulations as to how each was to be served, a form of group rights. The results were both additional burdens on the poor and increased expenses for the institutions performing charity. Examples of the former include requirements such as written petitions instead of oral ones to lodge complaints and requirements for legal representation neither of which the very poor, who were charity's focus, could afford. Associated with these changes was a massive increase in paperwork which increased expenses. One example comes from Florence, where a critic of reforms there noted that now "every three or four months, the required paperwork now filled four 500-page volumes, whereas previously two volumes of 200 pages each had sufficed"[24]—a 400 percent increase in effort and corresponding cost.

These reforms had another consequence: they created an incentive to cheat. As a result, fraud and abuse grew as those responsible for decision making were more distant from those receiving assistance, while receiving assistance itself was made more difficult and more expensive, often putting it beyond the means of the very poor these institutions were intended to serve. Problems included fraudulent claims, not providing services for which individuals were paid, and continuing to receive benefits after a recipient's death. The result was a further increase in regulations in an attempt to stop the fraud and still greater expenses for the institutions. Doesn't this sound like it could have been written today? History merely repeats itself when its lessons are not learned and kept in the forefront of our minds and acted upon.

The Relationship Between Governance and Religion

Before proceeding with the Enlightenment, let's take a few moments to reflect on the relationship between governance and religion, and how it also changed over time. Initially, during the state religion societies these two spheres were largely seen to be one and the same, as shown below, as political and religious power were closely connected. Note the Church and State did not exist at this time as we know them today.

```
        ┌─────────────┐
        │  Political  │
        │    Power    │
        │             │
        │  Religious  │
        │    Power    │
        └─────────────┘
```

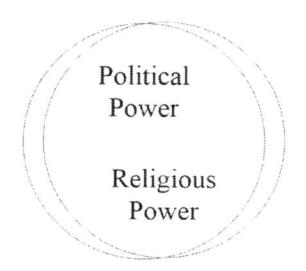

The relationship between political and religious power was emphasized by generally having the palace located close to the temple. The state was not what we think of when we use the word today, but instead was based on the *polis* of Greek philosophy, a local civic community broadly characterized by the Greek city-states. Religion, too, was not the same as today. Instead of worshippers, the temples had clients for whom they performed rituals as mentioned earlier. Both of these structures were generally built together on the highest point within a city, an acropolis. It was not unusual for the ruler and priest to be related or at times be the same individual. In addition, the rulers of these states often came to be considered gods themselves. If man can create the gods, or make themselves into gods, then isn't religion just the creation of man?

Augustine discussed this point in his *City of God*, where he spent several chapters reviewing the work of Marcus Varro, one of the brightest minds of his day who wrote a forty-one volume set on man and the gods of Rome. Even Varro implied that religion was the creation of man.[25] If everything came from the State, including religion, then rights, liberty, and the degree of freedom possessed by individuals all lie within the dictates of the State, and perpetuating the State becomes the single most important task for any society.

This view changed radically with the teachings of Christ as contained within the New Testament. One basis for this different view can be found in Mathew 22[26] where the Pharisees asked if it was lawful to pay the poll-tax to Caesar. What developed, in part from his response, was a notion that the state and religion were two separate—but equal—spheres within society as shown below.

38   Chapter 2

```
        Political                
         Power              Religious
                             Power
```

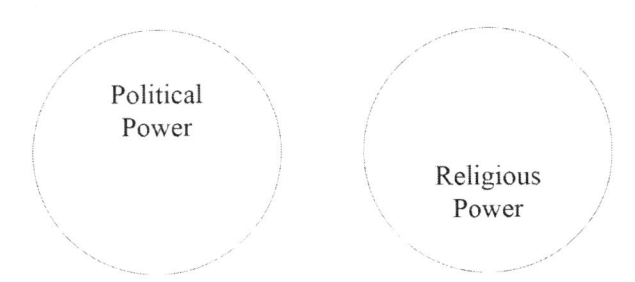

During the Middle Ages and the Renaissance, these two spheres often contested for dominance within society, with each serving as a counterweight to the other. Often they contested with each other to promote their own views and interests, or to hold and increase their own power. At times both spheres protected the people, and at times both attempted to use them. For example, the vacuum created by Rome's fall at times put the local bishops in the position of also acting as the local political power. This led to corruption between the political and religious spheres by once again combining Church and State. Attempts to reform the church and remove the corruption were undertaken by several popes, including Leo IX and Gregory VII.

Also during the Middle Ages rulers often established churches and monasteries, which they did out of a belief that it was the right thing to do for both them and their people. However, oftentimes these same rulers came to view the organizations they had funded as "their church," another form of corruption between church and state. This culminated in the contests between King Henry II of the German Republics and Pope Innocent III in the twelfth century. These power disputes resulted in the church's power being placed over that of the state, and set the stage for the mingling of church and state power under the Medici and Borgia popes beginning in the fifteenth century.

It was the removal of this corruption that Machiavelli wrote about, the removal of the church's power so the state would be free to fully exercise its power. However, Machiavelli was wrong. Removing a ruler from the philosophy underlying religion is not a valid solution. All it does is remove the learning of virtue and morality from the ruler. In the end, this approach has never worked. Also, the diagram above is not a complete view of the proper relationship between these two spheres. This view would be true if the preceding were the only recorded statement Christ had ever spoken concerning this relationship. But it is not.

Some additional biblical verses state that all the law hinges simply on two things: loving your Creator and loving your fellow man as yourself.[27] In other words, we are to be pointed to Him first, and once we have a right relationship with Him, then by extension we are in a position to be in a right relationship with our fellow men. As the spheres of government and religion are made up of men, then it follows that these two spheres are to also be oriented in a like manner and for the same purpose. There is another related verse within Mark that states that those who wish to be first must be the servant of all.[28]

The relationship between man and his Creator comes from His Word and provides the basis for our morality, and this morality requires the existence of virtue within each of us *both as individuals and as a people*. If this is true, then it must be that religion's underpinnings are intended to exert an indirect influence on both religious and political power, as it is through the Word contained within religion that the basis for morality and examples of virtue are received. These lessons in virtue are enhanced through the study of history, among other areas, by examining the success of virtue and the failure of vice.

So while these two spheres are indeed intended to be separate, if there is to be any wall between them as some assert, *it must be a wall which prevents one sphere from directly controlling the other. However, the indirect influence of religion on the character of the people through the morality it teaches is intended to be an influence on both spheres, and it must be so*. It is only when one sphere turns away from its purpose that it attempts to impose its will upon the other and there becomes the need for a wall. Any wall is to be a secondary structure put into place for times when the primary structure of man's morality fails and his orientation drifts from its intended purpose. It is the same for the existence of the means of governance. While religion is always needed in order to transmit and teach morality and virtue to a people, government exists only to administer justice when people fail to live in a moral way – to abide by the morality taught through religious ideas. This is borne out by several passages within the *Old Testament* which state that justice is to be meted out by judges impartially and in righteousness, "for the judgment is God's."[29]

By the end of the High Middle Ages and Renaissance, however, we were once again at the point where the powers of the Church and State were largely one. Notice that it is no longer religion represented by one of the spheres, but an organization which represented the ideas expressed by religion—the church. Additionally, at this time the states were largely Christian instead of pagan. This remerging of the spheres came about in several ways. First, there was a large desire to return to the "glory days of Rome" among rulers: the divine right of kings to rule all. Second, as rulers within Europe were Christian, some believed that they had a moral duty to help take care of the disadvantaged within their kingdoms.

We've already outlined the results of this later force as it resulted in municipal associations assuming control, not only of charities, but at times and in places the State's determining who would occupy positions within charitable organizations and even the church itself. This culminated in the complete assumption of the church by Henry VIII within England, and the creation of the Anglican Church. So once again we had come full circle back to a place very much like the one from which we started, but this time religious and political powers are represented by the organizations that we know as the Church and State.

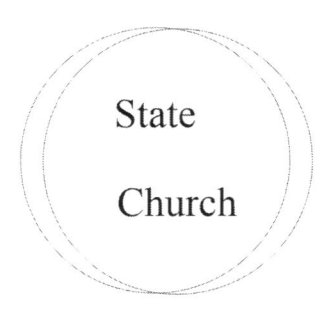

State

Church

The Enlightenment and the First Great Awakening

In reaction to some of the changes which took place during the Renaissance, a stream of thought aimed toward greater individual freedom and liberty (individualism) led to documents such as *Vindicae Contra Tyrannos* (France), *the Act of Abjuration* (Netherlands), the *Petition of Right* (England), and the *Mayflower Compact* and *A Model of Charity* (American Colonies). At the same time, a separate contradictory thread of thought aimed at increasing the power of the State (collectivism), or at least removing the influence of the Church from it, also continued to develop. By the early 1700s, the writings of Machiavelli, Spinoza, Hobbes, Newton, and Locke had been published. With the merging of state and church noted during the Renaissance came the persecution of people on religious grounds within Europe.

Many of those coming to the New World colonies did so to flee the religious persecutions occurring within their own countries. Within the American Colonies, the First Great Awakening occurred during the 1730s and 1740s. It was a religious revival which began in the northeast and spread throughout most of the colonies. This event, along with the traditional notions of English liberty, served to set the stage for the War for Independence a few decades later.

This awakening occurred in both Europe and America. Some of the leading figures within this event included John Wesley, George Whitefield, and Jonathan Edwards. Edwards was one of the most prolific preachers of this time. He is generally known for his work "Sinners in the Hands of an Angry God."[30] However, much of his writings focused on the equality of man's nature, his purpose, and the subject of charity. He also wrote several sermons directly addressing the role of governance in society, and the roles of religion and state. It is these that we will focus on in the rest of this section. For those who wish to cut to the chase, a summary is provided toward the end of this section.

We can summarize his relevant ideas into the following topics and will briefly discuss each in turn:

- Who do we belong to, how, and why?
- Is governance a part of creation, and if it is, then what type of governance should exist?
- What roles should exist within this governance and what are their purposes?
- What qualities should exist within those who govern?
- What happens when we choose not to obey?

To Whom Do We Belong?

The first item stems from the knowledge that there is nothing which has been created that our Creator did not create. If that is true, then "the Creator of the world is doubtless also the Governor of it. He that had power to give being to the world, and set all the parts of it in order, has doubtless power to dispose of the world, to continue the order he has constituted, or to alter it."[31] There are two senses in which we belong to Him, for "God hath made all things for himself."[32] The first is through our creation by Him. In this sense of belonging, we have no choice.[33] The second sense of belonging is through our obedience to Him as Governor, and in this sense we do have a choice, for we have free will (freedom) in the actions that we take.[34] And through our choice of obedience we are "not merely to be his subjects and servants, but to be his children."[35] As one knows their parents, they are intended to know their Creator.

This choice has been given to us for a specific purpose: to assist us on our journey. For "you are placed in this world, with a choice given you, that you may travel which way you please; and one way leads to heaven."[36] While there are many places that we can travel and many concerns we can choose to pursue in life, we should go beyond these to consider the underlying motive for choice. "All men have some aim or other in living. Some mainly seek worldly things; they spend their days in such pursuits. But is not Heaven, where is fulness of joy for ever, much more worthy to be sought by you? ... No man is at home in this world, whether he choose heaven or not; here he is but a transient person."[37] These thoughts are almost exactly the same as those expressed by Clement of Alexandria in his work *Stromata* over fifteen hundred years before. This ability to choose is a gift from our Creator, to enable us to fulfill our purpose of coming to know Him just as children learn from their parents.

Governance

Edwards expressed several additional ideas that came from accepting our Creator as our Governor. The first is that heaven is our native country.[38] The offered proof of this is that we all speak the same language (the Word), and profess the same doctrines.[39] Second is, as noted above, that we do not belong to this world but are merely sojourners here, so why should we pursue material possessions that we will be unable to take with us on our final journey? Third, we "are under the same government. The Christians are one society, one body politic; and therefore, as here the church is represented by a nation, so oftentimes it is called a city. They are subject to the same King, Jesus Christ. He is the head of the church, he is the head of this body politic. Indeed all men are subject to the providence and power of this King."[40]

As we are all under the same government, we "are all governed by the same laws, and all subject themselves to the same rules. The commands of God that are obeyed by the saints are the same all over the world. There is the same method of government, there are the same means of government, the same outward and visible means, the same officers, gospel, and gospel ministers, in like manner appointed and sent forth by the head of the church, the same visible order and discipline appointed for all. And there are the same inward and special means of government. Christ governs his people in a peculiar manner. He immediately influences their wills and inclinations, and powerfully brings them to a compliance with God's commands and rules. They are a society united in the same public interest and concerns."[41]

As everyone lives under the same rules, laws, and methods of government, then everyone must be treated in the same manner and therefore everyone must have the same rights and nature. As to how we are to treat each other, it is through "charity, or expressions of Christian love in gifts to others."[42] We are to "be ready to distribute, willing to communicate, and do good; consider it as part of your office thus to do, to which you are called and appointed, and as a sacrifice well-pleasing to God; pity others in distress; be ready to help one another; God will have mercy and not sacrifice."[43] These are the same requirements described by Scipio for defining a people. That a people must have both a common set of mutually agreed upon rights, and have a shared commitment for the common good.

So what does this government look like? Edwards draws meaning from I Peter 2:9,[44] which is that we are to be a "priesthood of kings."[45] "The two offices of king and priest were accounted very honourable both among Jews and heathens; but it was a thing not known under the law of Moses, that the same person should sustain both those offices in a stated manner ... Those who were kings by divine appointment in Israel, were of another tribe from the priesthood."[46] However, we are called to be both a kingdom (a people) and priests, and not simply a kingdom of priests, the former being exemplified by Melchizedek, king of Salem.

The reference to a kingdom applies to both this world and our future state as "the reward of the saints is represented as a kingdom, because the possession of a kingdom is the height of human advancement in this world, and as it is the common opinion that those who have a kingdom have the greatest possible happiness."[47] The happiness Edwards refers to consists of honor, possessions, and authority, but is also a different happiness as it "is far greater than that of the kings and greatest potentates in the world."[48] Second, the reference to being a priesthood consists in what we are to offer, how, and why. We are to offer up our own hearts in sacrifice; in dedication to our Creator. This sacrifice consists of praise, obedience, charity, liberality, bounty to the poor, and faith.[49] In short, the building and practice of virtue by each and every one of us. Again, we are to "be ready to distribute, willing to communicate, and do good; consider it as part of your office thus to do, to which you are called and anointed, and as a sacrifice well-pleasing to God; pity others in distress; be ready to help one another; God will have mercy and not sacrifice."[50]

This nation is open for all to join: "So now is there free liberty to any to come and join themselves to this nation, and they shall be received and admitted to the same rights and privileges, and be in all respects treated as the same people ... This nation is governed by the most wise and righteous laws ... This nation is a free people. The happy government under which they live, is most consistent with freedom; it does not in the least infringe upon the liberty of the subject, there is nothing like slavery within the kingdom of God. The law of this nation is a law of liberty ... There is not a nation that dwell in such love and peace as this holy nation enjoys. The happiness of a people very much consists in its peace; a nation is never more miserable than when it is rent by civil wars, or disturbed by intestine broils."[51] Can you hear the echoes of these words within the *Declaration of Independence* written only forty years later?

Governance Roles

This governance is to have a moral foundation. Edwards exclaims that there is a great difference between our Creator's moral governance and that of his creatures. His moral governance; its nature, design, and ends are "secret things that belong to God. ... But it is quite otherwise with respect to God's moral government of a kingdom or society of intelligent and willing creatures; to which society he is united as its head, ruling for its good."[52] This later form of governance requires communication between the governor and those governed. As we are intelligent agents, possessed with free will, there must be some promulgation to promote the declarations, methods, rules, and enforcements for governance. This understanding is necessary *in order for us to choose obedience.* Further, this communication to the governed must take place in a way that is

> agreeable to their [creation's] nature; that is, by way of voluntary signification of their mind to the governed, as the governed signify their minds voluntarily one to another. There should be something equivalent to conversation between the rulers and ruled; and thus the rulers should make themselves visible. The designs and ends of government should be made known; it should be visible what is aimed at, and what grand ends or events are in view, and the mind of the rulers should be declared as to the rules, measures, and methods, to be observed by the society.[53]

This conversation with our Creator, First Cause, requires revelation: "Yea, notwithstanding the clear and infinitely abundant evidences of his *being*, we need that God should tell us that there is a great being, who *understands*, who *wills*, and who has made and governs the world ... On the supposition, that God has a moral kingdom in the world, that he is the head of a moral society, consisting either of some part of mankind, or of the whole; in what darkness must the affairs of this moral kingdom be carried on, without a communication between the head and the body; the ruler never making himself known to the society by any word, or other equivalent expression whatsoever, either by himself, or by any mediators, or messengers!"[54]

This is why the writings of those such as Machiavelli, Spinoza, Hobbes, and others that rely on the foundation they have built all fail. Their notions of first being do not consider revelation and its relationship with moral governance, so they are left with man alone. Edwards asserts that all moral agents are (1) conversable agents, and (2) social agents, as "affairs of morality are affairs of society."[55] "The ground of moral behavior, and all moral government and regulation, is society, or mutual intercourse and social regards."[56]

Governing Qualities

So what qualities are needed by its rulers? Edwards stated rulers were to be the strong rods, people of virtue, for their respective communities.

> One qualification of rulers whence they may properly be denominated strong rods, is great ability for the management of public affairs. This is the case, when they who stand in a place of public authority are men of great natural abilities, men of uncommon strength of reason and largeness of understanding; especially when they have a remarkable genius for government, a peculiar turn of mind fitting them to gain an extraordinary understanding in things of that nature. They have ability, in an especial manner, for insight into the mysteries of government, and for discerning those things wherein the public welfare or calamity consists, and the proper means to avoid the one and promote the other; an extraordinary talent at distinguishing what is right and just from that which is wrong and unequal, and to see through the false colours with which injustice is often disguised, and unravel the false and subtle arguments and cunning sophistry that is often made use of to defend iniquity.[57]

Rulers are the image of their people, and those which are strong rods possess a largeness of heart, and a greatness and nobleness of disposition. They are individuals in possession of honor and eminent fortitude; stability and firmness of integrity, fidelity, and piety in the exercise of authority. They are men "of strict integrity and righteousness, firm and immovable in the execution of justice and judgment."[58] Strong rods create an environment promoting virtue and unity as a people. Weak rods promote vice and division. Strong rods "are like the main springs or wheels in a machine, that keep every part in its due motion ... Their influence has a tendency to promote wealth, and cause temporal possessions and blessing to abound; and to promote virtue amongst them, and so to unite them one to another in peace and mutual benevolence, and make them happy in society, each one the instrument of his neighbours' quietness, comfort, and prosperity."[59]

With the ability to choose comes both great opportunity and great responsibility. Strong rods are needed as not all men will choose the type of obedience being discussed. "Government is necessary to defend communities from miseries from within themselves; from the prevalence of intestine discord, mutual injustice, and violence; the members of the society continually making a prey one of another, without any defence from each other. Rulers are the heads of union in public societies that hold the parts together."[60] Government exists primarily in order to protect those who choose to support moral governance from those who do not. "As government, and strong rods for the exercise of it, are necessary to preserve public societies from dreadful and fatal calamities arising from among themselves; so no less requisite are they to defend the community from foreign enemies ... Thus both the prosperity and safety of a people under God, depends on such rulers as are *strong rods*."[61]

Choosing Disobedience

As stated earlier, rulers are a reflection of the people that they rule. What happens when a people rejects their ruler, in this case their Creator and the moral governance described above and freely offered by Him? "In the case of a people broken off from their king, the maintaining of intercourse by conversation is in no wise in like manner requisite. The reason for such intercourse, which take place in the other case, do not take place in this. In this case, society ceases; i.e. that union ceases between God and man, by which they should be of one society ... Moral governance in a society is a social affair; wherein consists the intercourse between superior and inferior constituents, between that which is original, and that which is dependent, directing and directed in the society."[62] Without our Creator, man is left to his own devises. Strong rods no longer rule, and the things they promote—virtue and morality—eventually cease to exist within society. It becomes a society where its members no longer look out for each other, but only for themselves. What we have been describing is a moral society whose end is morality and virtue; whose end is love. In the absence of morality and virtue come iniquity and vice, which leads to division, jealousy, and hate. Compare these words to the path we are on as a nation today.

So how do we know what kind of government we currently possess? Edwards used the state of local governance from his own time to discuss this point. The following passages are from his work *The State of Public Affairs*.[63] Although written over two hundred and seventy-five years ago, it could just as well have been written today. In describing the state of the Massachusetts colony society of his day, Edwards opens with a description of two possibilities:

> The public [common] good here mentioned is a settled, the calamity is an unsettled, state of public affairs. While public affairs are in an unsettled posture, they are continually liable to be shifting and altering; and this [is] a great calamity to the land. But when the public state is settled and prolonged, and remains unshaken and undisturbed, this is a great blessing to any people.

Edwards's states that the cause of an unsettled state of affairs is "by a land's 'having many princes' ... often changing its princes, often changing the persons governing and the forms of government that it is under." That the calamity is the result of "the state of public affairs of a land being in a changeable posture, whereby a people are exposed to lose their rights, privileges, and public blessing which they enjoy by virtue of the present establishment." This is because the

> Rulers are not so deeply engaged in seeking the public good. They don't act with that strength and resolution, their own circumstances being unsettled and uncertain. And rulers, not being united among themselves, don't assist and strengthen one another, but rather weaken one another's hands.

> Such an unsettled state is commonly attended with abundance of strife and contention, with jealousies [and] envyings. Rulers are divided into parties, and so the whole land with them. The distemper becomes general, so that the devil hereby gets a great advantage to promote his kingdom amongst one to another. And while all are engaged in contention, justice and righteousness is neglected. The suppressing of vice and wickedness is neglected, and they take advantage and prevail without restraint.
>
> Rulers, instead of discouraging and suppressing vice, do rather encourage it by their own unchristian behavior in their heats and debates. And commonly at such a time the wealth of a people is greatly wasted and consumed. While a state is unsettled, its strength and wealth consumes, as the health of the body natural under a sore disease.
>
> And such an unsettled state, if continued, tends to a people's ruin. It tends to its ruin from within and from without. The commonwealth is exposed, to become a prey to the ambition and avarice of men in its own bowels, of those that should be its fathers.[64]

This state comes about because, in the absence of virtue, vice arises to take its place as men begin to think that they have been elected to rule instead of to serve. "Sin tends to the temporal ruin of particular persons, but much more inevitably to the ruin of a public society; not only as it directly hurts the particular members, but as it weakens and breaks the bonds of union instead of making a people subservient to one another's good, which is [the] end of society."[65] Further, a people subject to vice "lose their power and influence, and so lose their honor and expose themselves to contempt and the insults of their neighbors; and often by this means are reduced from a prosperous and flourishing state, to become subjects and slaves to foreigners' honor."[66] This is because "humanity, civility, common decency and religion are so near akin that if one prevails, the other will prevail, and if the one languishes, the other will decay with it ... Education will be neglected, and children will grow up like the brute creatures, without instruction, and will be answerably barbarous in their manners."[67] The absence of virtue puts society on a downward spiral which will infect not only the present generation, but future ones as well. It is only when a people attempt to acquire and grow in virtue that the blessings of moral governance are realized.

Summary

Edward's thoughts can be summarized as follows:

1. We belong to our Creator as we are a part of His creation. However, we have a choice of whether or not we accept His governance.

2. Under His governance, heaven is our native country.

    a. We speak the same language and believe the same doctrines.

    b. We are a part of the same society and body politic.

    c. We are all under the same laws, rules, and methods of government.

    d. We are all ruled by the same ruler. Under His governance, we already have a single world government.

3. There must be communication between governor and the governed. In the case of divine governance, this occurs through revelation.

4. This governance is open to all.

    a. Each has the same rights and privileges, and is to be treated as the same people. It is a nation of free people.

    b. Governance is to have a moral foundation.

    c. The offices of ruler and priest are separate.

    d. Rulers should possess and promote virtue, and strive to bring unity and prosperity among their people. These are Edward's strong rods.

    e. We are called to be both a people and priests, not a people of priests.

5. We are each to build and practice virtue. We are to be ready to perform charitable acts and thereby do good. It is a part of the office to which we are called, to help others.

6. Rulers are a reflection of the people they govern.

    a. When man rejects his Creator's governance, the union between man and Creator ceases, and man is left to his own devices.

    b. People on their own turn inward. Rulers become weak rods. Division and strife increase, leading to society's fall if they do not change their direction.

It was the writing and teaching of leaders such as Edwards that shaped the basis of knowledge for the Founders of our own country. This knowledge provided them with the understanding necessary to restore the relationship between church and state. They had seen first-hand the corruption which occurred when the state assumed control of the church. This notion was not one of separate and equal, but instead one where the existence of the church was necessary to provide the moral basis for society, which in turn would have an influence on the state. The protections put into place were to protect the church from the state, especially as there was no dominant religious denomination within the American Colonies at the time of the War for Independence. They wanted to prevent the same situation that had occurred in England. So once again we have a form of separation between the Church and the State.

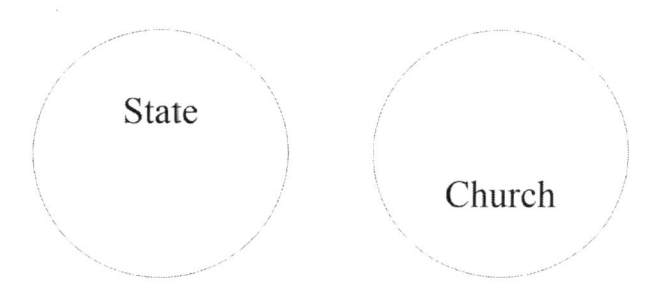

```
        State
                    Church
```

While the above diagram is accurate, it is still incomplete. As no single denomination dominated within the colonies, the thought turned to how to encourage all denominations to participate—in short, to create a religious marketplace. Although this idea has not always been realized, it was and is the vision to be strived for. This was necessary if the moral basis necessary for society's success was to be perpetuated. Education was a critical component for citizens to learn and understand truth, and this education needed to include both reason and faith.

If the notion that the church must be protected from the state is true, and education is critical in order for a society to be successful, then it follows that the state must be excluded from education so that a complete and well-rounded education can be provided to students. Madison and Jefferson both struggled with the use of public funds in education when creating the University of Virginia during their later years. They were unable to create a satisfactory solution. Instead Jefferson thought that the choice came down to either (1) having state supported institutions which private religious educational institutions could use, or (2) having the state institutions provide access to materials around religious ideas, but offering no direct courses on things related to theology.[68] We'll discuss the role of education more in a later chapter.

So what is missing from the diagram above? It is simply this.

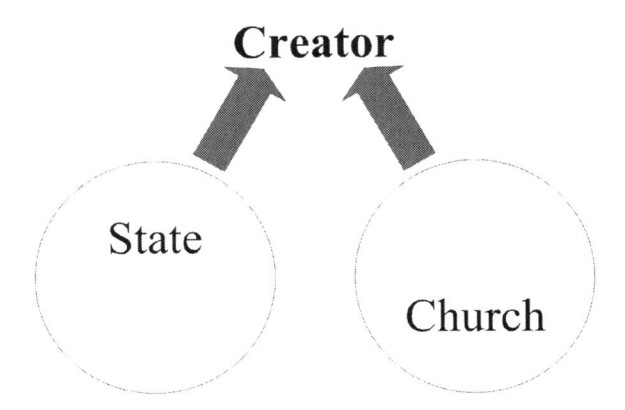

Creator

State   **Church**

Our Founders understood that there is only one supreme power, and it does not reside on this earth. That proper governance can only occur when both spheres are oriented toward Him, and not contesting with each other for earthly dominance. This basic belief is why the *Declaration of Independence* opens in the way that it does. That we are each "endowed by [our] Creator with certain unalienable Rights ... That to secure these rights, Governments are instituted among Men, deriving their just powers from the consent of the governed." Both spheres are necessary, they must remain separate in their functions, and education is a key component for any society's long-term success as the virtue and morality developed through religion influences both spheres. We will go into much greater detail about the above relationships from a collectivism perspective in the next two chapters, where we will take a closer look at some of John Locke's writings.

So why does all of this matter? It seems to me that we are once again repeating the mistakes of the Renaissance and returning to a place where the spheres of Church and State are merging into one. Consider the following:

- The secularization of the education in our public schools. Virtue is no longer taught to our children, unless they receive it at home, and even then does society support those teachings or actively work against them? Does society still celebrate virtue or once again revel in promoting vice? Consider the protests around the deaths in Ferguson and Staten Island, and the protesters calling for the deaths of policemen. Those protests were supported by the mayor of New York City, and the environment he created contributed to the execution of two policeman by a mentally unbalanced individual. And oh yes, we can also count among the many contributions of the state: the takeover of our mental healthcare systems, which has served to reduce the resources required to care for those who are in need of those services. This helps to demonstrate the point that large government is only capable of exceling at incompetence. It is the Renaissance all over again. *Only when governance is kept closest to the people it serves, and a complete education is offered, can society thrive.*

- At the core of issues as far apart as rap music and abortion, isn't the real issue about putting self above others? We've moved from sacrificing for others to focusing on ourselves—our rights over our responsibilities. We should ask ourselves whether just because we are able to do something, should we choose to do it? Consider also the media. While this chapter was being written, on Christmas day of 2014, on the op-ed pages of *The New York Times* there appeared two pro-atheist opinion pieces; there were no opinions supporting any other view. We can also look at our federal government and the extent to which it now performs what should be acts of charity. Unemployment benefits, welfare, child care, rent assistance, social security, education loans and grants (sometimes in return for services after completion), Obamacare, housing assistance, food stamps—the list simply goes on and on. What is worse is that even the perception around these benefits has shifted. Previously they were viewed as a last resort for those who could no longer care for themselves. Now there is a sense of entitlement, a belief that if I meet the rules, the benefit is mine. I simply deserve it. Is there any virtue present in such a notion?

- Finally, we can look at the shift in the roles of the church and state. The State is using the Supreme Court's declaration of "separation of church and state" to forcibly remove the presence of Judeo-Christian values from the public arena—as the State is present, the church cannot be—whether the State has the right to the role it has assumed or not. Some of our leaders have actively advocated for a "freedom to worship" instead of the freedom of religion we were founded with. Collectivists of all stripes are pushing for the state as the be-all and end-all for the solutions to all of our problems. It is man turned once again toward man. It is the return to the rule of the Roman Empire and the divine right of an elite to determine what is in our best interest, because we are incapable of doing so ourselves. They simply point to all of the havoc caused by the very programs they have created for us as examples to justify why those actions are necessary. This is crazy, sheer lunacy. It would be laughable if the stakes were not so high.

Fortunately, it is not too late, but to change things for the better we must first reorient ourselves. We must change the things that we have control over: our actions, our values, and our principles. Once we do that we can make better decisions and begin the work necessary to undo the damage that has been done to our society. That was the purpose of *Do You Want To Be Free?* It was to remind us of what our orientation is meant to be as both individuals and a single people. This work is about what the outcomes of a shift back to our purpose should look like and why. We'll next take a brief look at the biblical basis for charity.

Charity's Biblical Basis

We've looked at charity from philosophical and historical perspectives, and along the way we've mentioned it fulfilling divine law. So what does scripture say about charity? In looking at the *Old Testament*, we can find at least three different forms of charity being defined. These are the following:

1. Giving of first fruits (tithing)

    a. Things from the land (Gen. 4, Exodus 22, Deut. 18, 26)

    b. Livestock and wool (Gen. 4, Exodus 22, Deut. 18)

    c. Sons (Exodus 22)

2. Caring for the widows, orphans, foreigners, and others who are disadvantaged

    a. Not oppress or afflict them (Exodus 22, Lev. 19, Deut. 24)

    b. Not be partial to the poor in administering justice (Exodus 23, Lev. 19)

    c. Will not be unjust toward them (Deut. 24)

    d. Leave some crops in the field so others can glean them (Lev. 19, Deut. 24)

    e. Provide them food and clothing (Deut. 10)

    f. Provide whatever they lack (Deut. 15)

    g. Not take their pledge (security) when lending to the poor (Deut. 24)

      h. Give to them after your tithing (Deut. 26)

3. Years of restoration

      a. The Sabbatic years (every seven years)

           i. The land is to rest (Lev. 25)

           ii. Your kinsmen are to be set free with provisions (Deut. 15)

      b. The year of Jubilee (every fifty years)

           i. Property is to be returned (Lev. 25)

           ii. The poor who have sold themselves, and their families, as slaves, are to be freed (Lev. 25)

           iii. Debts are to be remitted (Deut. 15)

The above is certainly not an exhaustive list, but it is sufficient enough to begin to see several principles emerging. First that we return a portion to our Creator of whatever we have received. This is an acknowledgment that as Creator all things belong to Him. It is also a lesson teaching us the proper value of gifts with which we have been entrusted, that they are really only ours in the sense that we've been given the responsibility for their use. In a word, stewardship.

Second, we are to care for those who do not have enough from our own abundance. This is just an extension of the first lesson above, the fulfillment of the second part of divine law to give to others out of love, just as our Creator gave things to us out of His love for us. As things have been entrusted to us as individuals, giving is therefore an action that must be performed primarily by individuals. "The act of distributing common goods is the office of him who is their guardian ... note that distributive justice may be from the common goods of the family, not the State, and this dispensing can be done by the authority of a private person."[69] Both of these first two ideas have as their primary focus individual sacrifice for another, "wealth redistribution" is merely the by-product of an action—actions based upon voluntary individual actions of charity. Redistribution without voluntary sacrifice produces no virtue, and society is worse off on a number of levels.

Third, there were to be occasions where things were to be restored to those to whom they were originally entrusted. A lesson in mercy from our Creator that specific individuals should not always be in need. Note this was not simply the giving of things to someone like we do today through our entitlement programs, but endowing them with the *means to provide for themselves*. For the Israelites, this restoration was represented by land, freedom, and debt forgiveness. It is not much different for us today. Freedom and debt forgiveness help provide the means, ability, and opportunity to make economic choices for oneself. Land is somewhat different today in the developed world. The similarities are that land still represents a form of wealth, not only in itself but in what it is capable of producing; that is, through our production activities upon the land—our labor—we often create value. More on this as well in the next chapter. Further, the Israelites were the land's stewards, as are we. The primary difference is that for the ancient Israelites, much of what they needed to live came directly from the land: crops, wine, water, meat, leather, clothing, wood, and metal. Today, many of us can earn a living without ever having a direct stake in land. We can create value independent of the land itself. We have also made it a matter of positive law that man should individually own property. Much good has been derived from that notion when it has been properly administered.

It would seem that this third item comes down not necessarily to just land, but rather to having the opportunity to produce those things needed to live. While the means of production can still be associated with the land itself, it could also be equated with the skills derived from education and experience that are the means for an individual achieving their purpose of effectively utilizing their gifts, talents, and abilities. Education has already been mentioned as one of society's most important responsibilities. Not only is this the primary means by which a society perpetuates itself, but it is today the primary means by which one acquires the knowledge, skills, and means of learning a trade or profession. It is very difficult for someone to provide for themselves today without it.

Some charitable organizations, Habitat for Humanity for one, provide a contemporary example of this principle. They provide individuals with the opportunity to acquire home ownership by working for equity and learning to be a responsible owner—in short, the opportunity to learn what it means to be a steward and the responsibilities that come with this role, or the self-transformation of the individual. Human-enlightened transformations lead to nations producing inequity, strife, and dependence. Self-transformation of individuals within the framework outlined above leads to individuals and nations producing greater equality, unity, and independence. But you can only choose one. The choices are mutually exclusive.

Charity within the *New Testament* is at one level very different and at another level similar to the *Old Testament*. Divine law in the *Old Testament* was represented by the outward acts as contained within the Ten Commandments. The *New Testament* boiled these commandments down into only two inward commands: the loving of both Creator and our fellow man.

Characteristics about charity within the *New Testament* include those in the following passages. These are also not exhaustive, but are representative of the *New Testament's* directives.

Charity should

- Provide for the poor/those in need (Matt. 6, 19, Mark 10, Luke 12, 18).
- Come from within (Matt. 5, Luke 11).
- Provide what is needed (Matt. 25).
- Give more than what is asked (Luke 6).
- Expect nothing in return (Luke 6).

- Be revealed by our actions (Matt. 7).

Some behaviors associated with charity include

- Forgiveness (Matt. 18).
- Sacrifice (Luke 21, Rom. 5, 2 Cor. 5, Eph.5).
- Obedience (John 14, 15, 1 John 2, 5).
- Concern with the welfare of all (Rom. 13, 15, Gal. 10).
- Love and compassion (1 Cor. 13).

Finally, charity

- Is recognized by its fruits (Matt. 7, 12, Luke 6).
- Occurs when we are connected to our Creator (John 15).

From the passages above, we are still supposed to provide to others from our abundance. However, it not only matters simply that we give, but the motivation for giving also matters. It is not just the ends but also the means that matters. The why and the how. As mentioned earlier, within the *Old Testament* the giving of land represented a means for providing resources given in charitable actions, and the land belonged to our Creator. Within the *New Testament* it is we who are like the land, by the fruit that our actions bear—and good fruit comes when we are connected with Him.

Summary

Before we leave this chapter, we should summarize some of the main points as they are related to the next several chapters. These were in the areas of charity itself and the relationship between the church and state and included the following:

1. The motivation for performing charity changing from an introspective to an active form.

2. The primary responsibility for performing charity shifting from wealthy individuals alone onto the middle class, and thereby onto the community at large.

3. Those who receive charity becoming a defined group that included travelers, pilgrims, and the poor: those in need. This was later expanded still further to include widows, orphans, the aged, and infirm.

4. The form and control of the charitable institutions changing. These began as many small institutions and evolved into larger ones throughout the Middle Ages and into the Renaissance. These institutions were formed by both religious and lay organizations, but all had a religious motivation for performing acts of charity. With the shift later to larger charitable organizations came a shift in control from individuals to governmental units.

5. The number of charitable organizations growing during the Middle Ages to the point where most towns had one or more charitable organizations to meet local needs.

6. The changes in 1-5 above were supported by the technological advances that occurred during the Middle Ages after the fall of Rome.

These changes to charity reflected shifts that came in the relationship between the spheres of the state and religion, starting with the state religion societies. Initially, the two spheres overlapped to the extent that they were almost one. They were closely connected, and this relationship was emphasized. This changed with the rise of Christianity to one where these two spheres were considered to be separate and equal. Each contested for supremacy over the other, and by the Renaissance these two spheres had once again merged to the point where they had largely overlapped each other, with the State being in control by the Renaissance and Enlightenment. Within the U.S., these spheres were again separated after the War for Independence, but the separation was on a different basis than before. The Founders realized that while these two spheres were to be separate, *the morality that religion instilled within society was necessary in order for society to be successful in the long-term.* In addition, it was necessary for any barrier that did exist to protect religion from the state as they had seen first-hand the corruption that occurred when the state began to control religion.

It appears these two spheres are once again collapsing into overlapping spheres largely controlled by the State. Today we have the Office of Faith-Based and Neighborhood Partnerships, started under the Bush administration, playing a larger role in the facilitation and participation of religious organizations in various efforts using government funding. We also have assistance payments for those deemed in need increasingly coming from the State. These include such income redistribution schemes as welfare, housing subsidies, food subsidies, childcare subsidies, education subsidies, healthcare subsidies, and Medicaid. These efforts go beyond supporting the poor to caring for groups such as the aged (Social Security) and disabled (Disabilities Act). Control once again appears to be passing to the State, but it is not too late to prevent repeating the mistakes of the past.

There were three recurring ideas underlying much of this chapter's contents. These notions were virtue, stewardship, and education. We will cover each of these topics, but first we will take a closer look at the relationship between power and purpose from John Locke's perspective, and the basis for the shifts in Church and State we see occurring in our society today. For if we do not get this relationship right, the rest of it simply will not matter.

Chapter 3: Purpose and Collectivism

> *It does not follow that, if everything be done by divine providence, nothing is within our power. For the effects are foreseen by God, as they are freely produced by us.*
>
> —St. Thomas Aquinas,
> 13th century

The last chapter discussed the belief developed during the Renaissance that the sphere of the State needed to be freed from the Church's influence so that the State could effectively perform its function. Machiavelli wrote that the ruler should secretly be an atheist, outside of the influence of religion, while religion itself was necessary to effectively rule a people. Hobbes wrote that religion should be a civic one, directly under the control of and subservient to the ruler. That ruler would decide doctrine, the contents of religious writings, as well as a service's rituals, contents, and structure. Right and wrong would be decided by the State, and any afterlife would be connected to obedience to the ruler.

We will spend a moment on Benedict (Baruch) Spinoza. Locke drew from both Hobbes and Spinoza in his writings, but Spinoza's thoughts are arguably more radical and the connections to Locke's works more subtle. Spinoza was a Jew who grew up in Amsterdam. A statement of excommunication (herem) was issues against him at age 24. So what were some of his thoughts? First, our Creator is not outside of creation, but is creation.[1] Believing Creator and creation are one is similar to the basis of many Eastern religions and ancient state religion societies; monotheism did not grow within these other religions because their gods were too inconsequential for it to develop. They were impersonal gods created by man. These gods were not able to answer the big questions we have, such as "Who am I?" and "Why am I here?"

Second, if Creator and nature are one, then human actions become displays of Him in action and not doctrine.[2] Creation of the State is the collective action of men, and therefore its most powerful expression.[3] The ends of all such social organizations are security and comfort,[4] and the creation of the State fulfills man's desire for the chief good.[5] The State becomes divine,[6] and its actions become our Creators.[7] Duty to country therefore comes first before all else.[8] Worship and piety alone belong to the individual as inalienable,[9] as man is only free to think and say whatever he thinks.[10] His actions lie within the State. The chief outward expression of religion becomes keeping the public peace and well-being,[11] tolerance, which is where we will pick up the discussion of Locke.

Spinoza's works are important as they provide a basis for today's liberation theology, and form the foundation for collectivism's expressions of social and economic justice. But there is a significant flaw in Spinoza's logic. Justice, including love of neighbor, receive the force of law only through the rights of dominion, solely on the decree of those who have the right to rule, a temporal ruler.[12] Underlying this idea is that our Creator is not sovereign until man acknowledges Him, which is foolishness. Either God is God, and therefore worthy of our worship and obedience, or He is not, in which case it doesn't matter.

All of these writers attempted to address a fundamental problem. They attempted to correct a corruption between the spheres of the Church and State. However, all the solutions just mentioned made the Church subservient to the State in different ways. As we have argued in the last couple of chapters, it is not the Church *or* the State, but the Church *and* the State. All of the thoughts expressed by the above authors are only variations of the elitism inherent in the societal structures provided by the writings of the Greek philosophers such as Plato and Aristotle. Locke selected a different path that lies somewhere between those of the authors mentioned above.

Unlike the authors above, Locke had some influence upon our Founders, although not as great an influence as Montesquieu appears to have had, and we will see that much of Locke's thoughts were variations of earlier writings. Those variations though, are of great importance. Locke relies extensively on the *Bible* in his writing, particularly about Christianity related topics. In addition, it appears that some of his thoughts have carried over into today's prevalent "ism," progressivism. But regardless of the label, it is still the same substance that lies beneath. It is merely a different way of reaching the same end as the others proposed.

There has been wide disagreement over the true nature of Locke's thoughts. One group takes the position that "Locke followed Hobbesian atheism and referred to the Bible exclusively with obscurantist intent."[13] A second group asserts he "was a pious Christian and meant every Biblical reference as they appeared."[14] However, this second group also believed Locke's writing could only be understood in the context of the time he wrote, and therefore wasn't applicable today. A third group asserts Locke's being religious, but rejects the notion that his writing is irrelevant today. The views of all three groups have some basis in truth.

In Locke's worldview, charity lies within the religious sphere, so understanding religious power and its relationship with political power, is relevant to understanding charity from his point of view. The next chapter examines Locke's thoughts on political and religious power, and the relationship between them. In this chapter, we will look at Locke's underlying assertions about Christianity's chief characteristic, man's nature, and the civil societies to be formed by man (commonwealths). These chapters are not meant to disparage Locke's writing, but instead to find the relevant truth within them and integrate it into the discussion at hand. One reason that Edwards' writings are directly relevant is that they were written approximately forty years after Locke's works were published. The main difference between the works of these two men is that Edwards's perspective is aligned with individualism while Locke's thoughts are aligned with collectivism.

Locke added little that was new in the way of governance's purpose, its structures, or man's purpose. Instead he leveraged ideas that had existed for centuries. However, it is not only an idea's structure but the root from which it springs that determines the outcome. We will see that the root of Locke's writing is simply a variation of the authors just mentioned. All of these writings stem from the belief that there can be only one supreme power on the earth. They ignore the idea that there is only one supreme power, this supreme power does not reside on the earth, and that all earthly powers are derived from and intended to be oriented toward this supreme power, regardless of their human source. As such they all start from a false choice. While Locke accepted a more traditional starting point, we will see the conditions he places on the Church also makes it subservient to the State, again making the State the supreme power on earth.

While much has already been written interpreting Locke's works, I prefer to go directly to his writings and let him tell us. These two chapters will therefore contain quotes from a few of his relevant works, and quotes from earlier writers who present positions either consistent or contrary to his. Once again, summaries of these materials will be presented at the end of both chapters for those who do not wish to go through the details.

John Locke lived during the last half of the seventeenth century, about one hundred years after the reign of Henry VIII and the creation of the Church of England. He attended Christ Church College at Oxford, and after completing his education took a teaching position at the university. He saw firsthand the conflict between the church and state, and the corruption that had occurred within England's church and government. A corruption that led to intolerance and persecution and led many, including Jonathan Edward's family, to leave England for the American colonies.

Locke's Works

We will look at three of Locke's works. All quotes containing italics are as they appear in the quoted sources. Locke's *First Treatise of Government*[15] is written to destroy all of the arguments then cited supporting hereditary rule by sovereigns, and he covers those arguments one at a time in fairly extensive detail. His *Second Treatise of Government*[16] outlines his vision of the proper role between civil and religious society. But this later treatise cannot be fully appreciated without referring to another of his works, *A Letter Concerning Toleration*[17] *(Letter)*, where he goes into more detail about his thoughts regarding religious society. Religious persecution was common in Locke's day, and he often quoted from the *Bible* in affirming his position.

These areas present a lot of ground to cover, but it is important to understand the similarities and differences between Locke's ideas and those of the early church fathers, as the former provides much of the basis for the collectivism policies we see today, and are merely a repetition of what occurred during the Renaissance. So often, history repeats itself. Isn't there a desire by an elitist group today to move to a single world governance where no state sovereignty exists and government performs charity's function? This is man looking to himself again and creating structures that are contrary to charity's—and therefore man's own—nature, limiting a people's ability to fulfill its purpose, and undercutting a society's moral basis, leading that society to fail in the long-run. In addition, as we saw in the last chapter, it ignores the fact that a single world governance already exists, one whose acceptance is voluntary on our part.

As many of the ideas expressed are somewhat complex, and at times contradictory, we will conclude these next two chapters with a summary and an extension of some of the materials presented in the last chapter.

Christianity's Chief Characteristic

This goes to the heart of our purpose. Locke's *Letter* is his response to a question he was asked about the importance of "mutual toleration of Christians in their different professions of religion." He answered, "I esteem that toleration to be the chief characteristical mark of the true church."[18] The definition of a characteristic is a trait. If Locke is correct that toleration is the chief characteristic of the true church, then that should be its chief or primary trait. He states that the outward characteristics such as antiquity of places, pomp in their outward worship, doctrines, rites, etc. are not the signs of the true church. Rather the business of the true church is "the regulating of men's lives according to the rules of virtue and piety,"[19] the governance of man's spiritual aspects, including instilling the virtue required for charity.

Virtue underlies all charity and if one "be destitute of charity, meekness, and goodwill in general towards all mankind, even to those that are not Christians, he is certainly yet short of being a true Christian himself."[20] For "No man can be a Christian without charity, and without that faith which works, not by force, but by love."[21] His opening remark in the paragraph above and the last remarks appear to contradict each other, for if one cannot be a Christian without exhibiting charity, then isn't charity the chief characteristic of the true church? And as we've already seen, charity is the expression of love; therefore, the true church's chief characteristic mark should be love and not mere tolerance. After all, if one loves then his love should express tolerance, but the reverse is not necessarily true. Just because one shows tolerance does not mean that it is shown out of love; it may simply be an action performed out of compliance or expedience while inside loathing the individual or group shown toleration.

What does Locke mean when he refers to charity? He gives us an idea in his *First Treatise*:

> But we know God hath not left one Man so to the Mercy of another, that he may starve him if he please: God the

> Lord and Father of all, has given no one of his Children such a Property, in his peculiar Portion of the things of this World, but that he has given his needy Brother a Right to the Surplusage of his Goods; so that it cannot justly be denied him, when his pressing Wants call for it. And therefore no Man could ever have a just Power over the Life of another, by Right of property in Land or Possessions; since 'twould always be a Sin in any Man of Estate, to let his Brother perish for want of affording him Relief out of his Plenty. As *Justice* gives every Man a Title to the product of his honest Industry, and the fair Acquisitions of his Ancestors descended to him; So *Charity* gives every Man a Title to so much out of another's Plenty, as will keep him from extream want where he has no means to subsist otherwise.[22]

This is a view of charity grounded in the *Old Testament*. Many of Locke's biblical references concerning property and charity are to Deuteronomy and Leviticus. As discussed in the last chapter, under this view all things belong to our Creator and man has been given stewardship of creation. Second, we are to care for those in want out of our own abundance; this notion is consistent with both St. Thomas's and Edwards's writings. Locke is silent, though, as to the charitable restoration of land mandated by the *Old Testament*. This is not surprising since at this point land ownership was a matter of positive law, a concept that was also expressed by Thomas. Finally this view looks upon charity as an entitlement, a view of charity characteristic of the High Middle Ages and Renaissance, the view that the community owed charity as a form of moral restitution. However, Locke's view ignores the change from the *Old Testament* concerning charity that action alone is insufficient, the motivation also matters.

He goes on to discuss those who are persecuted for their religious beliefs: "When I shall see them [the persecutors] thus express their love and desire of the salvation of their souls by the infliction of torments, and exercise of all manner of cruelties. For if it be out of a principle of charity as they pretend, and love to men's souls, that they deprive them of their estates, maim them with corporal punishments, starve and torment them in noisome prisons, and in the end even take away their lives, I say, if all this be done merely to make men Christians, and procure their salvation, why then do they suffer 'whoredome, fraud, malice, and such like enormities'?"[23]

This persecution was carried out in the name of charity, but it was of course not charity. Instead it was an extension of the Renaissance municipal governments assuming control of charities and directing their actions, the attempt to forcibly change a recipient's behavior as a condition for receiving charity, a direct result of the very control advocated by collectivism for the State over the Church, with our Creator's morality becoming replaced by man's. In this case the notion underlying the persecution had been enlarged to cover not only people's behavior, but their beliefs as well, a further corruption of the State and Church spheres. What has been omitted from this line of thought is the freedom of choice with which we have each been gifted. By taking away that freedom there can be no virtue, and without virtue there can be no charity. Instead what we have is vice parading as virtue because of its stated end goal, a hallmark of all forms of collectivism. We will talk more about this in the next chapter concerning the relationship between civil and religious power.

He next asks why, if true charity is professed to exist, do we have so many expressions of cruelties, torments, and corruptions present within communities that claim to be Christian?[24] This is a good question, and he lays out the problem as follows:

> Whosoever, therefore, is sincerely solicitous about the kingdom of God, and thinks it his duty to endeavor the enlargement of it amongst men, ought to apply himself with no less care and industry to the rooting out of these immoralities, than to the extirpation of sects. But if any one do otherwise, and, whilst he is cruel and implacable towards those that differ from him in opinion, he be

indulgent to such iniquities and immoralities as are unbecoming the name of Christian, let such a one talk ever so much of the church, he plainly demonstrates by his actions, that it is another kingdom he aims at, and not the advancement of the kingdom of God.

That any man should think fit to cause another man, whose salvation he heartily desires, to expire in torments, and that even in an unconverted estate, would I confess, seem very strange to me, and, I think, to any other also. But nobody, surely, will ever believe that such a carriage can proceed from charity, love, or goodwill. If any one maintain that men ought to be compelled by fire and sword to profess certain doctrines, and conform to this or that exterior worship, without any regard had unto their morals; if any one endeavor to convert those that are erroneous unto the faith, by forcing them to profess things that they do not believe, and allowing them to practice things that the Gospel does not permit; it cannot be doubted, indeed, that such a one is desirous to have a numerous assembly joined in the same profession with himself.[25]

I agree with the above passage: if love is truly present within the Church then we should find greater unity, not less. Instead, immoral means were used for achieving what was proclaimed to be a moral end. There are several examples we can cite from today that demonstrate this same practice of creating division by dictating doctrine is alive and well. These examples include the Occupy Wall Street and Black Lives Matter movements that attempt to stifle any deviation from their viewpoints. The difference is in this: these groups are not attempting to convert someone from one religious sect to another, but rather that they are attempting to impose a secularism where religion, and the morality the latter conveys, has no place. They purport to represent your betters and know what you should believe, because you simply are not capable of making correct decisions for yourself. It is once again vice proclaiming itself as virtue because of its stated end. This is pure arrogance and evil, a variation of the individual pointing toward faith and love while practicing vice. These do not reside within the city of God, but rather within the city of man, as Rome did and as arose again during the Renaissance.

From the preceding passage, Locke goes on to state that "everyone is orthodox to himself."[26] Orthodoxy is defined as correct belief. If Locke's statement is true, then can't an individual have whatever beliefs they wish? Aren't those groups mentioned in the previous paragraphs then just expressing their own orthodoxy, one which has a basis in truth? Of course this is not true, and Locke indicated as much earlier. In his *Second Treatise*, Locke repeatedly refers to the need to comply with the Law of Nature within the sphere of governance, and Locke defines the Law of Nature to be "the Will of God."[27] An individual's belief must therefore align with the will of our Creator. It is in understanding His will that man often fails by turning to his own needs and wants rather than his Creator's directives. What is up to each of us is whether we decide to obey.

But we can examine this same idea by another approach. Locke's statement about orthodoxy applied to the Church. What happens if we apply it to the State instead? After all, Plato in his *Dialogues* states that "the good are a law unto themselves."[28] So therefore, should not everyone be subject to their own rule? Of course not, this would be pure anarchy. But if this is rejected on that basis for man's governance, why would it be any different towards our Creator's governance? Surely that is even more binding as we are all a part of His creation—we belong to Him as Locke admitted.[29]

Locke also states that every man's soul belongs to himself, in respect to the decisions we each make: our free will. "Seeing one man does not violate the right of another, by his erroneous opinions, and undue manner of worship, nor is his perdition any prejudice to another man's affairs; therefore the care of each man's salvation belongs only to himself."[30] This is true. However, as Clement stated, our souls are shaped by the choices we each make. For "the individual man is stamped according to the impression produced in the soul by the objects of his choice ... the cause lay in his choosing and especially in his choosing what was forbidden. God was not the cause."[31] So while our choices are ours, orthodoxy is not; it belongs to the realm of our Creator alone.

The responsibility for our choices cannot be delegated to anyone else, even to someone in a position of responsibility. From Locke again: "Nor when an incensed Deity shall ask us, "Who has required these or such like things at your hands?" will it be enough to answer him, that the magistrate commanded them."[32] This view is echoed in Thomas Jefferson's words: "But our rulers can have authority over such natural rights only as we have submitted to them. The rights of conscience we never submitted, we could not submit. We are answerable for them to our God. The legitimate powers of government extend to such acts only as are injurious to others."[33] In other words, the powers of government extend to acts of justice. Neither the Church nor the State can have authority over what our Creator has commanded.

Locke makes a final point that there is a priority each man has in taking care of his soul: "The principal and chief care of every one ought to be of his own soul first, and, in the next place, of the public peace."[34] It is true that we each are responsible for our own soul, but I would suggest that the order between self and another is not an either/or priority, but is concurrent. It is by taking care of another first, through actions that are truly charitable, that we both truly care for another's soul and our own at the same time, by showing love. Locke's statement places self above others, an indication that his statement is not anchored in truth.

Locke's statements indicate a belief that we are only called as individuals to the tenets he has outlined for the true church, and that those beliefs are up to the individual to largely determine. However, this ignores the dual calling that we have as both individuals and as the people of God[35] from 1 Peter in the *Bible*. To be a people requires both an agreed upon set of rights and a shared commitment to the common good, as previously mentioned. In short, we cannot simply be orthodox to ourselves for we must also have a common set of shared precepts as a people that are based upon our Creator's will. Individual belief is a necessary, but insufficient, condition in itself. Being united as one people in alignment with our Creator's will is also required. This principle was outlined previously in Edward's works.

Man's Natural State

This is an important topic, because if man's nature or the relationship he has with his Creator or fellow man are not correctly stated, then any conclusions drawn from those arguments are not well supported. In this section we will look at Locke's statements about man's nature, and the implications of that nature, both between man and Creator and between one human being and another. Finally, we will briefly examine the related topics of freedom, law, private property, and why men choose to give up their natural state as described by Locke.

Locke's discussion of man's nature is grounded in Hobbes' State of Nature and is described in chapter two of his *Second Treatise* as follows: "We must consider what State all Men are naturally in, and that is a State of perfect Freedom to order their Actions, and dispose of their Possessions, and Persons as they think fit, within the bounds of the Law of Nature, without asking leave, or depending upon the Will of any other Man."[36] Locke asserts that this State of Nature is the natural state into which all men are born.

Recall that he defines the "Law of Nature" to be the "Will of God." Within this State of Nature, a State of Equality also exists "wherein all the Power and Jurisdiction is reciprocal, no one having more than another."[37] Further, "though this be a *State of Liberty*, yet it is *not a State of Licence*, though Man in that State have an uncontroleable Liberty, to dispose of his Person or Possessions, yet he has not Liberty to destroy himself, or so much as any Creature in his Possession, but where some nobler use, than its bare Preservation calls for it. The *State of Nature* has a Law of Nature to govern it, which obliges every one:

And Reason, which is that Law, teaches all Mankind, who will be consult it, that being all equal and independent, no one ought to harm another in his Life, Health, Liberty, or Possessions. For Men being all the Workmanship of one Omnipotent ... they are his Property."[38]

From the preceding passages we can draw the following principles. First, that we all have the same nature and ability to exercise it as no one has been given more power than another. Second, while we have the freedom to act in our own interest, we have an obligation not to destroy that which has been entrusted to our care, except in extreme circumstances where a nobler purpose exists. Third, our Creator's will governs over this *State of Nature*, that as we are a part of His creation we therefore all belong to Him and therefore should do no harm to another. Fourth, reason alone is the law that teaches all mankind.

As to the equality of man's nature, there is no disagreement; all have been given the same nature as we have all been created by the same Creator, and all are Adam's descendants. As to the second item, we are called to stewardship in regards to the things that have been entrusted to us. In the end, none of these material things are really ours under divine law. Even the land belongs to our Creator, its maker. It is only by positive law that man's ownership of things is derived, for man's benefit.[39] Locke is presenting only half the issue as labor alone is insufficient to change ownership from something held in common to private ownership, except as an addition to natural law as private ownership of material items is not inherent in nature itself.

There are certainly instances where we may need to destroy something to preserve ourselves or rid ourselves of some good because it is to our greater benefit, but this is not the most common situation that we find. Our real calling in this area is the preservation of material things, not just for ourselves, but for the good of others, both in the present and those to come after us. In discussing man's competencies for doing this, Thomas stated, "Man's other competence is to use and manage the world's resources. Now in regard to this, no man is entitled to manage things merely for himself, he must do so in the interest of all, so that he is ready to share them with others in case of necessity."[40] Again the focus is on self *and* others. Locke takes the perspective that charity is a moral entitlement, a focus on self, both from the perspective of the giver and receiver. This is the very opposite of what is taught in the Gospel and referred to by Edwards.

For the third item, everything that has ever been created has been created by our Creator. As Edwards previously stated, in one sense we belong to him as He is our Creator. However, in a second sense accepting His governance is something we must choose for ourselves. Both are needed, but Lock appears to be looking only at the first part, as though the second part either did not exist or that our Creator is not actively involved in man's affairs. But this cannot be true if His Providence is active taking even our bad choices and turning them to His good as expressed by both Clement and Augustine.[41] Locke appears to be expressing a form of deism.

Locke is largely silent on man's knowledge of His Creator. But in the words of Clement, "It is then, as appears, the greatest of all lessons to know one's self. For if one knows himself, he will know God; and knowing God, he will be made like God, not by wearing gold or long robes, but by well doing, and by requiring as few things as possible."[42] Man is not just to exist for himself, but for the benefit of others. That is his natural state. Aren't we called to sacrifice ourselves for another, even to the point of death if it is for the common good? Isn't that why people enlist in military service, police and firemen serve those in their communities, and even strangers at times sacrifice themselves to save someone that they do not even know? While it is up to each of us to decide our course of action, it would appear the higher course is to be willing to lay down one's life for the greater good if needed, simply out of love for another.

As to reason alone being sufficient for man, this assertion also appears to fall short. What of faith? Faith is belief in our Creator, a virtue as outlined in Chapter 1. In the words of Clement of Alexandria, "Virtue is a will in conformity to God and Christ in life ... a system of reasonable actions—that is, of those things taught by the Word—an unfailing energy which we have called faith. The system is the commandments of the Lord, which, being divine statutes and spiritual counsels, have been written for ourselves, being adapted for ourselves and our neighbours."[43] To rely on reason alone indicates that all things can be proven, but how can the infinite be proved by the finite? How can the Law of Nature be known without coming to know its Creator?

According to the model put forth earlier, all actions ending in charity begin as acts of faith. All virtues end in charity, but knowledge is required in the exercise of reason that leads to virtue's development, and all charity is fulfillment of law, our voluntary compliance with our Creator's governance. From Clement: "For he who is wise will live concentrating all his energies on knowledge, directing his life by good deeds, despising the opposite, and following the pursuits which contribute to truth. And the law is not what is decided by law (for what is seen is not vision), nor every opinion (not certainly what is evil). But law is the opinion which is good, and what is good is that which is true, and what is true is that which finds "true being" and attains to it."[44]

Truth comes from our Creator, He who governs our natural state. It is by coming to know Him that we acquire knowledge. He is the Good, First Cause, and therefore he cannot be demonstrated. Instead knowing Him requires both reason and faith, reason alone is insufficient to know Him. Our nature is such that we have the capacity to know Him, if we should choose to use it. We are not born with understanding this truth any more than we are born already possessing virtue, both must be acquired and integrated into the nature we've been given through knowledge and exercise: "The sure seal of knowledge is composed of nature, education, and exercise."[45] A nature grounded in love, an education in reason and faith, and the exercise thereof to develop virtue in the fulfillment of our purpose.

Man's Relationships

We can now turn to the second part of divine law, Locke's views on one man's duty to another. He states, "Every one as he is *bound to preserve himself*, and not to quit his Station willfully; so by the like reason when his own Preservation comes not in competition, ought he, as much as he can, *to preserve the rest of Mankind*, and may not unless it be to do Justice on an Offender, take away, or impair the life, or what tends to the Preservation of the Life, the Liberty, Health, Limb or Goods of another."[46] Further, "And that all Men may be restrained from invading others Rights, and from doing hurt to one another, and the Law of Nature be observed, which willeth the Peace and *Preservation of all Mankind*, the *Execution* of the Law of Nature is in that State put into every Mans hands, whereby every one has a right to punish the transgressors of that Law to such a Degree, as may hinder its Violation."[47] "[For] in transgressing the Law of Nature, the Offender declares himself to live by another Rule, than that of *reason* and common Equity."[48] "From these *two distinct Rights*, the one of *Punishing* ... the other of taking *reparation* ... comes it to pass that the Magistrate ... hath the common right of punishing put into his hands."[49]

The following principles are contained within the preceding paragraph. First, man is bound to preserve himself. Second, he is to care for others to the extent that it does not compete with the first notion. Third, he is not to harm another except to do justice, for the Law of Nature includes the preservation of all mankind. Fourth, the Law of Nature is placed within every man's hand, and therefore each man has the right of punishment and reparation. Fifth, that the preceding provides the basis for a Magistrate's punishment of another. These ideas appear to present a contradiction. On one hand, each man has the Law of Nature in his hand, and everyone is orthodox unto himself. But on the other hand, Locke refers to the Law of Nature as something singular, and we have only one Creator. You cannot have it both ways.

We have already briefly discussed the first two items. I would add here that Locke's view is bound up in self and only secondarily concerned with the welfare of others. This appears to be a form of individual elitism that is in direct contradiction to the ideas expressed above and the instructions provided in the *Gospels*. "For whoever wishes to save his life will lose it; but whoever loses his life for My sake will find it."[50] We are all sojourners and should assist others on the way to our final destination. Locke's words would seem to indicate that there is nothing beyond what we possess in this current life, although he also clearly argues this is not so. Let me also add this, not only does the Law of Nature include the rights of punishment and reparation, but also voluntarily accepting the obligation of obedience, another virtue.

The remaining ideas all have to do with justice. Justice is simply the virtue whereby each person is given what they are due. If everyone followed the Law of Nature Locke speaks of, there would be little, if any, need for justice. However, some people choose not to do what is right. They live according to themselves and not the Law of Nature, for our Creator is by definition just. From Clement: "God is good on his own account, and just also on ours; and He is just because He is good. And His justice is shown to us by His own Word from there from above, when the Father was. For before He became Creator He was God; He was Good."[51]

It is man's wrong choices, exercised through his own free-will, that result in the need for justice. In the words of Augustine, "For it is the wrongdoing of the opposing party which compels the wise man to wage just wars; and this wrong-doing, even though it gave rise to no war, would still be a matter of grief to man because it is man's wrong-doing. Let every one, then, who thinks with pain on all these great evils, so horrible, so ruthless, acknowledge that this is misery. And if any one either endures or thinks of them without mental pain, this is a more miserable plight still, for he thinks himself happy because he has lost human feeling."[52]

The exercise of justice in the *Bible* was given to judges who were to be selected from the people. They were to exercise righteous judgment and to pursue only justice.[53] The judge had the right of punishment granted to him, but it was a right given to him solely due to man's inability to live in righteousness, and the judge himself would be held in judgment for the justice he rendered. From Clement again: "For the judge must be master of his own opinion—not pulled by strings, like inanimate machines, set in motion only by external causes. Accordingly he is judged in respect to his judgment, as we also, in accordance with our choice of things desirable, and our endurance."[54]

Clement stated there are three causes of the need for punishment: (1) so that an individual may become better than their former self, (2) those who are capable of being saved by example may be driven back, and (3) that the person injured may not be despised and apt to receive injury.[55] The capability of punishment has been given to individuals chosen by the people, with powers delegated by the people, in order to establish justice in instances where someone chooses to act in an unjust manner. It is the primary purpose of law to prevent acts of injustice that cause harm to another. It is the primary purpose of justice to set things right, so far as we are able. Locke asserts the negatives of punishment, but does not mention the good that should also be derived from the need for its use.

Since Locke equates the "Law of Nature" with the "Will of God," it follows that natural law must proceed from divine will. This agrees with the church fathers. In the words of Thomas Aquinas, "Divine and natural law proceed from the divine will ... and hence cannot be altered by custom proceeding from the will of man; change can come only by divine authority. Accordingly no custom can acquire the force of law against divine or natural law."[56] There is also a distinction which must be made in regard to the natural rights arising from natural law as either divine or human law is required in its application.[57]

From Thomas again: "You speak of something being according to natural right in two ways. The first is because nature is set that way; thus the command that no harm should be done to another. The second is because nature does not bid the contrary; thus we might say that it is of natural law for man to be naked, for nature does not give him clothes;

these he has to make by art. In this way common ownership and universal liberty are said to be of natural law, because private property and slavery exist by human contrivance for the convenience of social life, and not by natural law. This does not change the law of nature except by addition."[58]

We have two sources of natural rights. The first arises from natural law itself as "nature is set that way." The second is a change that man himself makes to natural law, which can be by either addition or subtraction, but any change must be in accordance with the law of nature. Much of what Locke writes about is not the law of nature arising from nature itself, but the natural law *that has been developed by man because nature does not forbid it*. These are not the same things. And we can see some of man's additions lead to immoral acts; consider slavery.

Finally, in regards to man himself, Locke states that, "Truth and keeping of Faith belongs to Men, as Men, and not as Members of Society."[59] This is true in itself, but incomplete as collectively we are also called to be not only a people, but the People of God as discussed before. This means that we are to be a single people with respect to the law of nature. This idea is at the heart of some of the points made by Jonathan Edwards in the previous chapter. We are called to charity as individuals as well as a people. Individually keeping faith is also a necessary, but insufficient, condition for the long-term success of a morally just society.

Other Related Items

There are four more points that we will discuss before moving to the next topic of the Commonwealth. These are man and freedom, private property, the role of law, and why men form societies. In regards to freedom Locke states, "We are *born Free*, as we are born Rational."[60] We are each born with the freedom that comes from the free will with which we have been gifted. The rationality we have been given is our Creator's image. It is only a capacity, for we are not born with knowledge of what is rational. Just as with virtue, being able to exercise rationality requires education and practice; it requires attaining the virtue of wisdom.

Per Locke, we are also born with at least two rights: "Every Man is born with a double Right: First, *A Right of Freedom to his Person*, which no other Man has a Power over, but the free Disposal of it lies in himself. Secondly, *A Right*, before any other Man, to *Inherit*, with his Brethren, his Fathers Goods."[61] It should be noted again that this first right comes from nature, while the second right is man's addition to nature. Therefore, while the first is a right in itself, the second is only a right as long as it is in accordance with the law of nature. Thus it is that the practices of hoarding and poor stewardship are morally wrong as these prohibitions come to us through divine law (see Chapter 2).

While men are born free, Locke cites two exceptions whereby this freedom is restricted. The first is that of a servant, where an individual grants another some authority over him for some period of time in return for wages. This is usually a temporary condition, it does not result in the loss of all freedom, and it is limited in scope to the specific contract between the parties. The second exception is that of slavery: "But there is another sort of Servant, which by a peculiar Name we call *Slaves*, who being Captives taken in a just war, are by the Right of Nature subjected to the Absolute Dominion and Arbitrary Power of their Masters. These Men having, as I say, forfeited their Lives, and with it their Liberties, and lost their Estates; and being in the *State of Slavery*, not capable of any Property, cannot in that state be considered as any part of *Civil Society*; the chief end whereof is the preservation of Property."[62]

Is this true? It certainly is consistent with history and the writings of the Greek philosophers such as Plato and Aristotle, but as stated earlier it is not by nature but by man's making an addition to natural law that this condition exists. I would suggest that slavery is not in accordance with the law of nature. Slavery in the biblical sense was more akin to indentured servitude. It was only in the state religion societies, such as Rome, that the status of slavery existed, and within Israel after it had turned away from its Creator. It is only with the Renaissance's "enlightenment" that we again had a rise in slavery, a rise concurrent with Islam and the development of the Ottoman Empire.

There are also many passages within the *Bible* relating to the virtues of mercy and forgiveness that run contrary to the notion of slavery. Man makes just war on another when the other party has acted without righteousness and is turned toward self rather than their Creator. But if they repent and turn again toward their Creator, then are they not to be forgiven? "You have heard that it was said, "You shall love your neighbor and hate your enemy." But I say to you, love your enemies and pray for those who persecute you."[63] If the premise of Locke's statement is false, can its conclusion be true?

In regards to property, Locke states that our Creator gave to all men in common, and it is through man's labor that he has come to have property. "How Men might come to have a *property* in several parts of that which God gave to Mankind in common."[64] "Whatsoever then he removes out of the State that Nature hath provided, and left it in, he hath mixed his *Labour* with, and joined to it something that is his own, and thereby makes it his *Property*."[65] So why were these things given to us? According to Locke, they are simply for our enjoyment. *"God has given us all things richly ... But how far has he given it us? To enjoy."*[66] "And thus, I think, it is very easie to conceive without any difficulty, *how Labour could at first begin a title of Property* in the common things of Nature, and how the spending it upon our uses bounded it."[67] Is this true? It would be if this life were all that there is, an end state in itself. But it is not, and the *Bible* that Locke often uses to defend his position says so repeatedly. According to Clement, these things of the earth were all given for our use[68] to assist us on the way to our final destination.[69] As such, we are called to be judicious in our use of them and exercise stewardship so that there are sufficient resources for those who come after us, *a form of charity across time*.

As to the third item, Locke starts discussing the role of law by defining the type of equality that exists between men, as men are not equal in all ways: "*That all Men by Nature are equal*, I cannot be supposed to understand all sorts of *Equality*: *Age or Virtue* may give Men a just Precedency: *Excellency of Parts and Merit* may place others above the Common Level: *Birth* may subject some, and *Alliance* or *Benefits* others, to pay an Observance to those to whom Nature, Gratitude or other Respects may have made it due; and yet all this consist with the *Equality*, which all Men are in, in respect of Jurisdiction or Dominion one over another, which was the *Equality* I there spoke of, as proper to the Business in hand, being that *equal* Right that every Man hath, *to his Natural freedom*."[70] This law consists of the law of reason. "The Law that was to govern *Adam*, was the same that was to govern all his Posterity, the *Law of Reason*."[71] Locke further explains this as, "The *Freedom* then of Man and Liberty of acting according to his own Will, is *grounded on* his having *Reason*, which is able to instruct him in that Law he is to govern himself by, and make him know how far he is left to the freedom of this own will."[72]

Let's unpack this a bit. His first point is that all men are equal by their nature and the rights they have received. Second, the law of reason alone is to govern man. Third, that man's innate freedom is to be grounded within this reason. Locke asserts that freedom cannot exist without law. "For in all the states of created beings capable of Laws, *where there is no law, there is no Freedom*. For Liberty is to be free from restraint and violence from others which cannot be, where there is no Law."[73] This is not the same notion of liberty or freedom as defined by the early church fathers or this country's Founders. As our freedom is innate, it is more accurate to say that there cannot be justice without law, just as there cannot be justice without virtue. Our freedom does not come from any law but divine law. Freedom of choice always exists, it is just that the penalties prescribed by the law may be intended to constrain certain types of choices to a greater degree.

Our Founder's definition of liberty is a specific type of freedom from the oppression, tyranny, or domination of a governing force. In short, it is political independence. However Locke states, "For *Law*, in its true Notion, is not so much the limitation as the *direction of a free and intelligent Agent* to his proper Interest."[74] These statements about law appear to contradict Locke's earlier statements regarding man having freedom by nature, that free will is freedom. Instead it indicates once man enters into a society that freedom comes from outside oneself instead of from the innate free will we have each been gifted with by our Creator, a notion inherent in all forms of collectivism, and not individualism's model. It makes no difference as to whether it is labeled a "direction" and not a "limitation." As stated earlier, natural law is applied using either divine or human law. Divine law by its very nature is just as it comes from our Creator. Thomas stated the purpose of human law is to be useful to men as it should be, "consistent with religion as corresponding with divine law, that it agrees with good discipline as corresponding to natural law, and that it furthers our welfare as corresponding to human usefulness."[75] It is to aid in providing the common good, creating an environment supportive of individual charitable acts and not controlling it from without.

Also from Thomas regarding human law: "Human laws are either just or unjust. If they are just, they have binding force in the court of conscience from the Eternal Law from which they derive ... Now laws are said to be just on three counts; from their end, when they are ordered to the common good, from their authority, when what is enacted does not exceed the lawgiver's power, and from their form, when for the good of the whole they place burdens in equitable proportion on subjects."[76] "Laws are unjust in two ways, as being against what is fair in human terms and against God's rights. They are contrary to human good on the three counts made above; from their end ... from their author ... and from their form ... These are outrages rather than laws."[77]

Why are laws unjust? "Laws can be unjust because they are contrary to God's rights; such are the laws of tyrants which promote idolatry or whatsoever is against divine law. To observe them is in no wise permissible ... *We must obey God rather than men*."[78] So while human law does provide direction, it normally does this by placing a limitation on something which is either contrary to divine law, runs contrary to the common good, or exceeds the lawgiver's authority. Locke would seem to agree. "Obedience is due in the first place to God, and afterwards to the laws."[79] However, freedom does not come from obedience to law but rather obedience to Locke's law of nature—the will of our Creator. This is the direction, but it is subject to an individual's free choice.

So if all of the above is true, why do men form societies? According to Locke, "To avoid this State of War ... is one great *reason of Men's putting themselves into Society*, and quitting the State of Nature."[80] However, not all forms of governance lead to men's quitting the State of Nature, but only those formed with the consent of the governed. "For 'tis not every Compact that puts an end to the State of Nature between Men, but only this one of agreeing together mutually to enter into one Community, and make one Body Politick."[81] "It being reasonable and just I should have a Right to destroy that which threatens me with Destruction."[82] So men form themselves into a society in order to avoid the state of war, but thereby also leave the state of nature just described.

The section *Commonwealths and Civil Society* discusses the structure men place themselves under when leaving the state of nature. But before that a question: When do human beings define a threat? Is it when someone says they will destroy you, when they mass an army at your border, when they invade your country, or merely when you view them in your own mind as a threat? According to Locke's definition, all of the preceding would provide reasons for the destruction of another, but I would submit that at most only the first three cases should be considered a threat for a just war, and it would likely be difficult to support the first case where mere words alone are used to threaten. It would appear that words would also need to be supported by some meaningful action.

Finally, in terms of the power, "No body can give more Power than he has himself; and he that cannot take away his own Life, cannot give another power over it."[83] Locke makes distinctions between liberty and freedom where man is in his natural state or has placed himself within a society. "The *Natural Liberty* of Man is to be free from any Superior Power on Earth, and not to be under the Will or Legislative Authority of Man, but to have only the Law of Nature for his Rule. The *Liberty of Man, in Society*, is to be under no other Legislative Power but that established, by consent, in the Common-wealth, nor under the Dominion of any Will, or Restraint of any Law, but what the Legislative shall enact, according to the Trust put in it."[84] It would appear that man turns away from the law of nature to a legislative power created by his own consent when he enters into a society. Does this differ from Augustine's city of man if faith is not included, or unless divine law is either incorporated in its principles or looked at to guide a common-wealth's creation?

In regards to freedom, "*Freedom of Men under Government*, is, to have a standing Rule to live by, common to every one of that Society, and made by the Legislative Power erected in it; A Liberty to follow my own Will in all things, where the Rule prescribes not; and not to be subject to the inconstant, uncertain, unknown, Arbitrary Will of another Man. As *Freedom of Nature* is to be under no other restraint but the Law of Nature."[85] It is with freedom as it was above with liberty. Man turns away from the law of nature to human law. This is the city of man, no matter how it is dressed up. It is the acknowledgement of our Creator, but then turning toward ourselves anyway; otherwise, the distinctions Locke draws would not be needed. It is the same type of elitism found at the heart of Greek philosophy and must sooner or later lead to the same outcome.

But what does Locke mean by a commonwealth, what is it and from what does it derive its power? These lead to a discussion of a Commonwealth, which is next.

Commonwealths and Civil Society

So what is a commonwealth? First, it is not a democracy. "By *Common-wealth*, I must be understood all along to mean, not a Democracy, or any Form of Government, but *any Independent Community* which the *Latines* signified by the word *Civitas*."[86] Second, it is men living together where no force is made one upon another. It is a form of governance created by the mutual consent of those to be governed. According to Locke, it "is a society of men constituted only for the procuring, preserving, and advancing their own civil interests."[87] "Civil interest I call life, liberty, health, and indolency of body; and the possession of outward things, such as money, lands, houses, furniture, and the like."[88] "The possession of all outward goods is subject to his (the Magistrate's) jurisdiction,"[89] so civil interests are the domain of the State. This interest includes both a man's goods and his person. "By *Property* I must be understood here, as in other places, to mean that Property which Men have in their Persons as well as Goods."[90]

There are several implications that arise from men freely agreeing to form a commonwealth. First, "When any number of Men have so *consented to make one Community* or Government, they are thereby presently incorporated, and make *one Body Politick*, wherein the *Majority* have a Right to act and conclude the rest."[91] Second, Locke's State of War ceases to exist when men enter into a compact creating a commonwealth. This makes men the masters of their own person once again, and "He that is Master of himself, and his own Life, has a right too to the means of preserving it, so that *as soon as Compact enters, Slavery ceases.*"[92] "For no body can desire to *have me in his Absolute Power*, unless it be to compel me by force to that, which is against the Right of my Freedom, i.e. make me a Slave."[93] For in the state of nature, "Men being, as has been said, by Nature, all free, equal and independent, no one can be put out of this Estate, and subjected to the Political Power of another, without his own *Consent*."[94]

There are three underlying reasons why men are willing to unite themselves "into Commonwealths, and putting themselves under Government, *[for] the Preservation of their Property.* To which in the state of Nature there are many things wanting.

> 1. *First*, There wants an *establish'd*, settled, known *Law*, received and allowed by common consent to be the Standard of Right and Wrong, and the common measure to decide all Controversies between them …

2. *Secondly,* In the State of Nature there wants *a known and indifferent Judge*, with Authority to determine all differences according to the established Law ...

3. *Thirdly,* In the state of Nature there often wants *Power* to back and support the Sentence when right, and to *give* it due *Execution.*"[95]

It is man's deciding to unite into a single society that removes them from the state of nature and puts them into a civil society. "Where-ever therefore any number of Men are so united into one Society, as to quit every one his Executive Power of the Law of Nature, and to resign it to the publick, there and there only is a *Political, or Civil Society* ... And this puts men out of a State of Nature *into* that of a *Commonwealth*, by setting up a Judge on Earth, with Authority to determine all the Controversies, and redress the Injuries, that may happen to any Member of the Commonwealth; which Judge is the Legislative, or Magistrates appointed by it."[96]

A couple of items to note at this point. First, Edwards described Christians as a nation that has the same law, ruler, and judge. There are also provisions for the administration of justice within society. So haven't Christians put themselves by agreement into a commonwealth with their Creator? If men are to obey their Creator first, then aren't all human laws subservient to divine law? Second, and related, a commonwealth creates an appointed judge on Earth, but what law will be applied in judgment? Divine law has already established standards for true justice, but human justice is limited to what we can observe—its justice is incomplete. It is also from man's decision not to follow moral standards that there arises a need for a judge with the power of a community to support executing the virtue of justice.

We also have this distinction made by Locke concerning spiritual interests: "If they are persuaded that they please God in observing the rites of their own country, and that they obtain happiness by that means, they are to be left unto God and themselves."[97] This is consistent with Thomas whereby happiness "is to be found, not in any creature, but in

God alone."[98] "Happiness means gaining the Perfect Good ... That man has the capacity appears from the fact that his mind can apprehend good which is universal and unrestricted and his will can desire it. Therefore he is open to receive it."[99] The pursuit of happiness is the ability to freely pursue forming a relationship with our Creator so that we can each come to know Him to the extent that we are able. Locke is setting up a separation between the spheres of spiritual (Church) and civil (State) governance. Life, liberty, and property belong to the civil domain, while happiness is a part of the spiritual domain. I believe this our Founder's had the same idea with their selection of like, liberty, and the pursuit of happiness in our *Declaration of Independence*, as we will see in the last chapter. We will look at Locke's views on the spiritual sphere and the separation between them in the next chapter.

As to the need for a commonwealth, "The necessity of preserving men in the possession of what honest industry has already acquired, and also of preserving their liberty and strength, whereby they may acquire what they farther want, [that] obliges men to enter into society with one another; that by mutual assistance and joint force, they may secure unto each other their properties, in the things that contribute to the comforts and happiness of this life."[100] This is a somewhat inconsistent notion when compared to some of Locke's statements where it is the individual man alone that matters within the spiritual sphere, but within the civil sphere it is man within a society that matters. *I would suggest that both levels are relevant in both spheres; man as an individual and as a member of a single society—a people—are both required.* You cannot have one without the other and still be a people oriented toward our Creator. After all, what other need is there for both levels to be present unless it be that some choose to turn toward themselves, and away from their Creator, a point that Locke himself makes.

We will pick up the discussions of civil power, religious power, and the relationship between them in the next chapter. But before ending this chapter, here is a summary of Locke's positions on the topics discussed so far.

Summary

1. The religious sphere's purpose is to regulate man's virtue and piety.

2. In relation to Christianity:

    a. Tolerance is Christianity's chief characteristic, but one cannot be a Christian without charity.

    b. Charity is focused on material possessions—things necessary to keep one from extreme want. Charity must therefore be just another virtue equal to all other virtues. This directly contradicts the early church fathers and the *Gospels*.

    c. Justice gives man title to things produced by his labor and industry, charity entitles one to another's abundance to keep him from extreme want. Both are an addition to the law as all things were given to man in common for man to care for as steward.

    d. We are to comply with the Law of Nature (Will of God), but each man is orthodox unto himself.

3. Man lives in Hobbes' State of Nature.

    a. He has freedom as to actions, possessions, and person.

    b. No one has more power than another.

    c. Obligated not to destroy himself or any creature within his power.

    d. Reason alone is the law.

    e. All men belong to their Creator.

4. Man's duty to his fellow men:

    a. Preserve oneself first before others.

    b. Preserve others as long as his own preservation is not in competition.

    c. Has the power of punishment and reparation for transgressions. This right is the basis for a Magistrate's power.

5. Man's rights include the following:

    a. Freedom of person.

    b. Right of inheritance of possessions. This is consistent with the *First Treatise*, but is an addition by positive law again.

    c. Freedom can be restricted either by servitude or slavery.

    d. Property is created by labor and industry in order for us to enjoy. This ignores the call for stewardship we have, and its relationship to charity.

    e. Law is grounded in reason. Where there is no law, there is no freedom. This implies freedom comes from outside, what is given by another. This would be the State within the civil sphere.

Chapter 4: Power

> *All Power on Earth is either derived or usurped from the Fatherly Power, there being no other Original to be found of any Power whatsoever. For if there should be granted two sorts of Power, without any Subordination of one to the other, they would be in perpetual strife which should be Supreme, for two Supremes cannot agree.*
>
> —John Locke, 1690

This chapter extends the collectivism discussion from that last chapter and covers Locke's positions on civil power, the ends of civil (political) power, religious power, and the relationship between the two. We'll summarize the information and apply it to extend the Church/State discussion in Chapter 2, before concluding with briefly discussing two areas that have come up repeatedly: virtue and stewardship.

Civil Power

The above quote is the perfect place to start this chapter about power from a collectivism perspective. A civil power is created when a commonwealth is formed. Locke states that this "Civil power is the same everywhere."[1] The areas to which it pertains, and the extent of that control, does not vary across any society. The civil magistrate has the following responsibilities: "It is the duty of the civil magistrate, by the impartial execution of equal laws, to secure unto all the people in general, and to every one of his subjects in particular, the just possession of these things belonging to this life."[2] From this statement, the duties of civil governance would appear to consist of the following:

- Impartial execution of all of the laws;
- Laws that do not unfairly affect specific members of society, but treat all equally;
- Laws that are equally applied to all individuals within a society;
- This application applies both to each subject and the people in general;
- Limited to just possession of things, including one's own person.

These duties are consistent with the equality under the law concept upon which this nation was founded. Those in the position of governing do not have the authority, unless it has specifically been granted to them, to choose which laws they will enforce and which they will ignore. This is a dereliction of duty. The laws are to be evenhanded and applied equally to all members of society and to us as a people. They are not to prefer one class of citizen over another. Duty does not end with the magistrate, but with the people from whom all of their power is derived. Leaders are merely a reflection of the uprightness of the people they lead. It is the duty of each subject, through charity, to share from their abundance with those who do not have. However, can such a free society exist as a single people or be successful if only human-created law is looked to for society's benefit?

Civil power is limited to the civil sphere only, but Locke notes that the individuals acting within the civil sphere, as individuals, still have the same care for the spiritual sphere of those members of its society—those apply to all of us, and are not suddenly removed just because one is in office. "The care of souls is not committed the civil magistrate, any more than to other men ... because it appears not that God has ever given any such authority to one man over another."[3] "Magistracy does not oblige him to put off either humanity or Christianity."[4] These are akin to the strong rods referred to by Edwards.

The power of a magistrate is also limited to the civil sphere. "[A] Magistrate's power extends not to the establishing of any articles of faith, or forms of worship, by the force of his laws."[5] This contradicts Hobbes as "The civil magistrate's power consists only in outward force,"[6] while the spiritual sphere is an interior domain within man himself. "Though the rigor of laws and the force of penalties were capable to convince and change men's minds, yet would not that help at all to the salvation of their souls."[7]

Commonwealths, and therefore civil power, are formed to remove men from the state of war with each other. "The remedy of this evil (man's depravity) consists in arms, riches, and multitudes of citizens: the remedy of others in laws: and the care of all things related both to the one and the other is committed by the society to the civil magistrate. This is the original, this is the use, and these are the bounds of the legislative, which is the supreme power in every commonwealth."[8] With the distinctions that Locke has made, and the way they have been made, it would appear that this ignores the laws which come from our Creator. It is as though once man leaves Locke's state of nature the law of nature (will of God) no longer applies, but the law of nature is the basis of the natural law that Locke uses in creating his governance vision.

These laws, divine and natural, that come from our Creator are the basis by which a good life is led as Locke himself has already suggested. This integration is exactly what our Founders did. They took some of the notions related to a commonwealth's structure and infused divine and natural law concepts into its foundation. It should be noted that the idea of a commonwealth was not new. They were put forth by Thomas

Aquinas in the thirteenth century in his *Summa Theologicæ*. It should also be noted that Thomas's work did not express new ideas, but was intended to gather common knowledge to teach students; Locke merely replaced the divine underpinnings with a secular one. (See the later section on the relationship between the religious and civic spheres.)

The legislative may be the supreme power within a commonwealth, but it is not the supreme power. There is only one supreme power and that comes from the One who is the basis for all existence, morality, and knowledge, without which even life itself is not possible. Human law can only act as an addition or subtraction to natural law, as man is not infinite. The end of the legislative power is to enable and facilitate prosperity within a society, it cannot create it. Note that Locke does not use the term *happiness*. "What end the legislative power ought to be directed ... and that is the temporal good and outward prosperity of the society, which is the sole reason of men's entering into society."[9] This appears to indicate coercion comes only within the realm of property or persons, but Locke's own experience and earlier writing suggests that this coercion also occurs in the spiritual realm. While the civic realm can make no laws with respect to the spiritual realm, neither can it make ones that interfere with its existence or society's ability to participate in its beliefs.

If laws violating the common good are created, Locke suggests that individuals are not to obey those laws as they are contrary to natural law. "I say, that such a private person is to abstain from the actions that he judges unlawful; and he is to undergo the punishment, which is not unlawful for him to bear; for the private judgement of any person concerning a law enacted in political matters, for the public good, does not take away the obligation of that law, nor deserve a dispensation."[10] The limits of this power lie in two places. The first is in the terms of the pact which creates the society. The second is in those rights and responsibilities to which we are accountable to our Creator and cannot be delegated to another. "The private judgment, as I may call it, of the magistrate, does not give him any new right of imposing laws upon his subjects, which neither was in the constitution of the government granted him, nor ever was in the power of the people to grant; and least of all, if he makes it his business to enrich and advance his followers and fellow-sectaries with the spoils of others."[11] Finally, the exercise of this power is to be evenhanded in its application.

Political Power and Its Ends

So what is political power and what are its ends? Locke defines political power "to be a *Right* of making Laws with Penalties of Death, and consequently all less Penalties, for the Regulating and Preserving of Property, and of employing the force of the Community in the Execution of such Laws, and in the defence of the Common-wealth from Foreign Injury, and all this only for the Publick Good."[12] In other words, the power to make human law. He also leaves behind two powers he has in the State of Nature when entering a commonwealth. "The first is to do whatsoever he thinks fit for the preservation of himself and others within the permission of the *Law of Nature*: by which Law common to them all, he and all the rest of *Mankind are one Community*,"[13] and "The other power a Man has in the State of Nature, ... the *power to punish the Crimes* committed against that Law."[14]

A civil society only has power over persons through their possession of land, so by divesting ones property, they are free to move to another commonwealth. "But since the Government has a direct Jurisdiction only over the Land, and reaches the Possessor of it ... only as he dwells upon, and enjoys that: *The Obligation* any one is under, by Virtue of such Enjoyment, *to submit to the Government, begins and ends with the Enjoyment*; so that whenever the Owner ... quit the said Possession, he is at liberty to go and incorporate himself into any other Commonwealth, or agree with others to begin a new one, *in vacuis locis*, in any part of the World, they can find free and unpossessed."[15] This appears to set a distinction between the degree that a commonwealth has control over a person versus their possessions. A commonwealth appears to always have control over property once it enters a commonwealth, but the owners can remove themselves from a commonwealth's control simply by divesting themselves of any property under its control and incorporating themselves into another commonwealth. Locke's ideas bring into question the notion of citizenship as it appears to be associated with property ownership. It also brings the focus of property ownership into the present, for one's own enjoyment.

To Locke, the granting of power to a commonwealth is one-way and permanent, except when this power is abused to such an extent that the commonwealth is dissolved. "The *Power that every individual gave the Society*, when he entered into it, can never revert to the Individuals again, as long as the Society lasts, but will always remain in the Community; because without this, there can be no Community ... Or else by the Miscarriages of those in Authority, it is forfeited."[16] "But if a long train of Abuses, Prevarications, and Artifices, all tending the same way, make the design visible to the People, and they cannot but feel, what they lie under, and see, whither they are going; 'tis not to be wonder'd, that they should then rouze themselves, and endeavor to put the rule into such hands, which may secure to them the ends of which Government was at first erected."[17] When these bonds are dissolved, man again enters the State of Nature and potentially the state of War. "Whosoever used *force without Right*, as every one does in Society, who does it without Law, puts himself into a *state of War* with those, against whom he so uses it, and in that state all former Ties are cancelled, other Rights cease, and every one has a *Right* to defend himself, and *to resist the Aggressor*."[18]

So what is the end of governance employing political power? "The *end of Government* being the *preservation of all*."[19] No one is exempt from this requirement to wield political power for the good of all. "They (Princes) owe subjection to the Laws of God and Nature. No Body, no Power can exempt them from the Obligations of that Eternal Law."[20] As discussed by Thomas in his *Summa Theologicæ*, all are subject to the ultimate source of law: Eternal Law. "Law is nothing but a dictate of practical reason issued by a sovereign who governs a complete community. Granted that the world is ruled by divine Providence ... it is evident that the whole community of the universe is governed by God's mind. Therefore the ruling idea of things which exists in God as the effective sovereign of them all has the nature of law. Then since God's mind does not conceive in time, but has an eternal concept ... it follows that this law should be called eternal."[21]

With the distinctions that Locke has previously created, the people have no other choice when power is misused except to appeal to their Creator for relief. He has left them no other option. "The People have no other remedy in this, as in all other cases where they have no Judge on Earth, but to *appeal to Heaven*."[22] People are to follow the Law of Nature, our Creator's will, but when they fail to do so they are left with only appealing to Him if the commonwealth fails to exercise justice. There is no acknowledgement of our Creator's Providence. This view potentially allows the State to create laws contrary to its purpose, leaving those within it with no viable alternative to correct such an act. This is immoral. Power becomes concentrated without a balance to restrain it, despite the limits Locke places for it below.

In the words of the seventeenth century minister John Cotton, all power should be limited.

> Give him power to make laws, and he will approve, and disprove as he list; what he approves is canonicall, what hee disproves is rejected: give him that power, and he will so order it at length, he will make such a state of religion, that he that so lives and dyes shall never be saved, and all this springs from the vast power that is given to him, and from the deep depravation of nature ... It is therefore most wholesome for magistrates and officers in church and common-wealth, never to affect more liberty and authority then will do them good, and the people good; for what ever transcendant power is given, will certainly over-run those that give it, and those that receive it ... if there be power given to speak great things, then look for great blasphemies.[23]

So how does a commonwealth exercise its political power? "The *first and fundamental positive Law* of all Common-wealths, *is the establishing of the Legislative* Power; as *the first and fundamental natural Law*, which is to govern even the Legislative it self, is *the preservation of the Society*, and (as far as will consist with the publick good) of every person in it."[24] So the legislative power is to have the highest authority within civil society. The preservation of society using law was the same goal as expressed by both Plato and Aristotle.

So from the above, political power

1. Is the right of making laws for civil society.
2. Extends over persons only to the extent they own property, specifically land.
3. Once given is permanent, unless it is abused by the commonwealth to such an extent and over a long period of time, that the commonwealth forfeits that power, in which case it devolves back to the people and they are again placed in Locke's State of Nature.
4. Is aimed at the preservation of all through the establishment of a legislature, the supreme power within a commonwealth.

So what are some of the limitations of this power according to Locke?

1. "It is *not*, nor can possibly be absolutely *Arbitrary* over the Lives and Fortunes of the People …
2. "Their Power in the utmost Bounds of it, is *limited to the publick good* of the Society …
3. "The *Rules* that they for other Men's Actions, must, as well as their own and other Men's Actions, be conformable to the Law of Nature, i.e. to the Will of God, of which that is a Declaration, and the *fundamental Law of Nature* being *the preservation of Mankind*, no Humane Sanction can be good, or valid against it …

4. "The *Legislative*, or Supream Authority, cannot assume to its self a power to Rule by extemporary Arbitrary Decrees, but is *bound to dispense Justice*, and decide the Rights of the Subject *by promulgated standing Laws, and Known Authoris'd Judges* …

5. "The *Supream Power cannot take* from any Man any part of his *Property* without his own consent …

6. "There is danger still, that they (Legislative Power) will think themselves to have a distinct interest, from the rest of the Community; and so will be apt to increase their own Riches and Power, by taking, what they think fit, from the People …

7. "If any one shall claim a *Power to lay* and levy *Taxes* on the People, by his own Authority, and without such consent of the People, he thereby invades the *Fundamental Law of Property*, and subverts the end of Government …

8. "The *Legislative cannot transfer the Power of Making Laws* to any other hands."[25]

9. "There can be but *one Supream Power*, which is *the Legislative*, to which all the rest are and must be subordinate, yet the Legislative being only a Fiduciary Power to act for certain ends, there remains still *in the People a Supream Power* to remove or *alter the Legislative*, when they find the Legislative at contrary to the trust reposed in them. For all Power *given with trust* for the attaining an end, being limited by that end is manifestly neglected, or opposed the *trust* must necessarily be *forfeited*, and the Power devolve into the hands of those that gave it."[26]

10. "These *Laws* also ought to be designed *for* no other end ultimately but *the good of the People*."[27]

11. "*No Man in Civil Society can be exempted from the Laws of it.*"[28]

As a legislature is seldom in constant session, there is the need for someone to execute the laws that it has promulgated. This is the role of the executive, who is simply given the power to enforce civil society's laws when the legislature is not in session. The executive has no power to create law, but does have the power of exercising prerogative toward existing law. That *"Prerogative is nothing but the Power of doing publick good without a Rule."*[29] Different executives have differing degrees of prerogative that are allowed to them by the people, based upon whether the executive is a strong rod (where a greater degree of prerogative is allowed), versus a weak rod (where limited prerogative is given).[30]

This often tempts the executive to abuse their power. This abuse can arise from at least two sources. The first is when the executive places himself outside of the law, regardless of the reason. "Having the Force, Treasure, and offices of the State to imploy, and often perswading himself, or being flattered by others, that as Supream Magistrate he is uncapable of controul; he alone is in a Condition to make great Advances toward such Changes, under pretence of lawful Authority, and has it in his hands to terrifie or suppress Opposers, as Factious, Seditious, and Enemies to the Government." These are the weak rods described by Edwards.

The second is when the executive abandons his charge, such as when he refuses to enforce the laws that have been enacted by the legislature. "When he who has the Supream Executive power, neglects and abandons that charge, so that the Laws already made can no longer be put in execution. This is demonstratively to reduce all to anarchy, and so effectually to *dissolve the Government.*"[31] So the abuse dissolving a commonwealth can come from either the legislature or executive. Underlying Locke's whole notion of governance is that *"Where-ever Law ends, Tyranny begins*, if the Law be transgressed to another's harm."[32] However, from Locke's own words it appears that tyranny begins wherever power over some aspect of another has been given.

Religious Society

According to Locke, "The end of a religious society is the public worship of God."[33] The ability to worship is not the same as the ability to live in accordance with one's beliefs, the latter of which is freedom of religion. The former includes only thought and speech, while the latter addes to them choice and action. From Locke's own arguments, the end of all religious societies is the salvation of men's souls. "The business of true religion is ... the regulating of men's lives according to the rules of virtue and piety."[34] This can only be accomplished by man's voluntarily bending the will he was given to the will of God (natural law), by voluntarily choosing to become good.

A fourth work by Locke, *The Reasonableness of Christianity*,[35] provides some additional context around the end of religious society – what it is to achieve. There are the laws of faith and works. The law of faith "is for every one to believe what God require him to believe,"[36] which can be summarized as "believing Jesus to be the Messiah, and a good life."[37] This good life includes fulfilling "the law in acts of charity."[38] The law of works "is that law which requires perfect obedience."[39] Both are required.

Locke further states that "were there no law of works, there could be no law of faith,"[40] that where there is no obedience there is no belief. "For there count be no need of faith ... if there were no law, to be the rule and measure of righteousness ... Where there is no law, there is no sin; all are righteous equally, with or without faith."[41] However, faith is belief without proof, it is an act of will and therefore voluntary on our part, just as accepting His governance through our obedience is also voluntary. The acceptance of the first should lead to the second, and the fulfillment of divine law is the performance of charity as described in the first chapter, and not simply a competing right to material goods between the one having stewardship of them and the one who is in want. The latter is simply cheap charity, form over substance.

Religious society consists of the various churches within it. "A church then I take to be a voluntary society of men, joining themselves together of their own accord, in order to the public worshipping of God."[42] Further, "No member of a religious society can be tied with any other bonds but what proceed from the certain expectations of eternal life. A church then is a society of members voluntarily uniting to this end."[43] "The right of making its laws can belong to none but the society itself, or at least, which is the same thing, to those whom the society by common consent has authorized thereunto."[44] If this right is not present, then "By what means then shall ecclesiastical laws be established … if not proceeding from a thorough conviction and approbation of the mind, is altogether useless and unprofitable."[45]

So belonging to a religious society is a voluntary choice, it is united by the belief in an eternal life, and is self-governing within its sphere. This is certainly a Christian perspective on the role of the church. It is also a purely human look at the religious sphere as the right of making its laws belongs to its head, to our Creator. Membership in the true church is a voluntary social contract accepted by the individual. Anybody that is authorized by common consent to make rules for itself must in all instances comply with the laws of its head. While a part of this relies on men's minds, it is achieved with attempting to understand our Creator's will through the study of and reflection on His word – with the end of charity in mind. Otherwise we reside on our own and outside the influence of that which we claim to be in submission. Locke appears to agree as he wrote, "But how that can be called the church of Christ, which is established upon laws that are not his, and which excludes such persons from its communion as he will one day receive into the kingdom of heaven, I understand not."[46]

Locke asserts that if toleration were simply shown to all, that many other differences would disappear. "If the law of toleration were once so settled, that all churches were obliged to laydown toleration as the foundation of their own liberty; and teach that liberty of conscience is every man's natural right, equally belonging to dissenters as to themselves; and that nobody ought to be compelled in matters of religion either by law or force. The establishment of this one thing would take away all ground of complaints and tumults upon account of conscience."[47] I agree. *There is much more that unites us than divides us, and tolerance allows us to focus on what we share instead of what divides.*

The role of the religious sphere is limited and differentiated from that of the civil sphere. "The only business of the church is the salvation of souls, and it in no way concerns the commonwealth."[48] Further, "Nothing ought, nor can be transacted in this [religious] society, related to the possession of civil and worldly goods."[49]

The Relationship between Civil and Religious Societies

From what has been discussed so far regarding the civic and religious spheres, Locke concludes that, "The boundaries of both sides (commonwealth and religion) are fixed and immovable."[50] "For the civil government can give no new right to the church, nor the church to the civil government."[51] This is necessary as, "The civil power can either change every thing in religion, or it can change nothing."[52] There is no such thing as partial power. We can see the effects of this corruption today toward our churches through the policies that our Federal government is today enacting to force churches to bend to its will in the areas of taxation, green energy, and healthcare – just to mention a few.

As the religious sphere is separate and distinct from the civil sphere, "Nobody therefore, in fine, neither single persons, nor churches, nay, nor even commonwealths, have any just title to invade the civil rights and worldly goods of each other, upon pretense of religion."[53] Charity can only come from the one who has possession of an asset – an individual and not the church or government. This is consistent with Thomas as noted earlier. "In vain, therefore, do princes compel their subjects to come into their church-communion, under pretense of saving their souls. If they believe, they will come of their own accord; if they believe not, their coming will nothing avail them."[54] "Speculative opinions, therefore, and articles of faith, as they are called, which are required only to be believed, cannot be imposed on any church by the law of the land for it is absurd that things should be enjoined by laws which are not in men's power to perform."[55] "Further, the magistrate ought not to forbid the preaching or professing of any speculative opinions in any church, because they have no manner of relation to the civil rights of the subjects."[56] Compulsion within religion never works as man cannot be compelled as to what he inwardly believes. This leads Locke to conclude, "But there is absolutely no such thing, under the Gospel, as a Christian commonwealth."[57]

This is of course true on its face. However, according to Thomas, "There are two things to be observed concerning the right ordering of rulers in a state or people. One is that all should have some share in government; this makes for peace among the people, and commends itself to all ... The other regards the kind of government, or how the rulers are instituted. There are various kinds of regimen ... but the principal ones are monarchy, in which one man rules as specially qualified, and aristocracy, that is the rule of the best ... Hence the best system in any state or kingdom is one in which one man, as specially qualified, rules over all, and under him are others governing as having special endowments, yet all have a share inasmuch as those are elected from all, and also are elected by all. This is the best form of constitution, a mixture of monarchy, in that one man is at the head, or aristocracy, in that many rule as specially qualified, and democracy in that the rulers can be chosen from the people and by them. This was the form established by divine law."[58] This passage was written by Thomas about 400 years before Locke.

Locke sees the outcome of his arguments as, "the unhappy agreement that we see between the church and the state. Whereas if each of them would contain itself within its own bound, the one attending to the worldly welfare of the commonwealth, the other to the salvation of souls, it is impossible that any discord should ever have happened between them."[59] This is true. If both spheres were properly oriented toward their Creator, each should function as intended. And when one of these spheres turns inward toward itself? "Who shall answer between them? I answer, God alone' for there is no judge upon earth between the supreme magistrate and the people."[60] Locke is not entirely in agreement with his own statement. A long train of abuses is one basis for the dissolution of a political society, and at the time a political society ceases to exist, the power it once contained devolves once again to its people. To think otherwise is to suggest that justice cannot exist in this world, but that is the primary purpose of governance.

Locke sees one answer as follows. "I beseech him, that the Gospel of peace may at length be preached and that civil magistrates, growing more careful to conform their own consciences to the law of God, and less solicitous about the binding of other men's consciences by human laws, may like fathers of their country, direct all their counsels and endeavors to promote universally the civil welfare of all their children."[61] I can only say Amen. But doesn't this require that religious sphere have an indirect influence on the civil sphere, as we suggested earlier, and also run counter to Locke's earlier ideas concerning the separation of the civil sphere? Locke appears to agree. He goes further to say, "A good life, in which consists not the least part of religion and true piety, concerns also the civil government: and in it lies the safety both of men's souls and of the commonwealth. Moral actions belong therefore to the jurisdiction both of the outward and inward court; both of the civil and domestic governor; I mean, both of the magistrate and conscience."[62] This goes further yet toward acknowledging the need for morality to be present within a society in both the spheres of religion and civic government. The conscience is our image of our Creator. Can one look to the image without also looking to its source? I would argue they simply cannot. Does this view contradict Locke's own statement that there can be no such thing as a Christian commonwealth? I think it does in that a commonwealth can be founded on Judeo-Christian principles, as ours is.

Summary of Locke's Writing

In summarizing the main ideas presented so far throughout this chapter, there is one thing that I want to reiterate. This chapter has not been intended to disparage Locke. He has presented some truth and we are looking at his thoughts to separate what is true from what is not, and determine where that truth lies and what conclusions we might draw from it. This is similar to Clement's review of Greek philosophy in trying to identify what truth might be found within it. His statement is as follows,

> The Greek preparatory culture, therefore, with philosophy itself, is shown to have come down from God to men, not with a definite direction but in the way in which showers fall down on the good land, and on the dunghill, and on the houses. And similarly both the grass and the wheat sprout; and the figs and any other reckless trees grow on sepulchers. And things that grow, appear as a type of truths. For they enjoy the same influence of the rain. But they have not the same grace as those which spring up in rich soil, inasmuch as they are withered or plucked up.[63]

So let us look to see what truth we may find. Locke's assertions are given at the start of each point, and any contrary thoughts are then presented after his in italics. The main points include:

Christianity's Chief Characteristic

1. Toleration is the chief characteristic of Christianity. *However, Locke's own arguments indicate charity to be superior. This latter view is consistent with that of the early church fathers who believed that a virtuous people were necessary for a moral society to exist, and that all virtues end in acts of charity.*

2. All individuals are orthodox unto themselves. *But how can this be if we all have the same Creator, all are his property and subject to His governance, all have the same nature, and no one has been given more authority (power) than another? It can only be our failings as human beings to always understand that leads us to differing views. None of us are perfect, and none us of has perfect understanding. This is where tolerance shown out of love should come into play. In addition, while we all share the same purpose, we have also all been given different gifts,*

talents, and abilities – we will each achieve our common purpose differently. The ends are the same, but the means will sometimes vary based on our gifts – no one size fits all cookie cutter approach will ever succeed. Because of our different perspectives, we are likely to see things differently – and those multiple perspectives may indeed be correct – as put forth by Augustine.

3. Men are responsible for the care of their own souls. We cannot delegate these choices to another, government or individual, as we are each responsible for them. *Nevertheless, he also states that the public peace should be pursued only after caring for one's own soul first. The biblical approach is others and self. We are called to voluntarily sacrifice out of love for our fellow man – simply because we share the same nature. We are also called not just as individuals, but also as a single people. Either alone is a necessary, but insufficient condition. This assertion carries over below into how one should conduct themselves in life.*

Man's Natural State

1. All men begin in a State of Nature and are subject to governance by the law of nature – the will of God. *Still, we are His in two ways, and not simply one as Locke asserts. We are His as we are a part of His creation as Locke asserts, but at the same time we have free will to choose whether to accept His governance. Simply forming human governance under human laws does not change His governance, and Locke later asserts we are to follow our Creator first.*

2. We are given material things solely for our enjoyment. *Then again, material goods are the means by which we are assisted by and assist others in achieving our purpose, a purpose that involves stewardship and assisting others – charity – and not simply in using them for ourselves and then maybe using some*

of it to help others. It is by their Creator intended use that we learn the proper place of material goods.

3. Reason alone is sufficient in life. *On the other hand, our purpose is to come to know our Creator, and that can only be accomplished by coming to know both the languages of reason and faith. The linkages between reason and natural law and human law are demonstrated repeatedly. However, the natural law Locke discusses is often an addition to natural law rather than one based upon nature itself. He expresses a form of deism, which can only be accepted if one denies the Providence of God – the very will he repeatedly expresses we are to follow.*

4. Man is to preserve himself first, and then others. *This is nothing more than a form of individualistic elitism that stems from the focus on self (a group of one) and ignores the call to be a single people under our Creator's governance. Locke extensively uses the Bible to support his notions regarding the individual, but ignores the same sources' call to also be a single people – specifically our Creator's people.*

5. The execution of justice is to prevent the violation of others rights or possessions. *True, up to a point. Yet the greater role of justice relies on its purpose and not simply its execution. These were identified by Clement as: helping an individual to become better than their former self, those who are capable of being saved by example may be driven back, and the person who was injured may not be despised and apt to receive further injury. It is not just about bad things using punishment, but also the opportunity for a society to improve.*

6. There can be no freedom without law, as the law restrains one from doing harm to another. *However, underlying this thought is a belief that man's natural state must be one of aggression and violence. This is contrary to the law of nature Locke cites. As our Creator is not only good, but the Good, all things that come from Him must be good. In the words of Thomas, 'one cannot give what they have not got.' Aggression and violence*

instead occur when man chooses not to place himself under his Creator's governance, but rather looks to himself instead. Locke's views in this regard are more consistent with those of Plotinus rather than the Bible he often references. This notion is further supported by Locke's views of liberty and freedom. One cannot claim the benefit from something and at the same time deny the source. His arguments in these areas appear to stem from effects and not causes.

Commonwealths and Civil Society

1. Commonwealth is to govern solely the civil interests – both the material possessions of man and his person. Men enter into a society to jointly enable each other in this effort. Man was given the cultural commission to create civilization in Genesis.[64]

2. Civil power is to impartially execute the laws, treat all members equally, and equally apply the laws to all individuals both as to the subject and the people in general.

3. The civil and religious spheres are separate and distinct. *While the civil sphere is to look after man's civil interest, the religious sphere is to look after his happiness. In the words of Thomas, that happiness 'is to be found not in any creature, but in God alone.'*

4. While the civil sphere is limited to the civil interests, the individuals acting within the civil sphere are still to have the same care for the spiritual sphere, both for themselves and other members of society.

5. Laws that are unlawful, contrary to what the individual views as unlawful, are not to be obeyed by the individual. *However, they are to submit to the punishment resulting from the breaking of the law. Given Locke's earlier assertions, these would appear to set the conditions not for freedom, but instead for tyranny or anarchy as orthodoxy is left to the individual to determine. Commonwealths would likely be short-lived under this notion.*

Political Power and Its Ends

1. Political power is the right to make all penalties and thereby preserve the civil interests. *The focus is on punishment alone. But justice is also a virtue where each is given their due and provides the opportunity for correction and improvement as noted above.*

2. Society only has power to act over persons insofar as they have property attached to the commonwealth.

3. This ceding of authority to a commonwealth is one way and permanent, unless by a long train of abuses that authority is misused. The end of political power is the preservation of all.

4. The legislative power is the highest power within a commonwealth and its purpose is the preservation of society. The executive power is to enforce society's laws when the legislative power is not in session. The executive has some prerogative in the exercise of its power, but prerogative varies with the ability and character of the executive.

Religious Society

1. The end of religious society is the worship of God. These are a voluntary society of men who join together of their own accord, the end of which is an expectation of eternal life. *This is true only if attending worship services alone is sufficient. But aren't we also required to act? In the words of Edwards again, we are to be 'ready to distribute, willing to communicate, and do good; consider it as part of your office thus to do, to which you are called and anointed, and as a sacrifice well-pleasing to God; pity others in distress; be ready to help one another; God will have mercy and not sacrifice.'[65] Again Locke sets up competing rights for possession within his notion of charity. Locke's notion of charity is confined to actions around material possessions – an incomplete view of charity when compared to the Gospels.*

2. The right of making its laws belongs to none but the society itself. *For human society itself, yes. However, there is a logical contradiction here. The right of making laws belongs to its head, as Locke admits. In this case that would be our Creator Himself as head of His church. Locke even agrees in another passage. As His governance exceeds man's basis, for He is our Creator, His law must also supersede man's.*

3. The only business of the church is the salvation of souls. *But what does that mean? From the first point above it must mean doing good, which is nothing more than trying, to the best of each of our ability, to become like our Creator. But this mens taking actions consistent with our Creator's laws.*

4. If toleration were simply shown to all, many of our differences would disappear. *Agreed, there is much more that should unite us rather than divide us. However, unvirtuous conduct destroys a society and should not be tolerated when contradicting natural law. This occurs when we turn toward ourselves. This is Augustine's city of man led by Edward's weak rods.*

The Relationship between Civil and Religious Societies

1. The boundaries of both the commonwealth and church are fixed and immovable.

2. Power can either change everything within the church or it can change nothing.

3. No one has just title to material goods on the pretense of religion.

4. There is no such thing as a Christian commonwealth. *True in terms of religion, but not in terms of a society's underlying moral precepts. Thomas asserted in the thirteenth century that while this form of governance was not advocated by scripture, yet all other forms were denied by it. This is exactly what our Founder's did. They did not integrate religion into the civil sphere, but rather the foundational principles of morality derived from Judeo/Christian tenets. As such we find the*

principles of faith, virtue, charity, equality under the law, and the biblical notion of justice within our founding documents.

5. An unhappy agreement exists between the Church and State. There is no judge on the earth between the magistrate and the people. *However, it is the balance between the Church, State, and people that matters. Ultimately all earthly power derives from the people itself – as Locke asserts in his discussion of man's natural state. For this balance to be kept, all must be oriented toward our Creator. Therefore the religious sphere must have an indirect influence on the civil one through the virtue and morality that is instilled in the people. If the people do not have this moral foundation, there can be no balance or justice. Virtue is only acquired through education that is internalized through effort and practice.*

We previously had the following relationships diagrammed between the spheres of the Church and State.

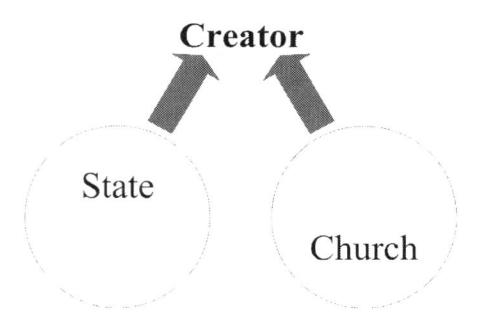

```
         Creator
          ↑  ↑
         ╱    ╲
    State      Church
```

The changes that Locke made to these relationships include: (1) delegating not only material goods but also the person to the State and the salvation of man's souls to the Church, (2) the State being oriented strictly to itself, with a further caveat that the people are to only obey those laws which individuals considered to be just, and (3) the Church was no longer a single sphere, but instead a grouping of smaller spheres representing each individual within a society as each is to be orthodox to himself. The Church is to remain oriented to His laws. These changes are shown as follows:

Collectivism and Charity

Creator

State

Church

Material Goods & Person

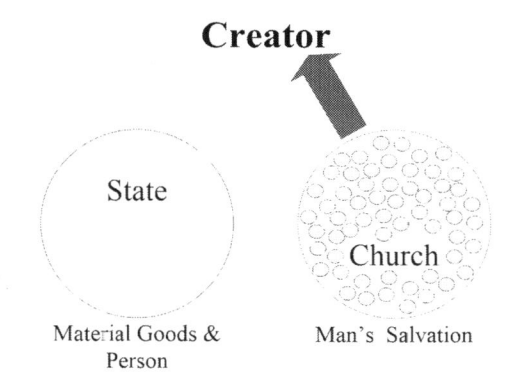

Man's Salvation

There is an obvious contradiction in the above diagram. Man's soul lies in the religious sphere, but his person and actions lie within the civic sphere. Can man be separated in this way? The early church fathers would say no. Our choices influence our soul, bad choices to its detriment and good choices to its betterment. This is a direct link that cannot be severed. Law understood in the manner that Locke asserts must assume these to be independent, thus the notion that the primary purpose of punishment is to prevent violation of the law.

However, our choices are connected to our being. In the end they define who we are and whether we are on the track of fulfilling our purpose. A purpose whose outcome is the performance of charity. The above differences in turn play themselves out in very different ways from the individualism model discussed in chapter one. That model, presented again on the left below, becomes the model on the right.

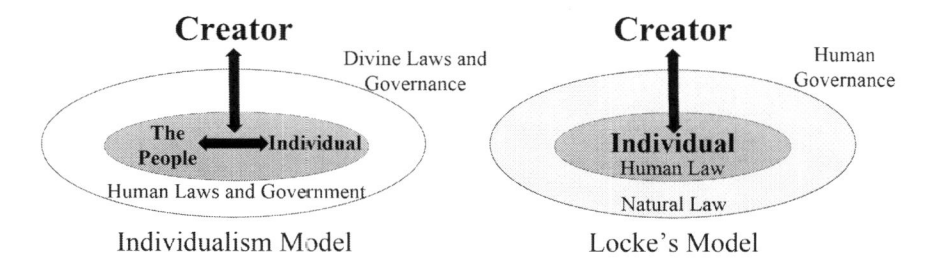

Creator

Divine Laws and Governance

The People ⇔ Individual

Human Laws and Government

Individualism Model

Creator

Human Governance

Individual
Human Law

Natural Law

Locke's Model

In Locke's world, once the people have determined what powers to grant to the commonwealth, they are largely out of the picture. Human governance is made up of human and natural law; the only reference to divine law is the appeal that one must make to our Creator when there is conflict between the two spheres of Church and State. It should be noted that the diagram on the left does include natural law. It is the area within divine law and outside of human law as natural law requires either divine or human law to enact it. The tension required between the people and individuals to remain properly oriented toward our Creator is missing in Locke's model, making it much easier for man to turn toward himself, and ignoring the commands of divine law in regards to how we are to live as a people – our underlying direction and purpose. How can an individual comply with those commands when they are not recognized? How can a society be successful if man uses reason alone, when faith is not given its due? Locke cannot answer these questions, except maybe by making an appeal to our Creator alone. While that appeal is not empty, it is also not how we were intended to live. One final point related to the beginning of this discussion in the previous chapter. Locke's notion of Church and State also places the State above the Church, but does so in a different manner. Whereas the other authors in various ways places the Church beneath the State, *Locke left the individual alone to face the State*.

Throughout the discussions in these last three chapters there are two topics that have come up repeatedly. Those are the subjects of virtue and stewardship, to which we now turn before closing this chapter.

Virtue

We'll start this topic by simply defining virtue. Early in this work we defined it as righteousness – moral uprightness. Thomas described virtue as follows, "It is clear that in the care of man the term virtue means a resource making a human act to be good. Any habit, then that is in every case the source of a good human act can be called a virtue in man."[66] In talking about virtue, Clement used truth and the search for it in his description. "One speaks in one way of the truth, in another way the truth interprets itself. The guessing at truth is one thing, and truth itself is another. Resemblance is one thing, the thing itself is another. And the one results from learning and practice, the other from power and faith."[67]

He further states, "If then we consider, virtue is, in power one. But it is the case, that when exhibited in some things, it is called prudence, in others temperance, and in others manliness or righteousness. By the same analogy, while truth is one, in geometry there is the truth of geometry; in music, that of music; and in the right philosophy, there will be Hellenic truth ... And each, whether it be virtue or truth, called by the same name, is the cause of its own peculiar effect alone."[68] Thomas concurs, "'Truth' can have two meanings. In the first it is the quality by which a thing is said to be 'true,' and it is not a virtue but the objective or the end for virtue ... In its second sense 'truth' can be taken as that by which a person speaks the truth; it is the reason for his being called 'truthful.' So understood, truth or truthfulness has to be a virtue, for to speak the truth is a morally good act and that which makes its possessor and his actions good is a virtue."[69]

We are not born with virtue, but "Above all, this ought to be known, that by nature we are adapted for virtue; not so as to be possessed of it from our birth, but so as to be adapted for acquiring it."[70] There are three things required for a virtuous act, it must be: (1) done knowingly, (2) performed from voluntary choice for a fitting end, and (3) done unwaveringly.[71] Virtue requires both education and practice on our part. "Use keeps steel brighter, but disuse produces rust in it. For, in a word, exercise produces a healthy condition both in souls and bodies ... For by teaching, one learns more; and in speaking, one is often a hearer along with his audience. For the teacher of him who speaks and of him who hears is one."[72] Virtue is necessary as "to the whole human race, then, discipline and virtue are a necessity, if they would pursue after happiness."[73] As to the end of happiness, "Now Plato the philosopher, defining the end of happiness, says that it is likeness to God as afar as possible."[74] The end of virtue is truth, a truth made strong by education and use. A truth which becomes unshakable because of the foundation it has been built upon – the virtue of wisdom.

Virtue is the path of truth, but not all paths lead to truth. "Virtues and sin do not arise from the same source. Sin springs form the desire for transient (material) goods; and consequently the desire for that good which helps towards the attainment of all other temporal goods is called the root of all sin. Virtue, conversely, derives from the desire for the changeless good; thus, charity, the love of God, is described … as the root of all virtue."[75] Vice (sin) and virtue are contrary to each other, therefore each virtue has a corresponding vice, each stemming from its own root. As these two things are contrary, an inclination towards one diminishes the other.[76] Locke's notions on civil society are grounded in material goods. Therefore it cannot achieve our spiritual end and must be detrimental to charity, as man cannot be separated from his actions.

Virtue is not the end in itself; for that end is only pleasing to man. From Augustine, "Philosophers,—who place the end of human good in virtue itself, in order to put to shame certain other philosophers, who indeed approve of the virtues, but measure them all with reference to the end of bodily pleasure, and think that this pleasure is to be sought for its own sake, but the virtues on account of pleasure,—are wont to paint a kind of word picture, in which Pleasure sits like a luxurious queen on a royal seat, and all the virtues are subjected to her as slaves.

"There is nothing, say our philosophers, more disgraceful and monstrous than this picture, and which the eyes of good men can less endure. And they say the truth. But I do not think that the picture would be sufficiently becoming, even if it were made so that the virtues should be represented as the slaves of human glory … [It] is unworthy of the solidity and firmness of the virtues to represent them as serving this glory … For their virtue,—if, indeed, it is virtue at all,—is only in another way subjected to human praise; for he who seeks to please himself seeks still to please man."[77] But the description Augustine provides is the same picture that Locke paints.

The above notions of virtue are true because we are not the author of our own nature. "Now, if we were the cause of our own nature, then, indeed, we would be the fathers of our own wisdom and would not need to get an education from our teachers. And if we were the source and the only object of our love, we would be self-sufficient and would need enjoyment of no other good to make us happy. But, in fact, God is the Author of the existence of our nature and, therefore, He must be our Teacher if we are ever to be wise, and He must be the Source of our inmost consolation if we are ever to be happy."[78] But as our Creator is First Cause, He is not demonstrable, "Faith is something superior to knowledge, and is its criterion … Knowledge, accordingly, is characterized by faith; and faith, by a kind of divine mutual reciprocal correspondence, becomes characterized by knowledge."[79]

Virtue is a moral uprightness that is grounded in truth. We are not born with virtues but are adapted to acquire them, and this requires education and effort on our part. These lead to happiness as they have their basis in the changeless good - our Creator. This is because "virtue most essentially consists in love"[80] – charity.

Stewardship

It is from the moral basis provided by virtue that man derives his capacity for exercising dominion over and the distribution of goods. Man does not possess this basis in and of himself, nor by his own nature. Without this underlying moral basis, which must be acquired, man would no longer possess the ability to exercise effective stewardship.

We can start with the nature of created things themselves, and the difference between man's creation and everything else. "For if the heavenly bodies are not the works of men, they were certainly created for man. Let none of you worship the sun, but set his desires on the Maker of the sun; nor deify the universe, but seek after the Creator of the universe."[81] Follow that with a question as to our final destination. Is this earth and this life all that there is, or is it merely the place where we journey to our final destination? If it is the former, then does anything really matter? If the latter, then understanding our purpose becomes critical so we are in a position to fulfill it. Clement asserts that it is the latter course we are on. "No one is a stranger to the world by nature, their essence being one, and God one. But the elect man dwells as a sojourner, knowing all things to be possessed and disposed of ... having care of the things of the world ... but leaving his dwelling place and property without excessive emotion ... and blessing [God] for his departure, embracing the mansion that is in heaven."[82]

As man was made differently from the rest of creation, in the image of our Creator, it follows that, "It is then, as appears, the greatest of all lessons to know one's self. For if one knows himself, he will know God; and knowing God, he will be made like God, not by wearing gold or long robes, but by well doing, and by requiring as few things as possible."[83] Clement embodies this approach to living in one he calls the Gnostic, one who attempts to know his Creator and His truth. It is the Gnostic's goal to live by well-doing, by performing virtuous acts – performing charity.

> After that which is reckoned perfection in others, his [the Gnostic's] righteousness advances to activity in well-doing. And in whomsoever the increased force of righteousness advances to the doing of good, in his case perfection abides in the fixed habit of well-doing after the likeness of God.
>
> The Gnostic is such, that he is subject only to the affections that exist for the maintenance of the body, such as hunger, thirst, and the like ... [One] who is incapable of exercising courage: for neither does he meet what inspires fear, as he regards none of the things that occur in life as to be dreaded; nor can aught dislodge him from this—the love he has towards God ... Nor is he angry; for there is nothing to move him to anger, seeing he ever loves God, and is entirely turned towards

Him alone, and therefore hates none of God's creatures.[84]

As to man's exercise of dominion over external things, Thomas states that there are two ways in which this can be considered. The first way is in the view of their nature itself, and in this way all things are subject only to our Creator's power, and not man's power – so this first way does not apply. The second way looks at man's competence through his use and management of external things and in this regard man has a natural dominion as: (1) he has a mind and will to use them, and (2) they seem to have been made for our use and support.[85]

This competence over material things is twofold. The first competence is the "title to care for and distribute the earth's resources."[86] Thomas expresses three reasons for this title. The first reason is because man takes more care for those things that are his sole responsibility. Second is because human affairs are much more organized if each person has their own duty to discharge, unlike what happens when many officials are involved. The third reason is men are able to live in greater peace with each other when everyone is content with their own tasks. The second competence is for the use and management of external things. "Now in regard to this, no man is entitled to manage things merely for himself, he must do so in the interest of all, so that he is ready to share them with others in case of necessity."[87] Note the difference here between what Thomas is espousing and what Locke has written regarding man's ownership and use of material goods.

As to the distribution of goods, it is "the office of him who is their guardian. Nevertheless distributive justice is also in subjects in that they are content with the fair sharing out. Yet note that distributive justice may be from the common goods of the family, not the State, and this dispensing can be done by the authority of a private person."[88] Because "The dictates of human law cannot derogate from natural or divine law. The natural order established by God in His providence is, however, such that lower things are meant to enable man to supply his needs. A man's needs must therefore still be met out of the world's goods even though a certain division and apportionment of them is determined by law. And this is why according to natural law goods that are held in superabundance by some people should be used for the maintenance of the poor ... At the same time those who suffer want are so numerous and they cannot all be supplied out of one stock, and this is why it is left to each individual to decide how to manage his property in such a way as to supply the wants of the suffering."[89]

Thomas, in discussing the giving of alms, relates moral actions to moral precepts, and states that "precepts are about acts of virtue."[90] Further, "As love of our neighbor is a matter of precept, whatever is a necessary condition to the love of our neighbor is a matter of precept also."[91] Reason around this giving "demands that we should take into consideration something on the part of the giver, and something on the part of the recipient. On the part of the giver, it must be noted that he should give of his surplus ... On the part of the recipient it is requisite that he should be in need."[92] Thomas cites Basil in bringing his argument to its logical end. "If you acknowledge them [your temporal goods] as coming from God, is He unjust because He apportions them unequally? Why are you rich while another is poor, unless it be that you may have the merit of a good stewardship?"[93] Compare this with the competing rights for material goods that Locke has created. It would appear difficult for the good stewardship over one's possession to develop in the world Locke created. And in looking at our society and governance today, that appears to be what is happening as we have transitioned from our Founders notion of society and charity to one closer to Locke's ideals.

Summary

In my previous work I wrote about two threads. The first thread stems from Plato's writings, and even though he did not understand the scriptures, he came closer than any of the other Greek philosophers to having an understanding. His was the framework the early church fathers used in responding to pagan arguments. The second thread was picked up by Aristotle, and this thread extends through the writings of Plotinus, Averroes, Machiavelli, Spinoza, Hobbes, Locke and many others. Locke was selected for these two chapters as his work came closest within this second thread to the writings of the church fathers. He used many of the structures from their writings, but confined faith, and therefore our Creator, from the public square by relegating it to a religious sphere and a right to worship whose responsibility is to merely care for a man's soul. Sound familiar? Locke's work sits squarely between those of Hobbes and Spinoza. If Locke's arguments come closest to those of the church fathers within this thread, but are deficient in some material respects, can any of these other writers work's supported? Machiavelli advocated that the ruler should be an atheist, but can the virtue of justice, the purpose of government, exist when the one administering justice is not turned toward his Creator – the source of all virtue?

What are some of these deficiencies? They include:

1. An orientation that leans toward man over a distant Creator. A form of deism.

2. We do not have a relationship with our Creator, except through the written word. Orthodoxy is left for each man to determine. For man to be oriented toward Him, we must know Him, and we know Him through

    a. His creation.

    b. Our coming to know ourselves as we were created in His image.

    c. What He has told us about Himself through the revelations He has provided to us.

3. He is not distant, or we could not know Him - we could not try to become like Him to the extent we are able. But we are called to become like Him to the extent we can, to become good. This requires acquiring virtue and exercising stewardship on our part, and understanding both reason and faith.

4. We have a calling both as individuals and as a single people. The latter is possible because of all of the things that we share when we have a Creator orientation, as outlined by Edwards in the second chapter.

5. While the State and Church are separate spheres:

    a. Both must be oriented toward our Creator.

    b. Morality within a society cannot exist without this orientation within both spheres.

    c. The end for the Church's sphere is the promotion of those things that underlie charity, and that of the Civic sphere is justice. It can be said that the first is provided from man's nature, and the second his actions.

In closing there are several cautions that Edwards provides us about mistaking some actions for true virtue. First, self-love is not true virtue, no matter the actions performed.[94] Further, that the "approbation of virtue and dislike of vice, is easily mistaken for true virtue, not Only because those things are approved by it that have the nature of virtue, and the things disliked have the nature of vice; but because here is a great resemblance of virtuous approbation, it being complacence from love; the difference only lying in this, that it is not from love to being in general, but from self-love."[95] A second reason is that for some actions there is "indeed a true negative moral goodness in them. By a negative moral goodness, I mean the negation or absence of true moral evil."[96] This occurs when goodness is not present, but there is also an absence of evil from the actions taken. This is because all vice (sin) has its source in selfishness – in self-love.

If a man believes that he is all there is, then there is no Creator active in his life, there is no downside in placing himself above all and putting his own private interest above others. In time such persons come to treat themselves as if they are all, and make all other interests give way to their own. This often occurs when one repeats acts of sin without any punishment, or at least the visible appearance of punishment. Vice becomes disconnected from punishment and self-justified.

This is something we see happening in our society today, in many forms. From the human created rights for abortion and same sex marriage to the placing of self above the law – as demonstrated by the legislation Congress passes while exempting itself, the calls of Black Lives Matter to kill police officers, the execution of non-Muslims by the likes of ISIS, and the calling on our college campuses for free speech – but *only* if your speech agrees with someone's preconceived notion. The trick is in this, "thieves or traitors may be angry with informers that bring them to justice, and call their behavior by odious names; yet herein they are inconsistent with themselves; because, when they put themselves in the place of those who have injured them, they approve the same things they condemn."[97]

Fully two thirds of this country feel that we are on the wrong track.[98] This is evident from the actions we see all around us, some of which were just mentioned above. The only way out of this mess is through education, an education grounded in both reason *and* faith. As we will see, there is no other way. The attempts to impose an education based on secular reason alone following the supreme court decisions to remove the *Bible* and prayer from the classroom – hypocritically in the name of religious freedom – has brought disastrous results, as has the subsequent creation of the federal Department of Education. The full effects of these actions are yet to be fully felt as it is only now that a generation subjected to secular instruction are entering society as adults. It is to that topic that we turn next.

Chapter 5: The Need for Education

> *It is He, then, who has given to the human soul a mind, in which reason and understanding lie as it were asleep during infancy, and as if they were not, destined, however, to be awakened and exercised as years increase, so as to become capable of knowledge and of receiving instruction, fit to understand what is true and to love what is good. It is by this capacity the soul drinks in wisdom, and becomes endowed with those virtues by which, in prudence, fortitude, temperance, and righteousness, it makes war upon error and the other inborn vices, and conquers them by fixing its desires upon no other object than the supreme and unchangeable Good.*
>
> —St. Augustine, 5th Century

We have been referring to education's importance for the last several chapters. It is now time for that discussion. This chapter reviews education's importance from both individualism and collectivism's perspectives. A large amount of data and statistics exist covering the time our federal government has increased its control over education. If collectivism's notion of education is as good as the government has stated it is, we should see positive results from these changes, but we will let the evidence speak for itself.

Why Education Matters

There is much agreement between the two perspectives about education's importance to society. One can find passages from Plato, Aristotle, Clement, Augustine, John Adams, Ben Franklin, and Thomas Jefferson, among many others on the subject. Some, such as Plato, stated that it was society's most important activity.[1] I would posit that its primary goal is to inculcate virtue within its students through the acquisition of knowledge in both the areas of reason and faith. In sum it is the examination of experiences, either your own and/or others, and not simply the acceptance of present customs, laws, or philosophies. This examination should be done in both a backward and forward looking manner. Retrospectively by examining classical texts which serve to illustrate both models and anti-models of behavior. Prospectively, building on that basis and instilling within a student the means to think what might happen as a result of one's own choices through studies in areas such as math, logic, music, and rhetoric.

So what is virtue? At its heart, as noted in the previous chapter, it is simply goodness or righteousness. Therefore, acquiring virtue is learning how to become good. Aristotle believed that the truly virtuous man would not be in need of law, and that possessing virtue was necessary in order to be a good citizen. Plato believed that a good education created good men, and that good men would be successful. Such an education led to victory, but that victory had the potential to lead to the loss of education through the growth of a society's pride, leading to other forms of vice. Virtue's presence was seen as inhibiting vice. In reading some of the more recent translations of Aristotle and Plato's works, I noticed the word formerly translated as *virtue* was now translated as *excellence*. This new translation is a poor word choice. Virtue is good, and virtue's opposite is vice. However, excellence merely refers to doing something well and can be applied to the performance of either good or evil, virtue or vice. The terms do not represent exactly the same thing, but the newer term is consistent with the moral relativism we see around us today.

So why does education, and the goal of virtue, matter? First, Aristotle believed that education was the means by which a state is united and made into a community, making individuals into a people. The Roman general and statesman Scipio defined a people as "a multitude bound together by a mutual recognition of rights and a mutual co-operation for the common good."[2] Being a people depended on the presence of virtue, for if there were no virtue there would be no justice, and without justice there could be no people.

Second, virtue was the unity of both reason and emotion, the proper ordering of both the head and heart—or the mind and the soul. This is a key difference between collectivism and individualism: "The argument for collectivism is simple if false; it is an immediate emotional argument. The argument for individualism is subtle and sophisticated; it is an indirect rational argument. And the emotional faculties are more highly developed in most men than the rational, even in those who regard themselves as intellectuals."[3] Collective arguments focus almost solely on the heart, while the individualism arguments place an ordering between the mind and the heart. In the latter, both are needed and the mind often comes first.

There is much agreement between the collectivism and individualism notions on the importance of education, but here is where the collectivism thread represented by those such as Plato and Aristotle, and their more modern contemporaries, separates from the individualism thread. Those such as Plato and Aristotle simply believed in education as the means by which the state was perpetuated. This is partially true, but the state is not the end. Those advocating the individualism thread such as Clement, Augustine, Thomas, and our Founding Fathers saw something additional which to them was more important. They understood that education provided the foundation for the acquisition and exercise of virtue, and by that process we become like our Creator—who is the Good—to the extent we can. This process of becoming good fulfills our individual purpose and in the process benefits society. It enables the creation of a society where progress is possible, and it can only happen in the presence of free will—freedom—where individuals are not coerced into making choices. Witness the technical developments occurring during the Middle Ages after Rome's fall as outlined in Chapter 2.

Within the individualism thread, just getting a good education is not enough. Education's contents cannot be limited to reason alone. Clement saw that both faith and reason were necessary in achieving our purpose of becoming good. This view laid the foundation for much of the later theological/philosophical thoughts of the early church fathers. There are two levels within individualism. We have touched on both previously several times. The first is at the individual level and is the act of fulfilling our purpose by becoming good. A good education is required as we are not born with virtues. The second level is as a people. We are called to be a people, and being a people requires virtue in order for justice to exist. The exercise of reason and faith requires individual choice: free will. Freedom. Coercion by the state directly conflicts with the achievement of our purpose and therefore our ability to be a people. In fact, we find that most who practice collectivism do so by dividing instead of uniting people, often in the name of righting some perceived wrongs. They often express a Robin Hood approach to problem solving using wealth redistribution –, based upon their (man's) view of justice. Witness todays arguments put forth about social justice and refugee resettlement.

The above individualism notions are echoed in the words of our Founding Fathers. In the *Virginia Act for Establishing Religious Freedom*, Jefferson said the following: "Well aware that Almighty God hath created the mind free; that all attempts to influence it by temporal punishments or burdens, or by civil incapacitations ... are a departure from the plan of the Holy Author of our religion, who being Lord both of body and mind, yet chose not to propagate it by coercions on either, as was in his Almighty power to do."[4] He further stated in his *Notes on the State of Virginia*, "But our rulers can have authority over such natural rights only as we have submitted to them. The rights of conscience we never submitted, we could not submit. We are answerable for them to our God. The legitimate powers of government extend to such acts only as are injurious to others."[5]

There is a limit to the power of what Locke termed the civil sphere, and that is the execution of justice. The rest is up to us. If man was destined to live in coercion under the state, our Creator could have easily set things up that way, but He did not. It was His purpose for us that we have and use our mind, reason, and the free will that each one of us was gifted with. We will and do mess up, but our Creator takes our mistakes and turns them to His good. "It is accordingly the greatest achievement of divine Providence, not to allow the evil which has sprung from voluntary apostasy, to remain useless, and for no good ... but especially to ensure that what happens through the evils hatched by any, may come to a good and useful issue, and to use to advantage those things which appear to be evils, as also the testimony which accrues from temptation."[6]

In addressing the continuance of political prosperity, Washington stated the following in his farewell address: "Of all the dispositions and habits which lead to political prosperity, religion and morality are indispensable supports. In vain would that man claim the tribute of patriotism, who should labor to subvert these great pillars of human happiness, these firmest props of the duties of men and citizens. The mere politician, equally with the pious man, ought to respect and to cherish them. A volume could not trace all their connections with private and public felicity. Let it simply be asked: Where is the security for property, for reputation, for life, if the sense of religious obligation desert the oaths which are the instruments of investigation in courts of justice?"[7]

Below is the diagram presented earlier on the relationship between justice and the notions we've been discussing.

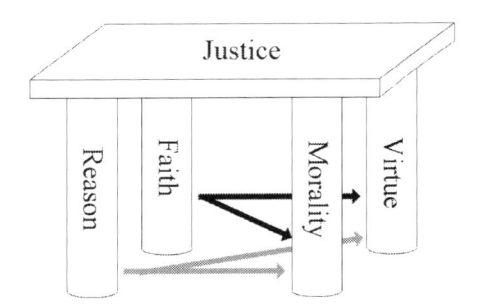

[Diagram: A table labeled "Justice" on top, supported by four pillars labeled "Reason", "Faith", "Morality", and "Virtue", with arrows from Reason and Faith pointing to Morality and Virtue.]

Reason and faith provide the basis for virtue and morality. The four together support justice, which provides society's foundation. Some, like Locke and George Mason, argued that reason alone was sufficient to produce virtue and morality. While it may be possible, I would suggest that this greatly weakens the structure of justice, because without faith society becomes centered on man. History has shown this never works in the long-run, just as Augustine chronicled Rome's demise from the same problem in his work *The City of God*. Both reason and faith must be present. These supports provide for the development of virtue and morality. It is only when all four pillars are present that the table of justice can exist and serve as a foundation for creating a people—and a successful society. Take any one of these four pillars away, and if left unattended, that society will eventually fail.

Collectivism and Individualism Differences

So far we've looked at the "why" and some of the "what" about education, from both collectivism and individualism perspectives. Both groups view education as one of the most important responsibilities within a society, as it is the means of perpetuating society, but for very different reasons. It is important to understand these differences as they shape the content of the education provided, its delivery, and who receives it. Within collectivism this amounts to the state perpetuating itself and the societal status quo. According to both Plato and Aristotle, the state is the lowest level within a society which matters. While their writings are ancient, their ideas are still relevant — there is nothing new under the sun.

The state's purpose is to bring people into harmony by either persuasion or compulsion[8], as the legislator's job is to not only write laws but to blend into them the explanations as to both what is respectable and what is not in regards to the perfect citizen, and bound its people by standards backed with legal sanctions.[9] The state is to decide what is best and to compel teachers to learn this material.[10] This material should include and be based upon information derived from various occupations, and includes control of words and the determination of what is good and bad.[11] Teachers are to be public instructors, and they are to be supported with public funds.[12] Finally, the children were to be given over to officials appointed for the purpose of educating them,[13] for the citizens did not belong to themselves; they ultimately belonged to the State.[14]

In short, the state is to determine what is good and bad, require teachers to learn this material, and use this material to educate all children who receive an education. It is also the state's role to enforce compliance with its standards of good and bad through the laws it sanctions and the penalties it enforces. This later is not much different from the views of the Hamiltonians and Jeffersonians in our own early history. The Hamiltonians believed that the state should rig the game so that only good behaviors would be rewarded from the state's view. The Jeffersonians, on the other hand, believed it was the state's role to prevent bad behavior, again from the state's view of what was bad. Both men and both views were wrong. It is disappointing that in the end even Jefferson could not place his faith in a paper constitution, or the ideas and people it represented. However, this does not mean that either men were collectivists—they were both very far from it, but in the end they were still just men. It is the modern collectivists who followed them who have perverted their ideas and words.

We see people starting to understand what collectivism truly represents today, and why it doesn't work. As the final edits were being made to this manuscript, the people of Great Britain voted to leave the European Union. Why? Because they felt they had lost control over decisions that mattered to them such as immigration. Instead decisions are being imposed upon them by faceless bureaucrats in Brussels. What has been the response of some political elites in Parliament? Calls to overturn the vote to leave as the elites know what is best. We see a similar movement here in the U.S. with the nomination of Donald Trump for president. His campaign has been focused on taking our country back from Washington - particularly in the areas of border security (immigration again) and the economy (trade, taxation, and regulation). This book expands those discussions and takes them to their ultimate end, charity versus entitlement.

So let's look at the other side of individualism. Clement, Augustine, and Thomas said very little about the state and education directly, only that education was vital and must include both the languages of reason and faith. Understanding both was necessary, and was embodied in the education generally given during the Middle Ages. That education included history in order to understand the past and derive what were good and bad models of behavior. In addition, education also needed to develop critical thinking skills in order for the student to develop the means of individually making good decisions going forward. It included the teaching of philosophy, rhetoric, math, and logic. Those addressed the aspect of education associated with reason. They also coupled history and the *New Testament* to teach about morality. Man alone is fallible. The inclusion of ideas based upon Divine and Natural Law was necessary in order to preserve society, as it is only within the context of our Creator that we have a basis for (1) existence, (2) morality, and (3) knowledge.

These components were necessary to learn charity: understanding the things of faith, creating the aptitude to make good choices (responsibly exercising freedom), and embodying morally righteous actions—virtues. An education in these matters is necessary if man is to fulfill his primary purpose, as an individual, of becoming good. That purpose can only be accomplished by individuals themselves using the drive they have from within. Morality imposed from the outside by another, including the state, ceases to be moral. This primary purpose has little to do directly with the state. Finally, it is only this education that provides the moral basis allowing man to self-govern.

But there is also a second purpose we are to fulfill within individualism: that of being a people. This purpose does touch upon the state, and I think that we can infer a few things about education and being a people from this perspective. First, that to be a people required two things: both a mutual recognition of rights and the mutual co-operation for the common good. The state's role is to administer justice when these rights are not observed or the common good is not upheld. These mutual rights would normally be defined within a constitution or social contract between those governing and the governed. Second, that morality and virtue needed to be present within any society if justice was to be present. After all, justice itself is a virtue. As stated earlier, virtues must be inculcated through education and exercise; we are not born with them. For morality and virtue to be present, either (1) those given to rule must be well educated, or (2) all the people should receive an education so that they are capable of participating in this second purpose. Collectivism professes the first approach, individualism the second.

Plato viewed society as being comprised of four levels, those who were either *gold* (those who governed, the guardians), *silver* (those who supported the guardians), *brass* (artisans and laborers), or *iron* (farmers). Slaves were not considered. Aristotle had more divisions, but his approach was basically the same. The structure of these societies resembled a pyramid. The guardians were the smallest group, their assistants were larger in number, and finally by far the largest segment of the population consisted of the remaining groups. These views were consistent with the structure of state religion societies like Rome and Greece.

This is because rule was to be held by the small number who excelled in virtue, the elite, while those who labored for a living were not considered capable of practicing virtue.[15] Citizenship could be obtained only by those who had been freed from such menial service, those considered to be gold or silver. The artisans and farmers occupied a level between the citizens and the slaves, freemen but without the full rights of citizenship. This lack of citizenship would exclude them from holding office, and from being included within society's elite. Once established, these classes were largely permanent, as it was believed that parents usually produced children like themselves.[16] Both men believed that education should be provided to members of society, and it was to be an education that prepared one for their future occupation. The best education was to be reserved for those who would most need it: those who would be citizens and participate in governance, and this education was to be paid for out of public funds.

Why is Public Funding a Problem?

Initially, public education in America had a Christian basis, grounded in the scholastic curricula of the trivium and quadrivium, the very education received by our Founders. Our present approach to public education began only about a century ago and is not very different from the views of Plato or Aristotle noted above. How? Few remember today that the original purpose of our current public education system was not to inculcate morality and virtue, but instead to produce skilled laborers for employment within factories by creating general skills in reading, writing, math, and a capacity to follow directions. In short, an education needed to prepare individuals for their future occupations, just as Plato and Aristotle believed. In addition, it was to be paid for with public funds, just as Plato and Aristotle believed. More advanced education was reserved for those who either had the means or exhibited great promise, just as Plato and Aristotle believed.

Our current system reflects the belief that it is the elite who can best determine the values to be taught and who they should be taught to—just as Plato and Aristotle believed. Don't think so? Look at the "health" mandates in support of "reproductive" rights, the "speech codes" at places like the Universities of Delaware or North Carolina, and the activities aimed at the forced acceptance of homosexuality done in the name of anti-bullying being performed in our public schools, just to name a few. It is the same root. Underlying it all is the bigotry that you are not capable of making your own decisions, and the movement away from individual virtue, morality, and responsibility towards a collective morality, just as Plato and Aristotle believed. When you lose your ability to make your own decisions, you lose your freedom. Period. My how far we've come to arrive at a place that looks very much like the one our Founders left behind.

With this change we risk losing what has brought us so far, and if we think that we will avoid the repercussions that have occurred to other civilizations before us who have thought the same things, we are sadly mistaken. Insanity is doing the same things over and over again, but expecting something different to happen. What are those things that have brought us so far in relation to education? First, that everyone within a society has the same nature, therefore, they should have access to, and the opportunity to receive, a common curriculum which teaches the languages of both reason and faith. The purpose is fourfold: (1) to inculcate morality in its students, (2) to learn from the past and develop critical reasoning skills so that they can achieve their purpose, (3) to fully develop whatever skills and abilities one has to go as far as they desire and are able, and (4) ensure they are equipped to govern themselves to prepare them for the gift of freedom.

A free society can only function if its members have acquired virtue and learned how to govern themselves. Freedom, in conjunction with virtue, enables a society to develop and flourish as each individual contributes what they are best at—fulfilling their purpose—which in turn results in progress being made within a society. One piece of evidence to support this: Florence, Italy was one of the early cities where freedom developed. As a result, by the tenth century it was a very prosperous city. Rodney Stark in his book *The Victory of Reason* cites a 1338 survey from that city which indicates that almost one-half of all school age children were engaged in some type of education. This is a level that would have been unheard of in Plato's or Aristotle's day.

Second, the control of this common subject matter is best left in the hands of those closest to the students, the community in which they live. We all learn differently. I taught 2–4 year-olds for a year in Sunday

School. I was most successful when I prepared two different approaches to a topic, one for those who learned best by listening and talking and another for those who learned by doing. Even then, each child had different aptitudes for specific kinds of information. Only a community is in a position to determine what its children need in terms of education, as they know them best. As for higher education, should this not then be left either in the hands of the individual college or university if it is privately funded, or in the hands of the community itself if public funds are used to provide that education? The question then becomes *Should public funds even be used for education?*

Madison and Jefferson believed learning the languages of both faith and reason were important, but struggled with how to incorporate religion and morality into public education. Both, like many of our Founders, believed this aspect of education was critical for society, but they also understood that government must be kept out of religion. Religion was to have an indirect influence on governance through the morality and virtue it taught the people, but the Federal government was to have no role in religion—including its teaching. That is the intent of our *Constitution* for the Federal government. Whether they would have extended this prohibition to the States is unknown, as nine of the thirteen Colonies had official State religions when the *Constitution* was ratified. It is doubtful that a *Constitution* with such a limitation would have been ratified at that time. Both men had seen firsthand the corrupting influences of state supported religion within the Colonies. Both also participated in a project where these issues were brought into focus.

Late in their lives, Jefferson and Madison served in creating the University of Virginia.[17] The university was publicly funded by the people of the Commonwealth of Virginia. Their first hire to head the school was a man by the name of Cooper. He was widely regarded as brilliant, but of at best questionable moral character. Such public pressure was brought to bear on the young institution that it was forced to release Cooper. This pressure included the threat of withholding public funds to the university as "it was not religious enough." In the end, they determined that religion should not be taught using public funds, but that an extensive collection of religious materials, both Christian and non-Christian, should be purchased with public funds, maintained at the University, and made available for all students *who should be encouraged to study them and learn on their own, instead of being taught.*

I believe they made a mistake in advocating using public funds for education. Is there any clearer argument against their use for this purpose than the example above? Wouldn't a better choice be using the philanthropy of the individuals within a community itself to fund the education of its own young? Most schools, colleges, and universities during this country's founding were in fact privately financed. If both the languages of reason and faith must be taught to develop morality and virtue, but the federal government is to be kept out of religion, what other answer could there be? It should be stressed that this does not mean that religion per se should be taught, but rather the underlying moral code and philosophy should be incorporated into education.

Third, beyond this set of core subjects, the choice of whether to continue an education, and its direction, should be left in the hands of the individual student. It should not be decided by an "elite" or based upon the occupation of one's parents. Otherwise how can each individual fully understand and use the talents, skills, and abilities that they have received? If they do not achieve their potential, how can a society succeed? Underlying this notion is the belief that things can be better tomorrow than they are today. It is a uniquely Judeo-Christian perspective, rooted in the virtue of hope. But this hope, as a virtue, requires individual effort and responsibility to achieve.

Augustine realized the need for this type of education. To close this section, I'll simply cite a quote from his *City of God*, written in the fifth century over 1,500 years ago. It reads as follows: "What wonderful— one might say stupefying—advances has human industry made in the arts of weaving and building, of agriculture and navigation! With what endless variety are designs in pottery, painting, and sculpture produced, and with what skill executed! What wonderful spectacles are exhibited in the theatres, which those who have not seen them cannot credit! How skillful the contrivances for catching, killing, or taming wild beasts! ... Who could tell the thought that has been spent upon nature, even though, despairing of recounting it in detail, he endeavored only to give a general view of it? In fine, even the defence of errors and misapprehensions, which has illustrated the genius of heretics and philosophers, cannot be sufficiently declared. For at present it is the nature of the human mind which adorns this mortal life which we are extolling, and not the faith and the way of truth which lead to immortality."[18] Perhaps because it represents the alignment of mind with our purpose.

How Well Are We Doing?

I will present two arguments. The first will be a logical one. Its basis is that, at its core, collectivism believes that all people are not created equal, or more precisely, that some are created more equal than others. Groups comprised of those who share common traits exist for the purpose of determining rights and obligations; the fewer groups, the greater control the State can exercise. This is captured by both Plato's and Aristotle's thoughts on the relationship between the state, education, and citizenship. Their relevant thoughts can be summarized as follows:

- Rights come only from the State and can be changed by the State at any time based upon its determination of a society's needs and goals.
- Man is to be ruled by his superiors, those who excel in the ability to govern, who they believed would excel in virtue. We are therefore not all equal. There exists at least one elite class.
- It is the elite who decide the State's needs and goals.
- All the people cannot be citizens, that status is reserved only for the elite.

- Education should be publicly funded and received by all, as it is the state's means of perpetuating itself. Therefore, education is intended to serve the state, but the education received would depend upon the group to which you belong.
- In Aristotle's view, the underlying notion is that man is self-sufficient; that there are many goods and many truths (moral relativism). These goods and truths have their basis in man alone.

Think these are not true today? Take a look at what is happening within education. More and more funding is being provided and mandates being issued by the federal government concerning education. The goal is the standardization of education, a standardization determined by those in government, those who view themselves as the elite. Standardized testing is being required, first through No Child Left Behind and now a standardized curriculum created through Common Core. Our textbooks are being increasingly "purified" to remove any offensive materials or references to religion—at least to Christianity — with offensive being defined by those put in charge of the editing. Teachers' time is increasingly scheduled down to the minute as to the text they will use, what material is to be presented, and how it is to be taught. We have a federal government that is increasingly determining the curriculum, the materials to be used, how the class time is to be used, and employing testing to ensure that this material is learned. Along the way there are many strings attached and regulatory requirements to ensure compliance.

Now let's take a quick look from the other perspective using a few key thoughts from our Founders, through some of the documents they left behind. There are many we can look at, but we can simply use the *Declaration* and *Constitution* as these were intended to be public expressions of commonly held beliefs. The *Declaration* states that we have rights which come from our Creator, which include life, liberty, and the pursuit of happiness. Life is the most basic of all rights, for without this right none of the rest matter. It comes solely from our Creator. Liberty is the freedom from tyranny, or the right to be allowed to make our own choices. This is free will, a gift from our Creator and necessary in order for us to fulfill our purpose. The Huguenots and others equated the pursuit of happiness with property. In a primarily agricultural society such as existed at our country's founding, and during much of the Middle Ages when freedom developed, property represented not only wealth but for many people the means to their survival.

However, I do not think this was intended to be the primary reference for this last right. The Judeo-Christian philosophy/theology that our Founders had received through their education asserted that happiness follows from attaining what Greek philosophers called The Good—our Creator—to the extent we are capable. It appears to me that the pursuit of happiness is therefore also a reference to the freedom to fulfill our purposes, both as individuals and a people, which can only be achieved by coming to know our Creator. It appears that Locke at least agrees as he put happiness in the religious sphere. This view is not only consistent with the rights of life and liberty, but serves as an extension of them into what we choose—to become good. This point is expressed in the writings of Clement of Alexandria, Augustine, and Thomas among others. Even Plato stated that the end of happiness is The Good, and that every man should do his best to make his own character reflect His to the extent he is able.

As for the *Constitution*, we can simply look at the rights contained within the Bill of Rights, the first ten amendments to this document. The first amendment cited provides for the freedom of religion, the opportunity for each of us to know our Creator, to fulfill our purpose. This is more than the mere right to worship. Anyone who thinks those two ideas are the same does not understand their purpose. They are like lost sheep, or perhaps wolves in sheep's clothing. This amendment also contains the right to express ourselves by both the spoken and written word. In short, to communicate with one another. Without this freedom, we could not become, nor remain, a people. The remaining rights in these first ten amendments concern the purpose of government and the recognition of our equality as all being created in the image of our Creator. These later rights have been expressed in many medieval documents, and I would suggest that the *Declaration* itself is also a medieval document. Other such documents include the *Magna Charta*, *The Petition of Right*, *The Right of Abjuration*, and *A Defense of Liberty against Tyrants* among others. All of the rights expressed in these documents have their basis in Divine and Natural Law.

Now let us look at some of the more recent freedoms and rights created by our government. Roosevelt declared the rights of freedom from fear and want and Johnson a right to freedom from poverty. More recently we have the rights to education (Carter), home ownership (Clinton), equitable income and healthcare (Obama). These do not have their basis in Divine or Natural law, except by addition also expressed by Locke, and are merely government creations. In the words of F.A. Hayek, these are promises of security offered in exchange for some of your liberty. Aren't these the same promises made by the serpent in the Garden of Eden? Go ahead and take a bite, it won't cost you a thing and think of all you will gain. However, taking that bite cost Adam and Eve their relationship with their Creator and brought death upon themselves—a pretty hefty price, don't you think? It is no different with these later promises. Give us control over these things; we can protect you better than you can protect yourselves. We will help you; it won't cost you anything. However, in the end it costs you the ability to fulfill your purpose as you are no longer able to make your own choices. No matter how well intentioned, at its heart the elitism underlying all collectivism represents a type of bigotry, an assertion you are incapable of caring for yourself. Do you believe that is the case? As noted by Locke, either a government has the power to change all things within an area or nothing; there is no in between.

The two views above are contradictory; they cannot co-exist. In the end, each of us must choose one or the other, no one can serve two masters. Which one will you choose?

Some of you reading this probably will not accept the above argument. That is fine. We can also look at things from a purely economic viewpoint, from the view of stewardship. From a big picture perspective, we only need to look at three things: (1) the population to be served, (2) the resources being consumed, and (3) the results obtained from expending those resources on education. We next look at each of these in turn.

The U.S. Department of Education was created in October, 1979 under the Carter administration. Its purpose was to improve education. Improvement can come about in a number of ways. These include (1) increased output in terms of numbers or improved quality with the same amount of resources, (2) fewer resources being consumed to produce the same output, or (3) shortening the timeframe to achieve the same output while maintaining quality. To put this within the perspective of education, if improvement has occurred, we should see at least one of the following: (1) improvement in outputs such as test scores indicating subject proficiency in areas such as math or reading, (2) improvement in the graduation rate, (3) a reduction in the number of personnel necessary to educate the same number of students, or at least a reduction in the overall amount of resources necessary, or (4) attaining a specific degree within a shorter period of time.

Our analysis uses data from the last 50 years. This allows for a pre-Department of Education baseline that can be compared to results achieved during the Department's existence. Let's start by looking at the population to be served, the number of enrolled students. From 1970 through 2010, this population only grew by about 7.8%. In comparison, the entire U.S. population during this same time grew by just over 51%. Based upon the modest student growth, we should expect to see a growth in the number of teachers by about 8%, less if there have been increased efficiencies through the implementation of technology or improved teaching methodology.

However, during this same time period the number of teachers has grown not just by about 8%, but by 60% and the number of non-teaching staff by an astounding 138%. The percentage of teachers as a total of school staff has dropped from 59.9% in 1970 to only 50% by 2010, so now only 1 in 2 public school employees teach in a classroom. Instead of the expected modest growth in the number of teachers, the growth in the number of teachers is 7 times that of the growth in the number of students and it is 17 times greater for non-teaching staff.

Growth in Education Staffing Has Far Outpaced Student Enrollment

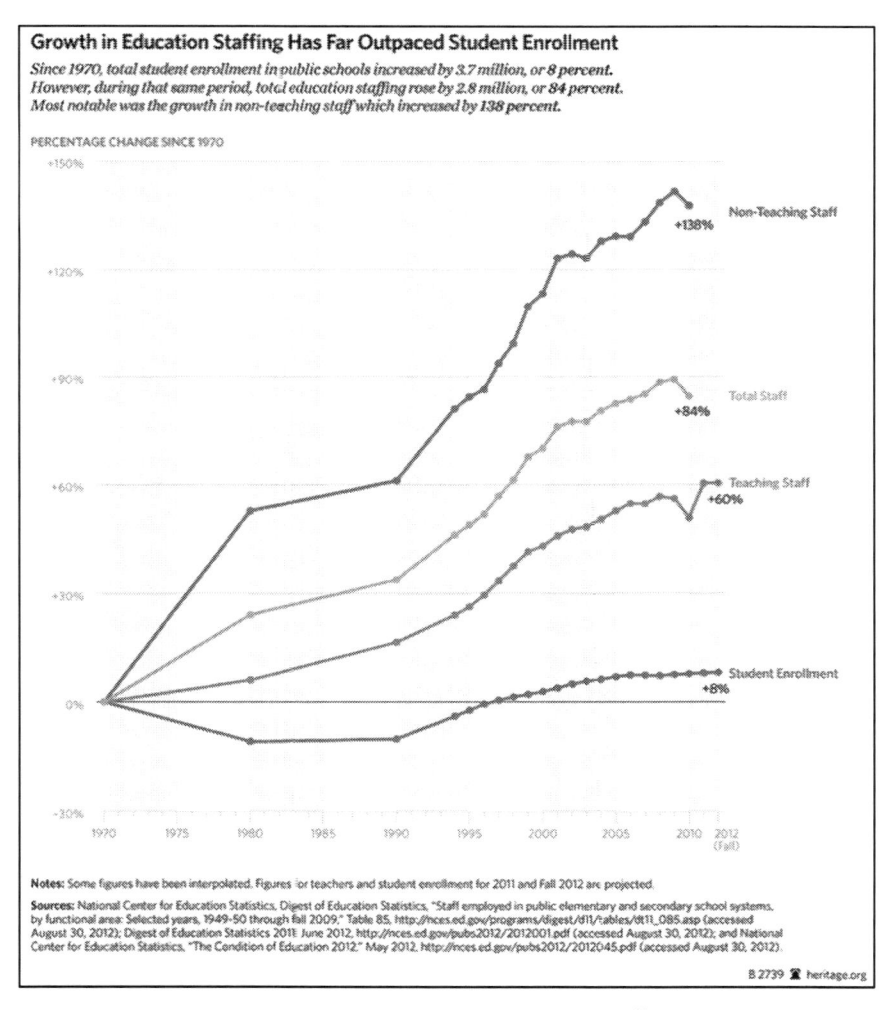

Since 1970, total student enrollment in public schools increased by 3.7 million, or 8 percent. However, during that same period, total education staffing rose by 2.8 million, or 84 percent. Most notable was the growth in non-teaching staff which increased by 138 percent.

Figure 1: Growth in Education Staffing[19]

This dramatic increase in personnel is reflected in the spending per student, where the U.S now ranks second only to Switzerland, spending more than $90,000 per student between the ages of six and fifteen. Further, the 13-year cost of public education for a high-school graduate in 2009 rose to about $149,000. This represents an increase of almost 200% from the $50,000 figure for the same education back in 1970. These figures are shown in the graphs below.

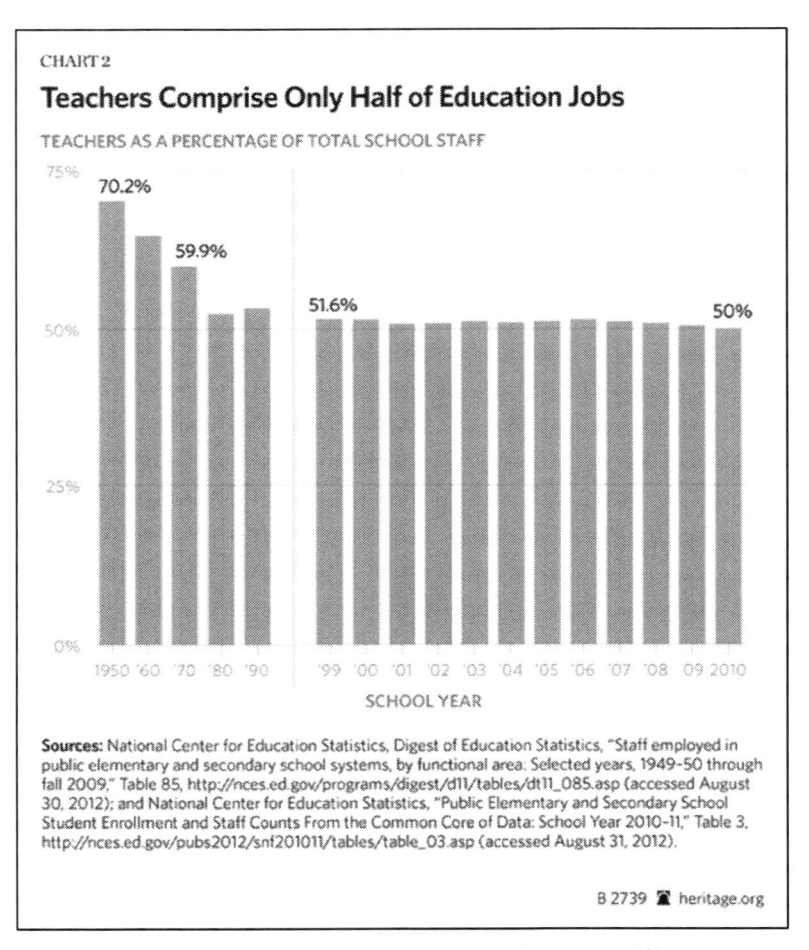

Figure 2: Teachers as a Percentage of School Staff[20]

K-12 Spending Per Student in the OECD

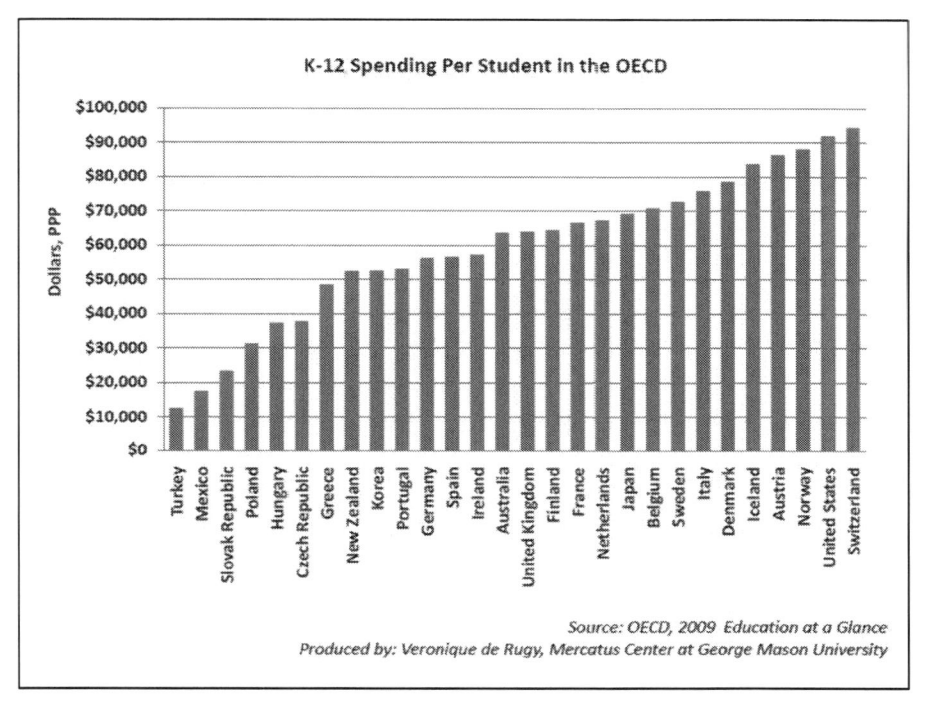

Source: OECD, 2009 Education at a Glance
Produced by: Veronique de Rugy, Mercatus Center at George Mason University

Figure 3: K-12 Spending Per Student in the OECD[21]

These data demonstrate that we have experienced a much more rapid growth in resources, and corresponding costs, to deliver the education necessary for a high school diploma over the last forty years. The savings generated by any process efficiencies have been more than offset by cost increases. So what about through-put in terms of the number of students graduating, or outputs in terms of the subject matter proficiency of high school graduates?

The usual reported graduation statistics include the number of students receiving GEDs, in addition to those receiving high-school diplomas. Such reporting overstates the number of actual high school graduates each year. Work by Nobel laureate Jim Heckman and Paul LaFontaine developed a measure based upon the actual number of high-school diplomas awarded. That information is presented in the graph below.

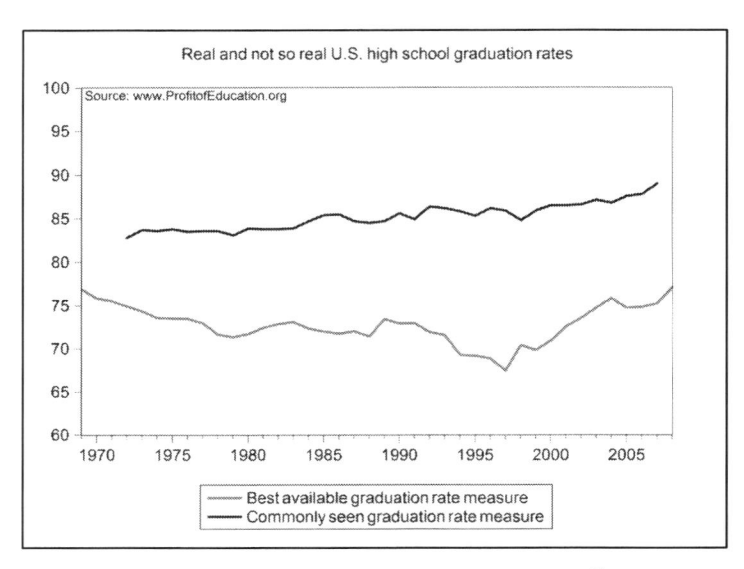

Figure 4: U.S. High School Graduation Rates[22]

The year 1969 represented a high-point in terms of the percentage of high-school students receiving a diploma. We can see that the percentage of high school students receiving diplomas actually declined for the next twenty seven years. It is only in the last ten years that the graduation rate improved. Even then it has only managed to return to where it was forty years ago when the Department of Education began. And it only took a 200% increase in cost per student to get us back to where we started.

Math and reading are two of education's basic building blocks on which all other subjects rely. The U.S.'s math and reading proficiency scores over the last forty years are presented below. These graphs show that both reading and math proficiencies have remained flat during the Department of Education's tenure, although there has been some minor improvement in the reading scores of the least proficient.

Collectivism and Charity 151

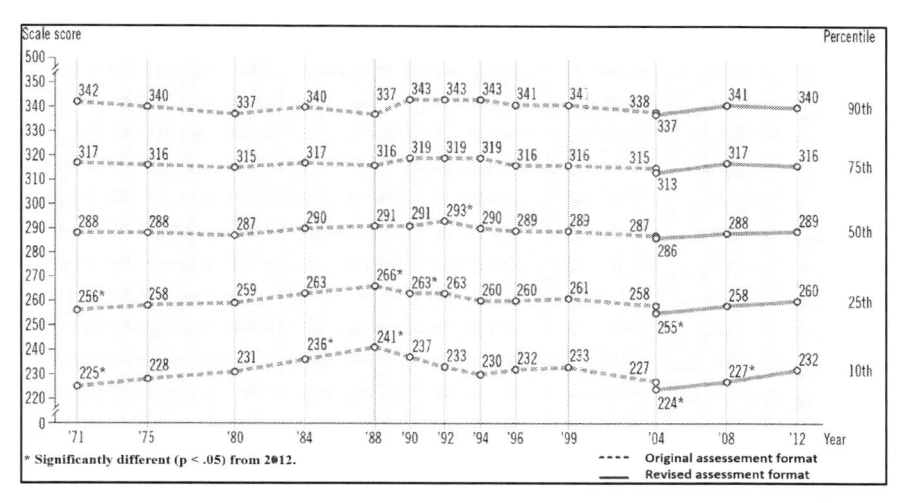

Figure 5: Trend in NAEP reading percentile scores for 17-year-old students[23]

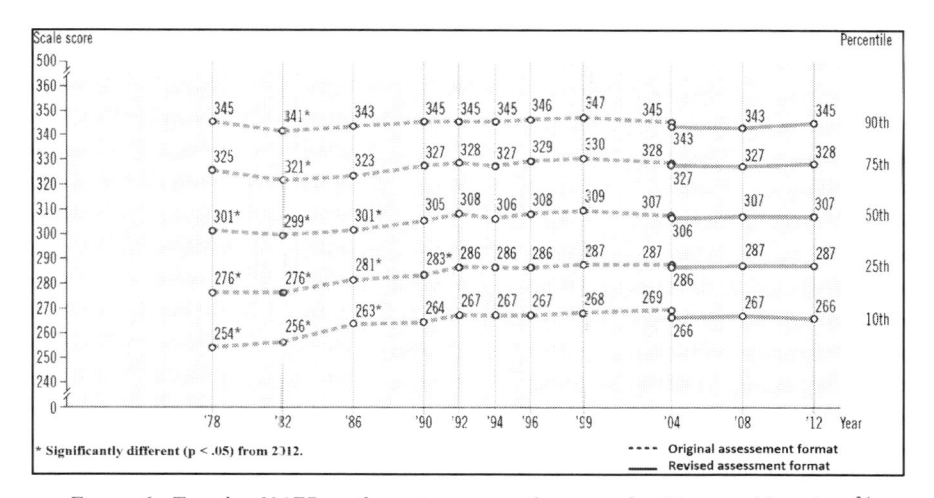

Figure 6: Trend in NAEP mathematics percentile scores for 17-year-old students[24]

In addition, I have reviewed the most recent International Programme for International Student Assessment (PISA) scores for the U.S.[25] Remember we spend more per student than every other country except Switzerland. What we've achieved is a ranking for reading of 17th out of the 65 countries participating in the program, and a ranking of 32nd in math. Massachusetts ranks first among the states in both scores within the U.S. and is the only state which scored above the proficiency mark for math. Only four additional states had a math proficiency score over 40 percent. Some of our most populous states, having some of our largest economies, scored below the U.S. average on both tests. These included California, Florida, Illinois, Michigan, and Missouri. Both New York and Texas were above average on one test score, but below average on the other.

We have almost tripled our per student expenditures for education over the last forty years and what have we obtained in return? We have gotten a decrease in students receiving diplomas for a large part of that time, stagnant scores in math and reading proficiency and ratings that lag further behind the rest of the world in both math and reading proficiency. Our Department of Education has clearly failed its mission, and more resources will not change its failure.

A Possible Solution

Education is such an important topic that, given what has been outlined so far, are there any recommendations that can correct the problems noted? I truly believe improving our education will require the following changes in some form.

First, there should ideally be no public funding of education, at least as we currently know it today. The Federal Government's involvement in education is inconsistent with the type of education a student must receive and, as outlined earlier, government involvement in education presents an incompatibility: it creates a conflict between government and those it was formed to serve, much like the conflict between governance and charity during the Renaissance. It is not a coincidence this is occurring today. Second, today's education is largely funded by state and local property taxes, with some block grants and other forms of assistance thrown into the mix. The means to locally collect revenue supporting schools and the mechanisms to administer these funds at both the state and local level already exist. Our Founders identified several taxation methods for generating revenue, which include income, consumption, assets, and wealth. Each basis has its pluses and minuses. What really matters is that only a single method is chosen and applied, so there is a high level of transparency in what monies are collected and how they are used.

One of the main problems today is that these monies are "transferred" from private individuals to the government. They "become" state or federal funds, reducing the level of accountability to the people the government has been formed to serve, just like the taking control of charitable organizations during the Renaissance reduced the accountability between those holding the funds (a municipal government) and those who were to receive them. Rather than continue our present system, these funds should be collected and held locally in trust on behalf of the student and their parents. It is the student, along with his or her parents, who should decide which school receives those funds based upon where they choose to send their child to school. As these funds would be held in trust, these funds would not become the governments. Instead, they would remain in the hands of individuals to whom the funds belonged or, more specifically, within the hands of the trustees charged with the fiduciary responsibility of looking after the student's, and their parents interests, and they would be legally liable if they failed in that duty; justice would be present.

Many of the items in the following list already exist for private schools that must be accountable to their students and their parents who pay the tuition. The recommendations in this list would extend some form of those same processes and procedures to the current public schools. These recommendations include the following:

1. Schools would continue to create their budgets and, at the same time, would maintain locally chosen performance metrics that would be used to provide cost and performance information to parents. The measures a particular school chooses would offer further information on its particular area(s) of educational expertise and how well it delivers on its goals.

2. A parent would apply for entry into a particular school when their child reached the age to begin attending it. As the monies used would not be government funds, but only funds held in trust for the parents and students, application for admittance could be submitted to any local school that would be paid using these funds.

3. Property assessments, if property were to be used as the taxing basis, would be collected at the local level based upon the stated funding needs of the schools within their jurisdiction. These amounts would be subject to agreement by the community, the schools would need to argue their case and demonstrate their ability.

   The sum total of these monies would be divided equally among all of the students within said jurisdiction. It would then be up to the parent and student to choose which school received those funds after their student had been accepted. Once a student is enrolled at a school, they would continue to attend that school unless the parent/student decided another school would better meet their needs, at which time they would need to apply to that other school.

4. There would likely be differences between the proration received by the parents for their child's education and the amount required by the school. In cases where the school's tuition is more, it would be the parent's responsibility to make up the difference. In cases where a school's tuition is less than the average provided to the student, those excess funds should be retained by the trust. At the end of the year, any remaining funds should be used as an adjustment in determining the amount of funding needed by the schools in the following year, and used in calculating the new assessments.

5. Scholarships could still be set up with outside funds and administered separately by schools, or other organizations, based upon their stated goals and objectives.

6. This approach has the following advantages:

a. It removes the government from education, which allows curriculums to be based upon what students need to be taught: both the languages of reason and faith.
   b. It removes the monetary strings from regulatory requirements associated with government funding, thereby reducing the overall resources needed. This should in turn reduce the overall headcount needed to provide education and put more focus back onto teaching headcount within schools, and away from administrative and other support personnel.
   c. Schools are held directly accountable to the student and their parents for education. If a school does a good job its enrollment will expand. If it does a poor job, enrollment will contract. If a poorly run school does not improve, it should go out of business. New schools would be created by the marketplace to serve needs that are not being met within the community.
   d. Schools would need to actively plan accordingly for the number of students they wish to serve, capacity planning, and take action accordingly.
7. This approach to a large extent removes the problem of geography associated with our current public education structure by allowing parents more freedom in choosing a school for their child, regardless of where they live. Unlike our present system, parents would have funds available to be applied to their child's education, providing them the capability of acting upon this greater freedom.
8. It allows teachers to decide if they want to belong to a union or not. If unionized teachers deliver a higher quality education, then the various costs associated with union membership will be acceptable to parents through the school selection they make for their child.

9. There would be an incentive for schools to provide efficiencies in educating students, which over time would lower the cost of education as schools would be competing in a marketplace. In turn, parents would pay less in tuition, and the community would benefit as it would see less collected from its constituents in taxes to meet school funding needs. These additional funds should find their way into the local economy through spending or increased savings, both of which would benefit the community. The primary driver of overall funding needs would shift to the increase or decrease in the number of school age children living within a county or municipality.

Second, as noted above, there must be a curriculum which teaches both the languages of reason and faith. It is only when an education in both of these areas is received that virtue and morality can exist over the long-term within a society. Without virtue and morality, justice cannot exist, and this is the primary reason for the government's existence. As the language of faith must be taught, and religion is to be protected from the influence of government, the only logical alternative, as noted above, is that government have no role in education. Citizens would need to make these decisions, in some cases through state constitutional amendments, but there is simply no other way. Any compromise would put us on a path that would bring us back to where we are today, and I would suggest that maybe this is one reason why performance indicators have not improved as government has become more involved in education. Maybe it is because the students realize that much of the education they currently receive is really not education at all but propaganda.

I'll admit that I have no hard evidence for this, but I do have one piece of anecdotal evidence. When our daughter was studying political policy at a very left-leaning East Coast college, she decided to switch majors late in her sophomore year. The reason, in her own words, was that she knew there was more than one perspective within the subjects being taught, but there was only a single view being presented in class and declared to be truth. She saw the focus of education she had been pursuing as not being valuable and changed her major. I am proud of her and her decision. I would suggest that she is far from alone in her realization.

Third, students should be responsible for their own education. A society can only present a student with the opportunity to learn, but make no mistake, an education is a privilege and not a right. No one can make another learn, or do much of anything else they do not want to do for that matter. Society does have a responsibility to offer its youth the opportunity to obtain a good education. Beyond that it is up to the student to take advantage of that opportunity by making effective use of the skills, aptitudes, and talents they have been blessed. The consequences of failing to apply oneself in education should rest on the student alone. Two quotes from the Bible support this position. First from Luke, "From everyone who has been given much, much will be required."[26] With talent and opportunity comes the need to work in order to succeed. Second from 1 Thessalonians, "For even when we were with you, we used to give you this order: if anyone is not willing to work, then he is not to eat, either."[27] With the ability to choose comes the responsibility for the choices one makes. To improve one's lot, one needs to learn to make good choices. That responsibility rests with the individual alone.

Fourth, we should eliminate both the Department of Education and all federal funding from our education system. The inculcation of morality and virtue are one of the primary goals of education. These require teaching the underpinnings of religion, and not religion itself; courses such as philosophy, rhetoric, logic, history, ethics, and morality incorporating examples from classical literature, including the *New* and *Old Testaments*. After all, it wasn't until man's enlightenment in the 1960s that the Bible and prayer were removed from schools. Our Creator alone provides a basis for existence, morality, and knowledge. Our purpose and the content required to fulfill it are therefore incompatible with a role for government. To remove content necessary for our children to be successful is a disservice to them. It is akin to Plato's noble lie, that it is okay not to tell the truth in order for the state to advance an agenda.[28] In addition, in terms of stewardship, the

Department of Education after more than thirty years has simply failed in its mission – it has failed dismally in the moral directive it was given. As government itself is not costless, the department and all its programs, should be dissolved. If any of them are worthy, a state(s) can pick them up on their own accord.

Fifth, States are free to make their own choices as to whether and how to fund education within their state. It is their people's right under their individual state constitutions, and the concept we were founded upon of government within government, for them to grant those powers to their state government. However, the federal government does not have such a right. The right exists within the people themselves, and in some cases those have been granted to their states by the agreements embodied within their individual state constitutions. The powers granted to the federal government were few and enumerated in areas where individual states simply were not the best vehicle to protect certain rights. The federal government cannot take from the states powers they do not possess. It is up to the people to directly determine when and how rights should change. Change is accomplished only by amending a constitution in the ways outlined within that document. It cannot be done by a group of people wearing black robes pretending to be the Creator, legislators proclaiming to know what is in our society's best interests, or an executive acting on his or her own accord because "the right" things are not being done; change effected by an elitist few exemplifies human arrogance of a type that a moral society should not allow.

In the end, the marketplace will decide, and people will vote with their feet if education is important to them and a state or locality is unable to deliver it. Before we end this work, there is a need to expand some of the arguments presented so far to demonstrate these thoughts are not limited to education alone. That is where we will go next.

Chapter 6: The Utopian Dream

> *The hereditary, indefeasible, divine right of kings, and the doctrine of non-resistence, which is built upon the supposition of such a right ... These notions are fetched neither from divine revelation, nor human reason; and if they are derived from neither of those sources, it is not much matter from whence they come, or whither they go. Only it is a pity that such doctrines should be propagated in society, to raise factions and rebellion, as we see they have, in fact, been both in the last, and the present reign.*
>
> —Jonathan Mayhew, 1750

So far, with the exception of education, we have largely looked at what should or should not be and why. We are now going to look at some other historical examples. But first, let's briefly look at the journey we've taken so far. We've presented the case for a particular relationship between what we've called the spheres of Church and State, and we've briefly reviewed some periods of history where that relationship has been undermined from both sides. The notion grew during the High Middle Ages and Renaissance that it was the Church that was the problem: it prevented the State from fulfilling its role. The solution was therefore to remove, or at least control, the Church's influence. It doesn't matter whether it was Machiavelli or Hobbes who intended their messages to be heard solely by the ruler; or Spinoza and Rousseau who intended their messages of state religion to be heard by the masses; or a message that lies somewhere in between, such as the privatization of religion and the subsequent removal of its effect on the State as espoused by Locke. The result is the same in each case. They are just different means of achieving the same end.

It doesn't even matter whether it is the State founded upon the notion of the *polis*, as used by the Greek philosophers, or the modern notion of the State as put forth by Machiavelli. It is a distinction which makes no difference. The stated problem was that the Church impeded the State from performing its function. Underlying this statement is the assumption that it is only the State's purpose to provide for and perpetuate society. If religion is to exist, it must be a religion created— or at least controlled by—the State. These are the notions which underlie the early state religion controlled societies, and all forms of collectivism, or statism if you prefer, that form the basis of modern liberalism. This thinking provided for a separation of Church and State, created a public square devoid of the trappings of religion, and sought a state that would be free to exercise its power for the benefit of its people. After all, society should be ruled by those who know best, those who have been endowed with the particular gifts that allow them to make the kinds of decisions that a state must make. This line of thought also believed that the masses are not capable of making decisions that are in their own best interests.

The above governance approach has always failed. It is interesting to note that when these efforts do fail, it was never understood that failure occurred because the underlying ideas were bad. Instead, the excuses were given that we the people were not committed enough to the cause. We either did not try hard enough, we were unwilling to sacrifice enough, we did not believe in the cause enough, or we did not spend enough. This is true for all forms of collectivism: communism, fascism, progressivism, and socialism. With the current level of spending and debt, the welfare states here and in Europe are on an unsustainable path, and all the while our leaders just pat our heads when we give voice to the problem saying that these efforts are required to implement social justice, that they know better, and if we only understood. At best their approach is poor stewardship, a wasting of resources by simply providing someone with fish instead of teaching them to fish, of increasing their dependence instead of *assisting them* in becoming independent. What happens when they succeed in their efforts, when they create their Utopia? This is the context for charity that we'll examine within this chapter.

First, let's acknowledge the arguments presented by those who believe in modern liberalism. Let's assume they could be correct. We are each free to believe what we want, for that is the gift of free will, freedom, that has been given to each one of us by our Creator. But that freedom must be exercised with wisdom if we are to fulfill our purpose. So let's examine a couple of periods from history where the State was successful in its attempts to override the effects of religion within their societies. After all, this is the stated fulfillment of modern liberalism. If it is truly the desired ideal, then we should see evidence from the fruit born during these periods.

First, we will look at Henry VIII's creation of the Church of England during the Renaissance. That is surely a period where religion was put under the power of the state, and similar events occurred in several other European countries. Second, we'll compare the American War for Independence and the French Revolution. These two events occurred within a couple of decades of each other, but their underlying bases were very different. The War for Independence was undertaken to restore the balance between governance and religion, while the French Revolution was undertaken to create a society where the State existed with a civil (secular) religion. Third, we'll look at government policy implementing the kind of social justice that modern liberalism states are its goal: America's own war on poverty. It was the Church that shifted charity to assisting the poor during the early Middle Ages, it was the State that assumed control over many charitable organizations during the High Middle Ages and Renaissance, and it is the State that has largely institutionalized that charitable role within America over the last fifty years.

The Renaissance and the Church of England

Henry VIII declared himself the head of the Church of England in the sixteenth century. He did so to extricate himself from a marriage that had produced no heir. Beginning in 1532, legislation was passed through Parliament "curbing the influence of the papacy in England, and appointing the king Supreme Head of the Church. Once the divorce and consolidation of power were achieved, the king moved to take control of much of the Church's property through the dissolution of the monasteries."[1] These events began a short fifteen years after Luther penned his theses in 1517. What is most amazing is that only a short time earlier the pope had given Henry the title of Defender of the Faith in the latter's defense of Catholicism against the Reformation. The pope during much of this time was Clement VII, the second of the popes coming from Florence's Medici family. Interestingly enough, Machiavelli had written *The Prince* in about 1513, but it was not published until after his death in about 1532, the same year that Henry took action against the church.

But to understand the events during Henry VIII's time, one must look back about four hundred years to the reign of Henry II. In that earlier time, "Kings took it as axiomatic that they were the directly anointed of God."[2] Kings appointed the church's bishops, as they were also barons[3], an indication of the church's subservience to the crown. On the other hand, the papacy held the keys to salvation. They crowned the Holy Roman Emperor. They also allowed arch-bishops to crown kings, an indication of the king's subservience to the church. Within England, "In the eyes of the Church, then, royal sovereignty stopped at the cathedral porch. In the eyes of the Angevin king, sovereignty was absolute within his realm."[4] In the words of Locke, there cannot be two supreme powers on the earth, and inevitably there arose conflict between the two spheres as described earlier, because both were focused on themselves and not upon service to others; they did not put their Creator or people first. It was during Henry II's rule that conflict between him and Becket over the roles of Church and State resulted in the latter's murder in December of 1170 within Canterbury's cathedral. Further, only forty-five years later, King John would be forced by his barons and nobles, under the leadership of arch-bishop Stephen Langton, to sign the Magna Carta. It is doubtful that this latter event could have occurred without Langton's presence and his conviction that the people came first over both the crown and the church.

But the notions of both Henry II and Becket came from reactions to earlier reforms implemented by Pope Gregory VII, one hundred years before. Those reforms were in part to make the act of bishop consecration clearly that of the church alone, to remove the State entirely from this act. These views were advanced further still by Bernard of Clairvaux in his *On Consideration*, written for Pope Eugenius III in the middle of the twelfth century, stating that the pope "was to be supreme over all authorities in the world."[5] These reforms were continued under Pope Innocent III, who appointed Langton as arch-bishop of Canterbury. However, by the end of the thirteenth century, King Philip IV of France humiliated Pope Boniface VIII by beginning to tax both the nobles and clergy, and at one point captured the pope and held him captive for several days. These events help set the stage for the later transfer of the pope's residence from Rome to Avignon for a time from 1378–1417 and brought to an end the church's supremacy claim.

But England was not the only country to experience such turbulence during this period. Our current notions of free societies have their roots in the Northern Italian states, where it then progressed through the Lowland countries and into England. These events began in the eighth century, over seven hundred years before the Reformation. Yet within one hundred years of Henry VIII declaring himself the head of England's church, the Northern Italian states and much of the Lowland countries were no longer free and their economies stagnated. So what happened and why? A quick look at some events in Spain, France, and the Holy Roman Empire (German Republics) provides insights to answer these questions.

King Charles I of Spain became Charles V of the Holy Roman Empire in 1519. He ruled a vast empire that included not only Spain, but portions of what is now Germany, the Netherlands, and Italy. Spain was a recently created country having formed through Ferdinand and Isabella's joining their kingdoms of Aragorn and Castile late in the fifteenth century. When the new country was formed, it had about 7.2 million people, roughly half the population of France. There was little manufacturing in Spain. What agriculture it had revolved around supplying the Italian City states with the fleeces the Italians had lost in England. The Spanish Mesta protected the sheep ranchers' interests, including the vast migratory routes across Spain used to graze the sheep, and prevented the development of other agricultural production. There were no limits on the crown's authority in this new country, and the upper classes held the elitist view that manufacturing and commerce were beneath them and their people.

Charles also inherited the great debt amassed by Ferdinand and Isabella. It was the need for money that caused the latter to gamble on Columbus and his proposed expedition. The amount of gold and silver that was brought back to Spain by its explorers was massive, but this new wealth also destroyed what little manufacturing remained within Spain. The new wealth was used to finance a large standing army of about 200,000 men in wars against the French, Dutch, Germans, Italian states, and England. However, as Spain had no manufacturing, it had to purchase weapons, cannons, powder, and ships from other countries on the continent, and these were generally inferior to what was being produced in England at the time.

Spain not only derived revenue from the New World's wealth, but its taxes were high as well, reaching rates of about one third of all income. In addition, Spain pressured the Catholic Church into obtaining a share of one third of all tithes it collected and the authority to tax church properties in order to fight the spread of Protestantism. All this wealth was not enough as Spain's rulers spent much more than they were able to take in, spending foolishly on armies, the purchase of outside goods, and buying allies. When Charles V retired and named his son Philip II as his successor, Spain had amassed a debt of 29 million ducats. Philip declared Spain bankrupt only a year after becoming its ruler. But within five years Spain was spending 1.4 million ducats a year on interest payments alone on new debt. Interest expenditures grew to 25% of the royal budget and annual expenditures were as much as twice its revenue. In 1575, only about twenty years after becoming Spain's ruler, Philip again declared bankruptcy on a royal debt of about 36 million ducats.

Spain's wars resulted in temporarily increasing its holdings within Italy, and along with France subverting portions of the Netherlands. It conquered the kingdom of Naples that made up the southern half of Italy below the Papal States and, along with France, also now effectively ruled over three of the four Italian states where freedom began: the states of Milan, Genoa, and Florence. These state's productivity suffered under Spanish and French rule. The imposition of taxes, along with the strength and rigidity imposed by the guilds, resulted in process stagnation, producing inferior luxury goods at relatively higher costs, and ignoring many markets that existed for lower quality goods for the masses.

But Spain was not the only country experiencing these developments. By the end of the Hundred Years War in 1453 with England, France had developed a large governmental bureaucracy. Like Spain, it was a new country, having been formed by a series of conquests and agreements with kingdoms between Spain and the Holy Roman Empire. There were no limits on the new country's taxing authority who exempted the clergy and the nobles from taxation until 1695. Its revenues consisted primarily of taxes on land, commodities, and headcount. As there were no checks on its taxing authority, it taxed its people to the point where their incentive was greater to produce less and hide it from the tax collector, rather than create the means to increase production.

Much of the revenues raised were spent on maintaining large armies and financing its court life, including the hiring of various relatives. France had the largest population in Europe, and also covered one of the largest land areas. As it was recently formed, there remained a strong pull toward local interests. The combination of taxation, incentives, and strong local interests created an environment rife with government corruption. This was compounded further by the sale of privileges, royal licenses that were essentially the granting of monopoly rights to the purchaser. These were renewable by making additional payments to the crown. In return, the purchaser often received an unlimited right to perform certain types of mining, manufacturing, or commerce. It was much easier for the crown to control a single source for a given commodity rather than regulate hundreds or thousands of small manufacturers or other business interests. This level of regulation over industry was maintained with the help of the French guilds. Byproducts of this approach included (1) the existence of scant property rights, (2) high import taxes to protect internal markets and prices, and (3) little to no incentive to reinvest in enterprises as most of the revenues went to other parties.

According to Rodney Stark, "Capitalism rests upon three factors: secure property rights, free markets, and free labor. France was quite deficient on all three … the French commercial and industrial economy consisted of licensed firms limited to given markets, subject to usurpation, and employing not workers but a guild."[6] The conclusion that can be drawn from the above examples is that there are different roads to despotism, but "despotic states are avaricious and devour much of the wealth that might go into economic development."[7] Despotic states create a set of conditions that reduce the incentives for expansion—they generate poverty and at the same time limit the resources that are available to a people for acts of charity. They very opposite of what we are called as individuals and a people to do.

So what was different about England? First, its ruler's power was not unlimited. It alone had the social contract of the *Magna Carta* that struck limits on the crown's power. Second, there was a long line of both noble and civic leaders who enforced the limits on the crown set forth in the Magna Charta. These included Simon de Montfort (1208–1265), Henri Bracton (1210–1268), Sir John Fortescue (1385–1479), Thomas Cromwell (1485–1540), and Edward Coke (1552–1634). It was Coke's battles with Elizabeth I's successors, King James I and his son Charles I (both self-styled Renaissance kings in the mold of Roman Emperors), that resulted in passage of the Right of Petition in 1628. It was not only power but wealth and military strength that was diffuse as well within England. Finally, the guilds did not obtain the type of power in England that they achieved on the continent. The wars and stifling of freedom on the continent led many of the best workers to relocate to England. This migration was enhanced by Henry VIII's generous tax policies allowing whole firms to move to England from the Italian states and Lowlands. They brought with them not only their skills, but their innovation as well.

Additional support for this position can be found in Charles V's rule of the Holy Roman Empire. He was much more lenient on the German republics who accepted Lutheranism, as he was dependent upon these princes to maintain his power. Such was not the case with the Dutch republics where he ruthlessly put down all attempts supportive of the Reformation. These policies were carried on by his son, Philip II, and resulted in the Dutch Revolt that began in 1568. This revolt resulted in the Dutch declaring their independence from Spain in the 1581 *Act of Abjuration*.

The Two Revolutions

The French and American revolutions can be looked at from the perspectives of both the documents and history produced by each. Many argue that Locke's works were a significant influence on our Founders' political thought. As we saw earlier, this is simply not the case. Instead, the War for Independence was waged not for some new philosophic political concept, but to reassert the Colonies' rights as Englishmen that had been usurped by the British government. Rights that had been documented within the Magna Charta, with the leadership of Stephen Langton and grounded in the writings of the church fathers, and reasserted later through the Petition of Right and Glorious Revolution. The War for Independence happened slowly and as a last resort. The time between the founding of Plymouth Colony and George Washington's inauguration is roughly the same amount of time as passed between Washington's and John F. Kennedy's inauguration, a period of almost 170 years. In addition, Jefferson wrote that the *Declaration* was not meant to express any new political thoughts, but was simply meant to be an expression of the American mind.[8]

Compare this to the French Revolution. France still had the largest population of any European country in the eighteenth century but, as outlined in the last section, it was both a relatively poorer country than England and its wealth was relatively concentrated. According to Edmund Burke, "The wealth of a country is another, and no contemptible standard, by which we may judge whether, on the hole, a government be protecting or destructive. France far exceeds England in the multitude of her people, but I apprehend that her comparative wealth is much inferior to ours; that it is not so equal in the distribution, nor so ready in the circulation. I believe the difference in the form of the two governments to be amongst the causes of this advantage on the side of England."[9]

We saw earlier that wealth and power were both concentrated among the nobility and church within France, as they were within Spain. Initially the nobility and clergy were exempted from taxation, but France's wars, including its participation in our War for Independence, had left it deeply in debt. In an attempt to raise additional revenue, its king decided to remove the tax exemptions. It should be noted that this decision was being duplicated elsewhere in Europe at this time, and was due to the adoption of enlightenment principles professed by those such as Machiavelli, Hobbes, Descartes, Spinoza, Voltaire, Locke, and Rousseau. The removal of these exemptions stirred resentment against the rulers within the nobility and church, and all sides attempted to find support for their positions amongst the subjects. Their rulers became the weak rods identified by Edwards, and created division and strife within their countries.

While there is still debate regarding the causes of the French Revolution, the following are commonly cited: (1) bourgeoisie resentment from the exclusion of political power and positions of honor, (2) peasant awareness of their situation and becoming less willing to support an outdated feudal system, (3) the new philosophes being more widely read in France than anywhere else, (4) French participation in the War for Independence that had driven it to the brink of bankruptcy, (5) crop failures in 1788 coupled with a long period of economic difficulties and unrest, and (6) a French monarchy no longer able to adapt to the political and societal pressures being exerted upon it.[10]

The *Declaration of Independence* and *Constitution* created vastly different structures than did France's *Rights of Man*. The *Declaration* acknowledged our Creator as the source of our rights and law as this sentiment had been expressed in the *Magna Carta*, but it was nowhere to be found in the *Rights of Man*. The creation of our legislature as a bicameral body represented the interests of both the individual colonies and the people. The French legislature did not. According to Burke, "Your new constitution is the very reverse of ours in its principle; and I am astonished how any persons could dream of holding out any thing done in it as an example for Great Britain. With you there is little, or rather no, connection between the last representative and the first constituent. The member who goes to the national assembly is not chosen by the people, nor accountable to them. There are three elections before he is chosen, two sets of magistracy intervene between him and the primary assembly, so as to render him, as I have said, an ambassador of a state, and not the representative of the people within a state."[11]

Burke goes on to state,

> It is impossible not to observe, that in the spirit of this geometrical distribution, and arithmetical arrangement, these pretended citizens treat France exactly like a country of conquest. Acting as conquerors, they have

> imitated the policy of the harshest of that harsh race ... to destroy all vestiges of the antient country, in religion, in polity, in laws, and in manners; to confound all territorial limits; to produce a general poverty; to put up their properties to auction; to crush their princes, nobles, and pontiffs; to lay low every thing which had lifted its head above the level, or which could serve to combine or rally, in their distresses, the disbanded people, under the standard of old opinion. They have made France free in the manner in which those sincere friends to the rights of mankind, the Romans, freed Greece, Macedon, and other nations. They destroyed the bonds of their union, under the colour of providing for the independence of each of their cities.[12]

In terms of religion, the War for Independence was a religious event. The ideas expressed by the Founders were shaped by the preachers of the First Great Awakening several decades before in the writings of those such as George Whitefield and Jonathan Edwards, among many others. Our Founders expressed the notion that religion was an indispensable pillar for a successful society, and these expressions can be found in the writings of Washington, Franklin, Jefferson, John Adams, Madison, and many others. Their reasoning is expressed by M. Stanton Evans: "Self-government required observance of the moral law, respect for rights of others, restraint upon the passions. Virtue was thus a necessary precondition to a regime of freedom."[13] Not so with the French revolution. Two passages from Burke point out the differences.

> First, In short, Sir, it seems to me, that this new ecclesiastical establishment is intended only to be temporary, and preparatory to the utter abolition, under any of its forms, of the Christian religion ... They who will not believe, that the philosophical fanatics who guide in these matters, have long entertained such a design, are utterly ignorant of their character and proceedings ... by a sort of education they have

imagined, founded in a knowledge of the physical wants of men; progressively carried to an enlightened self-interest, which when well understood, they tell us will identify with an interest more enlarged and public. The scheme of this education has been long known ... by the name of a *Civic Education*.[14]

***

Compute your gains: see what is got by those extravagant and presumptuous speculations which have taught your leaders to despise all their predecessors, and all their contemporaries, and even to despise themselves, until the moment in which they became truly despicable. By following those false lights, France has bought undignified calamities at a higher price than any nation has purchased the most unequivocal blessings! France has bought poverty by crime! France has not sacrificed her virtue to her interest; but she has abandoned her interest, that she might prostitute her virtue.

All other nations have begun the fabric of a new government, or the reformation of an old, by establishing originally, or by reinforcing with the greater exactness some rites or other of religion. All other people have laid the foundations of civil freedom in severer manners, and a system of a more austere and masculine morality. France, when she let loose the reins of regal authority, doubled the licence, of a ferocious dissoluteness in manners, and of an insolent irreligion in opinions and practices.[15]

While the War for Independence was a religious event, the French Revolution was an anti-religious event. As further proof, the *Northwest Ordinance* was a resolution passed by the Continental Congress in 1787 concerning the territory north of the Ohio River. Its first article states that "No person, demeaning himself in a peaceable and orderly manner, shall ever be molested on account of his mode of worship or religious sentiments."[16] The third article goes on to say, "Religion, morality and knowledge, being necessary to good government and the happiness of mankind, schools and the means of education shall forever be encouraged."[17] Here is a second example. During the War for Independence the Continental Congress in 1777 approved a resolution to instruct the Committee of Commerce to import 20,000 *Bibles* as they could not yet be reasonably created and printed in the colonies. The issue would come up again in 1781 when Robert Aitkin, a prominent colonial publisher, asked Congress for its recommendation of the Bible he had printed in the colonies. The matter was referred to a committee consisting of James Duane, Thomas McKean and Rev. John Witherspoon. The approval was granted in 1872 by the Committee, Revs. White and Duffield (chaplains of the United States Congress), and the United States Congress itself.[18]

Finally we can look at the history of both countries after their respective revolutions. The first five presidents of the United States were all Founding Fathers. Despite their disagreements over specific aspects of governance and policy, power was transitioned peacefully from one administration to another, and they all died peacefully. Compare that to the French Revolution, whose policies created internal revolts and wars with the other European powers. This revolution concluded in the Reign of Terror where at least 300,000 people were arrested, 17,000 were sentenced to death, and more died while incarcerated in prison. And in the end a military leader named Napoleon Bonaparte assumed power, just as Burke predicted would happen. The sources and outcomes of these two revolutions could not be any more different.

The American War on Poverty

In President Johnson's 1964 State of the Union address,[19] he urged the U.S. to embark on a war on poverty. Relevant portions of that message include the following:

- "It will not be a short or easy struggle, no single weapon or strategy will suffice."
- "Poverty is a national problem ... but this attack, to be effective, must also be organized at the State and local level and directed by State and local efforts."
- "For the war against poverty will not be won here in Washington. It must be won in the field, in every private home."
- "Our chief weapons ... will be better schools, and better health, and better homes, and better training, and better job opportunities to help more Americans, especially young Americans."
- "Our aim is not only to relieve the symptom of poverty, but to cure it and, above all, to prevent it."

It was, and is, a laudable goal. Reducing poverty would not be easy, it was a problem that we as a people must work to achieve, but the effort must be led and directed locally. The weapons used lie in creating better opportunities for all—access to those things which allow someone to *better themselves*. The goals are good ones; they are consistent with the individualism model as they aim for individuals and local communities to assist individuals become more independent and successful. They are consistent with charity as it has been defined in this work, voluntary actions performed out of love for another human being. But they were implemented with top-down federal programs such as employment legislation, food stamp programs, revamping existing programs insuring the uninsured, creating a national job corps, minimum wage laws, special school aid programs, housing programs, and health insurance programs. One of the biggest mistakes individuals make is trying to use collectivist means to achieve individualistic goals. This simply *never* works as both the ends and the means matter, and collectivism focuses on only the ends.

We saw in the last chapter the impacts this same approach had on our education system. We'll take a similar approach to examining the problem of alleviating the effects of poverty in the U.S. If poverty is effectively addressed, as put forth in Johnson's address, what should we expect to see happen? Some effects of reducing or eliminating poverty should include

- Fewer people in poverty, either in total or as a percentage of the population.

- A rise in income of those deemed to be in poverty, indicating that their lot is improving as they are better able to take care of their own needs; they may still need some assistance, but it should be less over time.

- In conjunction with the above, we should see the same or fewer resources needed to assist people in poverty as they become more independent.

- If efforts are led locally, then some ideas are likely to work better than others, leading to an improved delivery of the means to assist others become more independent, which over time should reduce the expenditures necessary to combat poverty.

So how have we done? First, let's look at the general population and the funds that have been expended in the war on poverty. The funds that have been included in the analysis are those defined by the U.S. Census Bureau as being included in public assistance directed toward relieving poverty as defined in President Johnson's address. These programs include means-tested assistance programs such as Medicaid, Supplemental Nutrition Assistance Program (SNAP), housing assistance, Supplemental Security Income (SSI), Temporary Assistance for Needy Families (TANF), and general assistance (GA).[20] The chart below shows the change in the total population, the population at or near poverty, and our annual expenditures for the mean adjusted programs providing public assistance.

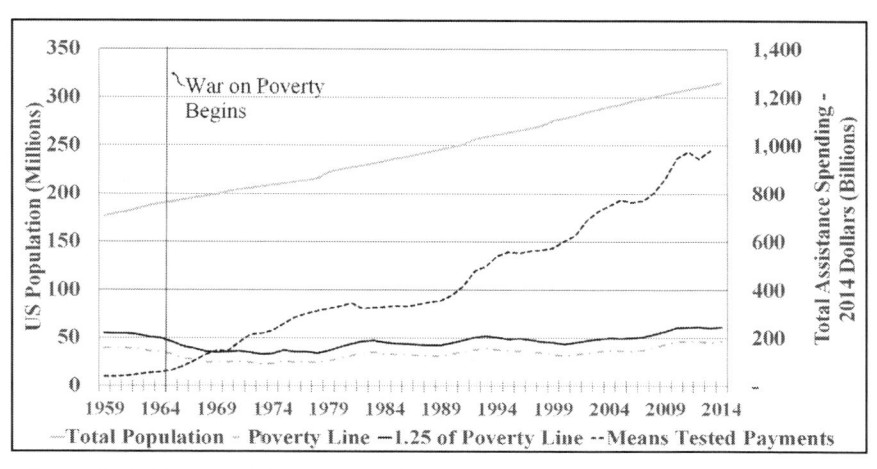

Figure 1: US Total and Poverty Populations, Annual Public Assistance Expenditures, 1959-2014[21]

The total population has almost doubled since 1959, but the number of people in or near poverty is almost unchanged over that same period. However, the number of people in poverty had actually decreased all ten years prior to the chart and that decrease continued until about 1969, the same year that many of the anti-poverty programs started to function. Since that time the number of people in poverty has slowly increased. While there was a small increase in the overall number of people in poverty, the program expenditures to combat it have grown from less than $50 billion a year (in 2014 dollars) to almost $1 trillion, a result similar to what we saw with government's education intervention. To put this in context, over $22 trillion have been spent on programs to fight poverty (not including Social Security or Medicare). This is three times more than has been spent on all military wars fought by the U.S. since the War for Independence.[22]

It should be noted that the program expenditures used to fight poverty do not represent the benefits provided but only the total program funding. More efficient delivery would translate into more benefits for those in poverty. That point will be touched upon later. We can take the information from the first chart and look at it in terms of percentages and averages, as shown below.

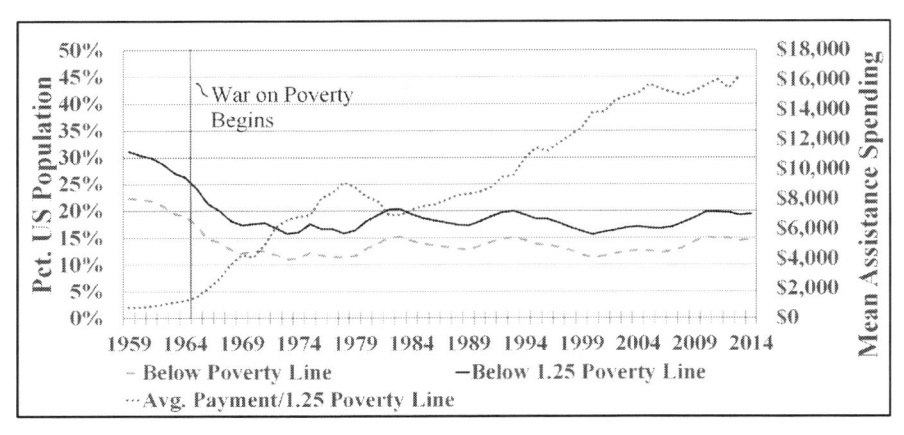

Figure 2: US Percent At or Near Poverty and Mean Assistance Spending, 1959-2014[23]

The figures show that those near poverty have hovered between 15 and 20% of the total population over the last 50 years, and those below the poverty line at between 10 to 15%. However, during that time, average program expenditures in real dollars (using 125% of the poverty line) have increased from less than $1,000 per year to over $16,000, an increase of over 2,000%. The population within 125% of the poverty line was used since (1) a substantial number of people above the poverty line also receive assistance, as we will see later, and (2) figures have been collected for this population. So just as with education, we have seen no significant decrease in the number of people in poverty, but there has been a substantial increase in cost outlays to provide support.

One possible explanation is that job opportunities are simply not adequate to support the population increase that we have seen in this country. The next chart shows the changes in the Civilian Noninstitutional Population, Civilian Labor Force, Employed, and Not Employed populations. The Civilian Institutional Population (CNP) is the population above 16 years of age. The Civilian Labor Force consists of those in the aforesaid population who are either employed or unemployed. The Employed line represents those working, and the gap between it and the Civilian Labor Force represents the government's unemployment measure until about 2009. The government has revised their unemployment measure so that only those continuing to look for work are now included in the measure. The Not Employed line represents the total of those both unemployed and those not in the labor force.

The chart's data show the workforce excluding those 65 and older to remove the effects of those in retirement, as this group has a workforce participation rate of less than 20% versus the rest of the population which historically has been between 65% and 75%. This gives us a population measure to compare those that produce most of the revenue used to finance the public assistance programs with those receiving the assistance.

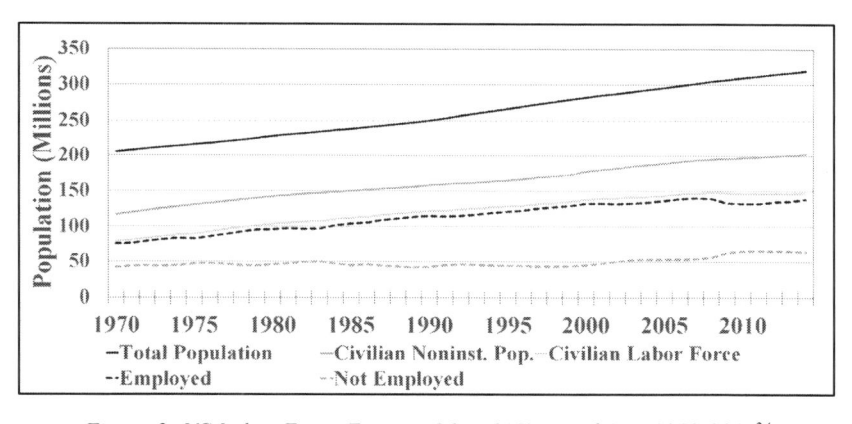

Figure 3: US Labor Force Figures, 16 to 64 Years of Age, 1970-2014[24]

While the CNP grew by 74% during this period, the civilian labor force and employed numbers grew by 86% and 84% respectively, indicating that job growth more than absorbed the population increase. The number of individuals not employed grew by only 47% during this same period. More interesting is that the number not employed was essentially flat from 1970 through 2002, increasing by only 11% during that thirty two year period. That is a remarkable achievement. Most of the increase in the not employed population has occurred since 2009, fueled by the housing bubble collapse and the irresponsible increase in national debt that had occurred before that time. It should be noted that the housing bubble was also created as a result of government policies implemented during the 1990s.[25]

From this graph we see a total of about 50,000 people who are not employed. That roughly corresponds to the figure of those below the poverty line. I am not inferring that they are the same population, but it would be interesting to obtain demographic information about this group versus the rest of the civilian labor force to see what differences may exist. It does not appear that job opportunities are the source of the problem, although education could be one cause if people in the not employed group do not have the skillsets necessary to compete in the current job market.

We've now looked at poverty with respect to the general population. What about the program expenditures and the people receiving assistance? To answer those questions we will look at (1) the total number of assistance program recipients, (2) the number of people receiving some form of assistance, and (3) the number of individuals above and below the poverty line receiving public assistance.

The first graph simply compares the number of individuals enrolled in each of the major means tested public assistance programs versus the general population. The CNP is used as it represents a measure of those providing the funding used/transferred to those in the programs receiving funds.

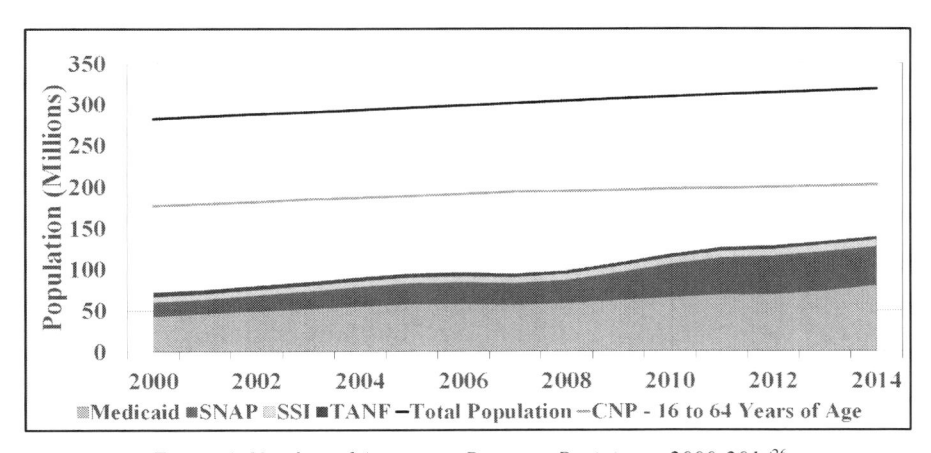

Figure 4: Number of Assistance Program Recipients, 2000-2014[26]

The data show the total number of program recipients has grown by more than 92% during the fifteen year period while the total population and CNP have only grown by about 13% and 14% respectively. In addition, the total number of program recipients is about two-thirds of the entire 16 to 64 age CNP. All other things being equal, more instances of providing assistance are being required. This indicates that people in poverty are becoming more dependent and not less. If the present program growth continues, it will not be too many years before there will be more total program recipients than workers to support the programs. This is not sustainable. To be fair, this does somewhat overstate the issue as many individuals who receive assistance receive it from more than one program, another indication that those in poverty are becoming more dependent and not less.

To account for individuals receiving assistance from more than one program, we can look at the most recent Survey of Income and Program Participation (SIPP) study performed by the Census Bureau. This study identifies individuals who receive public assistance from one or more sources. As before, the program assistance figures will be compared to the CNP between 16 and 64 years of age.

The following chart looks at the percentage of individuals receiving public assistance. As assistance from more than one program is often received, the figures do not reflect the total number of recipients enrolled in each program, although the relative size of these means tested assistance programs is retained.

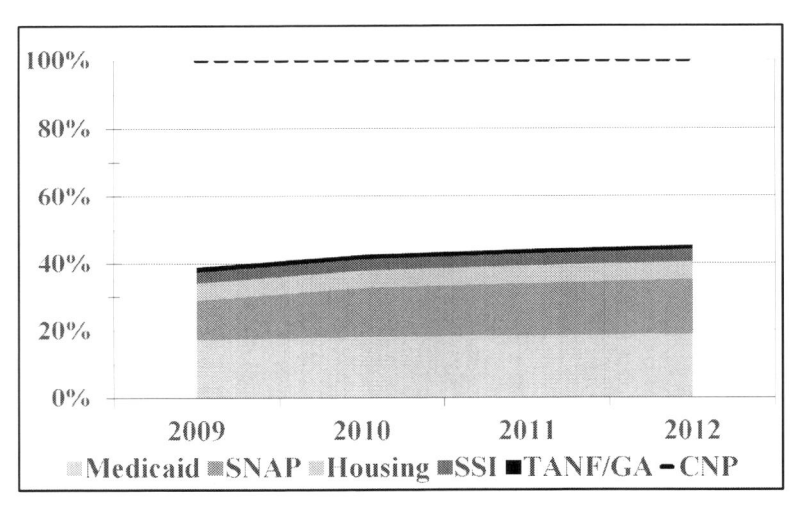

Figure 5: Percentage of CNP, Ages 16 to 64, Receiving Public Assistance, 2009-2012[27]

The number of individuals receiving public assistance grew by 4.5% during this four year period to over 45% of the CNP. As this is a longitudinal study, there are breakdowns available that show how long households received assistance. Over 72% of those below the poverty line received assistance for 36 to 48 months of the study, compared to only 30% for those above that measure. Those with less education had both higher rates of receiving assistance and received assistance for a longer period of time. The program participation rate was about 45% for those not completing high school, but fell to about 13% for those having at least one year of college. Almost 50% of those not completing high school received assistance for 36 to 48 months while 43.5% of those with at least one year of college only used assistance for 12 months or less.[28]

We can also take into account the relative income of those receiving assistance. As these programs were created as part of the war on poverty, we should expect most of the benefits to go to those below the poverty line. This data is presented in the following graph.

Collectivism and Charity 181

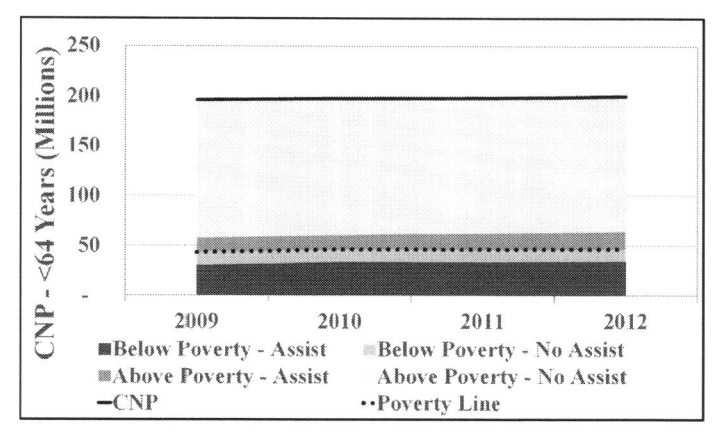

Figure 6: Portions of CNP Receiving Assistance versus the Poverty Line[29]

The study indicates that about 72% of those below the poverty line receive assistance from at least one program compared to 18% of those above the poverty line.[30] This sounds reasonable. However, it translates into an average 33,000 recipients below the poverty line receiving assistance and about 15,800 above the poverty line. *Only about 66% of those receiving public assistance from one or more programs created to end poverty were actually below the poverty line.*

The wealth transfers to program recipients are also not included in their income—they are not recognized as resources that they have available to meet daily living expenses. This understates their resources. The next graph takes the mean family income by quintile and adds a figure representing the average assistance program expenditures for each family in that quintile. It is assumed that all of the assistance program expenditures support the families in the first and second quintiles, and that those expenditures should be roughly split two-thirds to the bottom quintile and one-third to the second quintile, based on the results in the preceding paragraph.

The assistance program expenditures are averaged across the entire group as the aim of the war on poverty was to eliminate it, and those most in need should receive the support. In essence it is treated as a revenue transfer to the families in those two quintiles, a negative tax if you will. The family data comes from the US Census Bureau.[31] The results are shown below.

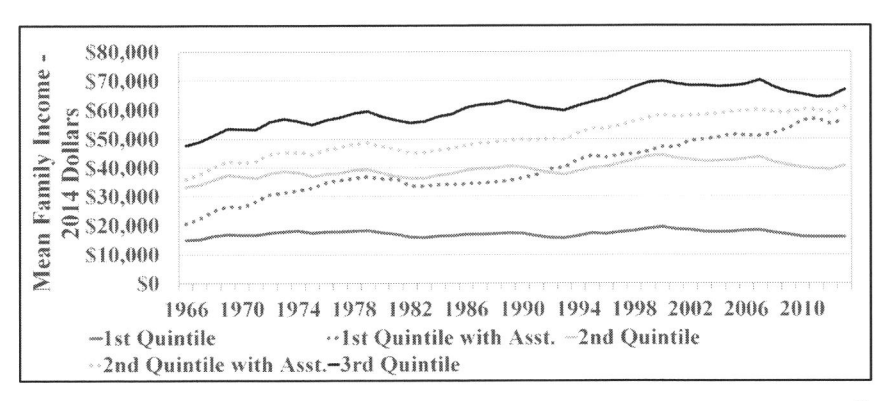

Figure 7: Mean Family Income, with Assistance Expenditures, by Quintile, 1966-2013[32]

The chart above indicates several things. First, that the average incomes for the Bottom, Second, and Third quintiles have grown by about 7%, 22%, and 40% respectively. There has been a widening of the gap between those at the bottom and those in the middle. Second, it was the purpose of the war on poverty to eliminate that gap. Toward that end the average assistance program expenditures for the bottom and second quintiles have increased by 173% and 69% respectively. Third, and most importantly, if there were no costs associated with these wealth transfers, and the program's expenditures were given to every family in the bottom two quintiles, there would only be a $1,300 (about 15%) gap between the bottom and third quintiles. From a strictly monetary perspective, the war on poverty would be essentially over.

But wealth transfers are not costless, because government is not costless, and this brings us back once again to stewardship. The intent of the war on poverty was to eliminate poverty by helping people become more independent, and to accomplish that task at the individual and local community level. This approach is the only way such an effort can be done successfully.

So how well does government act in the capacity of a charitable organization? How effective a steward is it? In a study by James Roth Edwards, for every dollar budgeted for government assistance, on average, 70 cents goes not to the poor, but "to the members of the welfare bureaucracy and others serving the poor."[33] That means that on average only 30% of budgeted expenditures go to the recipients. If a private charity were that negligent in their operations, you could rest assured that the organization would be shut down and its leaders tried for fraud or malfeasance. By any stretch of the imagination this approach is poor stewardship. Incidentally, this same study found that 70% of charitable organizations spent at least 75% of their budgets on programs and services. We will talk more about stewardship in the next section.

The previous chart is presented again below. Only this time two adjustments have been made to the average assistance program expenditures. First, they have been adjusted to 30% as noted above, representing the amount of budgeted government expenditures that typically go to recipients. Second these same figures have been adjusted to 75% consistent with the average effectiveness of private charitable institutions.

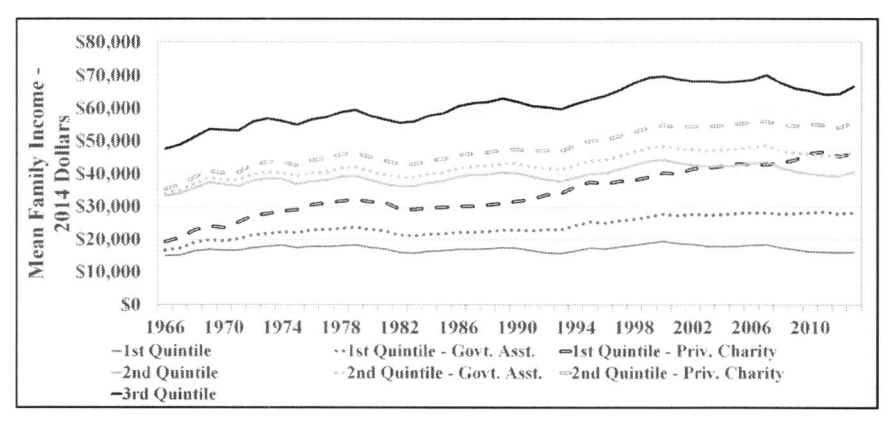

Figure 8: Mean Family Income, with Adjusted Assistance Expenditures, by Quintile, 1966-2013[34]

The change in outcomes is significant. Much of the government program expenditures are lost to the recipients. A 75% increase is achieved for the bottom quintile when the government administers the expenditures, but an increase of over 185% is achieved with the same expenditures using the service rate for a typical private charity. This puts the bottom quintile income above that of the second quintile, and within about 30% of the average income for the third quintile, a significant difference. The point here is not to say that these results are reflective of the actual program benefits that would be received by their recipients, but rather to show the difference that effective stewardship makes in performing charity. I for one would be happy to donate the portion of my taxes used to support assistance programs directly to families in need, instead of the government, as long as those families had the opportunity to receive the kind of education necessary to allow them to stand on their own.

We must also remember that whatever benefits are realized come at a great cost. Over $22 trillion has been removed from the economy, a sum which could have been used to grow it and provide the additional opportunities necessary to enable this change to become permanent. Opportunity through education and work provides an incentive to learn to fish. Just providing material goods is simply giving someone fish. An action that once again increases dependency, instead of leading to independence.

There is one additional aspect we should explore. So far we have discussed what is spent, how, and on whom. As alluded to above, where do these funds come from? After all these are wealth *transfers*. It must come from somewhere, and if it goes to the government then it is not available to those from whom it is taken: taxpayers. The following figures represent the average that Americans in the third quintile will give to their government for *each additional dollar they earn*, funds that are used to provide assistance and other government services.

Federal Income Tax	25.0%
Social Security Tax	12.4%
Medicare Tax	2.9%
State Income Tax	5.8%[35]
State Sales Tax	7.3%[36]
Total	53.4%

Both the employee and employer portions of the Social Security and Medicare taxes are included as the employer's portion does not impact the cost of labor (i.e., the employee would receive this amount in additional income if it were not paid to the government). State sales and income taxes are weighted averages based upon the current rates and state populations. While not every transaction in every state is subject to sales taxes, there are many more taxes that are not listed as they are not so easy to identify. These include real estate taxes, personal property taxes, gasoline taxes, fees and taxes on utilities, and all of the taxes paid by the companies who produce the things you buy: their corporate taxes, sales taxes on their purchases, real estate taxes, etc.

These are taxation levels similar or beyond what was reached during the late Roman Empire and in Spain and France during the Renaissance. And just like those periods the taxation and programs for the poor are used in an attempt to control behavior. This is immoral and contrary to our purpose. Moreover, the results are the same as experienced in those earlier periods. Again, there are different roads to despotism, but despotic states are avaricious and devour much of the wealth that might go into economic development. Opportunity is senselessly squandered. History merely repeats itself if we are not vigilant enough to remember its lessons. That responsibility rests with each one of us, both as individuals and a people.

So in closing this section on the war on poverty, we will go back to the questions initially asked at the beginning of this section.

- Have the number or percentage of people in poverty been reduced? *No.*

- Have incomes increased for those in poverty? *No for the bottom quintile, but there is a minor improvement in the second quintile.*

- Have the resources available to those in need increased? *Yes, somewhat more for the bottom quintile than the second quintile.*

- Are people needing assistance more independent? *No.*

- Are the same or fewer resources needed to assist those in need? *No.*

- Has delivery of services to those using them improved? *No.*

Again, what little improvement there is has come at great costs. We are repeating the mistakes made during the Roman Empire and the Renaissance. The poor have generally become more dependent, and we have exercised poor stewardship in relation to the resources used in the war on poverty. We have abdicated our responsibility as a people, and some individuals within our society have abdicated their personal responsibility as well, a kind of 'I gave at the office' mentality. True charity can only take place where there is a connection between the giver and receiver, where virtue is built by both, where love is present. This cannot happen when there is a faceless bureaucrat between the giver and receiver. There is no connection, nor is there virtue; it is replaced with the vice of entitlement. There is no love, and we miss an opportunity that would take us a step closer to fulfilling our purpose.

We noted above that some private organizations financially do a reasonable job of performing charity. It is to that issue we turn next before closing with a few final thoughts.

What Role Should Charitable Organizations Play?

To answer this question, we need to look again at the origins of charitable organizations. Performing charitable acts originally was the domain of individuals. This was true during Rome's rule and early in the Middle Ages after its fall, as noted in Chapter 2. The development of charitable organizations began with efforts by the Church itself, but these efforts were only partially successful. Many more organizations were also started by various lay groups. One thing that both sets of institutions had in common is they were largely local community responses to needs that overwhelmed an individual's resources. It was more effective in some instances for them to pool resources to meet specific needs locally, than for each individual to do so on their own. It came at a loss of efficiency in delivering charity, but as long as relationships remained within the community those inefficiencies were manageable.

Remember that originally charity was largely not about money. Instead it was about the things needed to survive: food, clothing, shelter, and safety. These initial institutions were often set up to provide safety and shelter to pilgrims; they practiced the virtues of hospitality and liberality in areas where it was not safe or there simply were not adequate supplies of food, water, or shelter. These are the hospitals, hospices, and bridge brotherhoods described earlier. Their primary purpose was to offer their services for a very short period of time to all who passed through. It wasn't until much later that the roles of these organizations expanded to include the sick, orphans, widows, the elderly, etc. The services provided to these additional groups generally required longer term commitments in response to local conditions and catastrophes such as demographic changes, economic collapse, weather events, plagues, and famines.

By the High Middle Ages "most villages and rural locales came to possess one or more of these institutions."[37] It was the efforts of both the church and municipal governments that attempted to consolidate these local institutions under their control that led to the increase in institutional size, budgets, and distance between a charity's supporters and those receiving its services. Why does this matter? I think that it is simply a matter of both stewardship and achieving our intended purpose as human beings.

According to Fidelity Investments, there are four phases to disaster relief that touch upon charity.[38] The phases are Immediate, Intermediate, Long Term, and Disaster Preparedness. The goals of the first phase are to perform triage and restore order—to stop the bleeding so that healing can begin. Large disasters can require massive amounts of human resources and material. The focus of the second phase is the stabilization of the situation, and the third rebuilding.

For the first phase there would appear to be a role for large charitable organizations that have the capabilities to deliver the amount of assistance necessary to meet the immediate needs. However, after the immediate response, the *control and responsibility* for completing the task should return to local resources, whether they are individuals or local charitable organizations. Local individuals and organizations "have valuable relationships and a unique understanding of the affected area in which they operate, enabling them to offer applicable and efficient solutions."[39] They have knowledge which should make them better stewards, and their voluntary initiation of charitable actions leads to greater independence and to the development of virtue within their people. They are fulfilling their purpose by expressing love for their neighbors. What greater gift is there?

We have numerous examples today of churches in America still supporting ones they helped start overseas in places like Africa, and in some cases supporting those organizations for more than 100 years. This is what happens when people are not allowed to learn and become independent, regardless of who provides the funding.

In terms of stewardship, consider the following. If someone asks me for something that they need such as food, gas, clothing, help with some kind of repair, etc., it usually costs me just whatever the services cost in time and/or money. There is virtually no transfer costs as it is a direct transaction between a giver and receiver. With charitable giving to an organization, there is a transfer cost. The average amount going to services is about 75 cents on the dollar for most large American charitable organizations.[40] The 25% not going to services is split between fundraising (10% on average) and administration (15%).

Well run organizations can and do achieve results of 90% or better of contributions going to services, and there are also those who do much worse than the averages noted above. The point is that less of your contributions go into services when they are given to charitable organizations, and that is offset by these organizations having access to sufficient resources to effectively respond to their recipient's needs. It is up to each of us, as stewards of those resources that we have each been blessed with, to make good choices in giving to those in need, whether we do it ourselves or through a charitable organization. After all, none of those material things are ultimately ours, we cannot take them with us when we go. This is charity as defined in the *Old Testament* and expanded upon in the *New Testament*.

We can contrast the above with government entitlement programs, which currently serve as a proxy for all types of charity as was noted in the previous section and the last chapter. According to several multi-year studies, "public income redistribution agencies are estimated to absorb about two-thirds of each dollar budgeted to them in overhead costs, and in some cases as much as three-quarters of each dollar."[41] The reason for this? Private charities are under strong pressures to operate efficiently in order to maintain their donation stream.[42] These pressures are absent from public programs where Congress sets funding using compulsory taxation. There is no ownership. No accountability. No stewardship. In addition, any private charity that performed this poorly would likely be charged and prosecuted for fraud, something which does not happen with government agencies. From a stewardship perspective, there is no credible means to justify the use of public funds for charitable acts. Just as in the Renaissance, it leads to inefficiency, waste, fraud, and dependency. There are at least two things large unaccountable organizations excel at, regardless of which sphere they reside in: incompetence and corruption.

As individuals it is our purpose to become good, and the performance of charity is the way in which we do that as posited at the beginning of this book. That is why we feel good when we give. We know inside ourselves that we are doing what is right, we are fulfilling our purpose. Charity relies on the performance of voluntary actions that are virtuous; they require the freedom to act, or not act, and are grounded in moral uprightness. Without a virtuous society, it is unlikely that as many charitable acts would be carried out as virtue would be replaced by vice. People would not regard service to others as an important component of their life's purpose. Instead, they'd seek to fulfill their own needs. They would become selfish and prideful. The lie is in this claim that larger organizations bring both an increase in resources and efficiency in service delivery. While the first is sometimes true, the latter has never been shown to be the case.[43]

This becoming good is not a one-time effort. It requires exercise and practice to become better tomorrow than we are today, it requires us to change — transformation. None of us are perfect or good by our own nature. It is only by being oriented toward our Creator that we succeed, performing efforts to fulfill our purpose. Performing acts of charity are key to that success as they fulfill His law.

Final Thoughts

Throughout this work, we have looked at charity, its nature, how it has changed over time, how it relates to our purpose, and therefore how it relates to society. At the core of these thoughts is that to be one people requires both a single set of mutually agreed-upon rights and a shared commitment to the common good. Some might think that the ideas expressed here are intended to drive us apart. Nothing could be further from the truth. These ideas are intended to help us understand the issues so that we can change course and solve the problems that we face such as truly helping the poor, and runaway spending—both public and private—including entitlements.

However, I would assert that we are currently not a single people, and that in fact we have not been this divided as a nation since the time just prior to the War Between the States. We currently do not recognize a single mutually agreed upon set of rights, and while we may still have a shared commitment to the common good, we no longer agree on what the common good even is.

Some still believe that our rights come from our Creator, and that those are inalienable; they cannot be taken away or absolved. Others believe that our rights come from the state, just as in the days of the state religion societies. Progressivism has caused a regression to the past. What are some of the specific differences? Below are a few quotes that summarize some of the differences.

Area	Individualism	Collectivism
Rights	That they are endowed by their Creator with certain unalienable rights, that among these are Life, Liberty, and the Pursuit of Happiness.	The principle of all sovereignty resides essentially in the nation. No body nor individual may exercise any authority which does not proceed directly from the nation.
Man's Nature	We hold these Truths to be self-evident, that all Men are created equal.	Men are born free and equal in rights. Social distinctions may be founded only upon the general good.
Man's Dominion	No man is entitled to manage things merely for himself, he must do so in the interest of all so that he is ready to share them with others in case of necessity.	God has given us all things richly ... But how far has he given it to us? To enjoy.

Area	Individualism	Collectivism
Man's Purpose	Man is made principally for the knowledge of God.	Every one as he is bound to preserve himself, and not to quit his Station willfully; so by the like reason when his own Preservation comes not in competition, ought he, as much as he can, to preserve the rest of Mankind.
Freedom	The good man, although he is a slave, is free; but the bad man, even if he reigns, is a slave, and that not of one man, but, what is far more grievous, of as many masters as he has vices.	For in all the states of created beings capable of Laws, where there is no law, there is no Freedom.
Education	Neither is knowledge without faith, nor faith without knowledge.	The Freedom then of Man and Liberty of acting according to his own Will, is grounded on his having Reason, which is able to instruct him in that Law he is to govern himself by.
Governance	The guidance of human conduct required a divine law besides natural law and human law.	All are equal before the law … The will of the people shall be the basis of the authority of government.

Area	Individualism	Collectivism
Faith	No person, demeaning himself in a peaceable and orderly manner, shall ever be molested on account of his mode of worship or religious sentiments	No one shall be disquieted on account of his opinions, including his religious views, provided their manifestation does not disturb the public order established by law.
Charity	Virtue … derives from the desire for the changeless good; thus charity, the love of God, is described … as the root of all virtue.	So Charity gives every Man a Title to so much out of another's Plenty, as will keep him from extream want where he has no means to subsist otherwise.
Focus of Actions	If anyone wants to be first, he shall be last of all and servant of all.	The principal and chief care of every one ought to be of his own soul first, and, in the next place, of the public peace.

We mentioned above that every right has an underlying responsibility, which cannot be decoupled from the right. One of the problems we face today is an overwhelming focus on what our "rights" are, and in the process we fail to examine or understand our responsibilities. For example, with the right we each have to property, we have an accompanying responsibility to be good stewards. If we focus only on our own enjoyment, then we may deprive someone of their livelihood now or sometime in the future. This does not mean that we cannot use our resources, for they have been given to us by our Creator, rather it means we should use only what we need and out of our abundance we should share with others. By voluntarily accepting the right, we also voluntarily accept the responsibility(s) that come with it.

Likewise, when someone wrongs us, they are denying the equality of rights we each possess due to the nature that we both share. This is corrected, to the extent humanly possible, through the virtues of justice, mercy, and forgiveness—all forms of charity. By voluntarily accepting the right of an equal nature, we are also voluntarily accepting the responsibility of submitting to justice, showing mercy, and acting with forgiveness. Looked at in this way, if we voluntarily acknowledge and accept the rights that our Creator grants to every one of us, then we are obligating ourselves to become and stay virtuous; otherwise, we will simply not be successful. This is one foundational principle upon which our society is based. Our Founders understood and accepted this without any argument, as it was a part of their heritage. We have forgotten this linkage, and in recent years many man-made impediments have been set against even learning these ideas.

This brings us to the notion of the common good, and I would assert that we do not currently share the same ideas here either. Those who submit to rights being granted by our Creator (individualists) do not recognize the same rights or source as does collectivism. This leads to differences in what is the common good. Some of the main differences are summarized as follows:

1. Individualism's goal is to create independence. Its aim is to assist another in developing their strengths so that they are able to fish for themselves, just as a parent teaches and assists a child. Eventually most children grow to become independent adults.

2. Collectivism's goal is to provide security. This is done by creating entitlements to even the playing field, to create some artificial and humanly contrived equality of outcomes. This results in

    a. Less choice, and therefore increasing difficulty in achieving our purpose.

    b. Dependence as individuals/groups are simply provided with fish instead of being taught to fish, being taught to become self-sufficient.

    c. The breeding of weaknesses, vulnerability, and vice. The emphasis is shifted from service and caring to receiving my "fair share" of material possessions, and all of the envy, greed, and strife that result from this inclination.

We are facing a perilous time, both from within and without. However, it is not too late to change course. But changing will take effort on our part. We must recognize where we are, determine what and how we need to change to do better, and then commit ourselves to bring those changes about, each taking care of what lies within our own control. It will require educating ourselves, as our present system does not teach us what we need to be successful as a society, and working to acquire virtue. Neither is easy, but both are doable. We were made for them. It is up to each one of us, but to be successful we must be willing to acknowledge to whom we belong, submit, and be transformed. What will you choose?

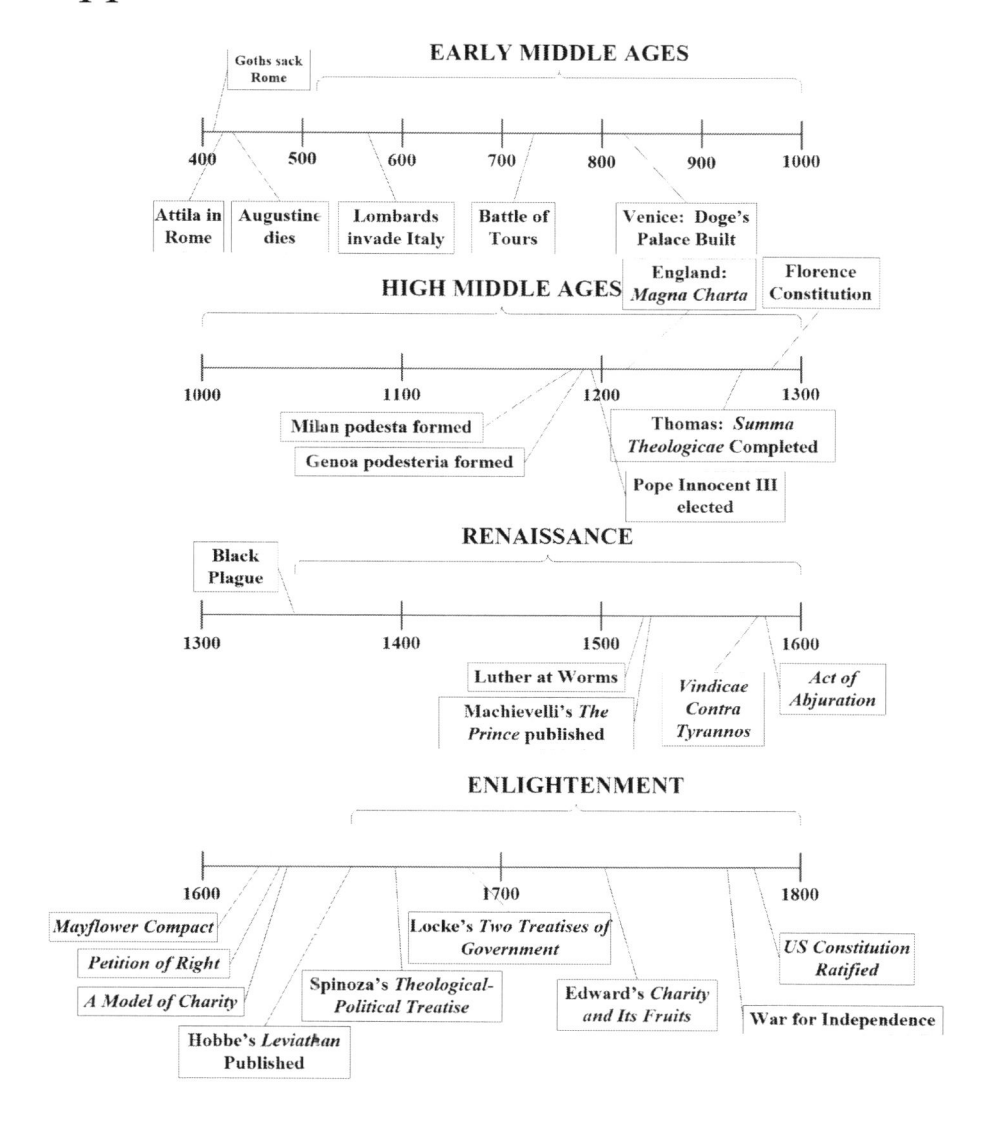

Appendix A: Timeline of Events

EARLY MIDDLE AGES (400–1000)
- Goths sack Rome
- Attila in Rome
- Augustine dies
- Lombards invade Italy
- Battle of Tours
- Venice: Doge's Palace Built
- England: *Magna Charta*
- Florence Constitution

HIGH MIDDLE AGES (1000–1300)
- Milan podesta formed
- Genoa podesteria formed
- Thomas: *Summa Theologicae* Completed
- Pope Innocent III elected

RENAISSANCE (1300–1600)
- Black Plague
- Luther at Worms
- Machievelli's *The Prince* published
- *Vindicae Contra Tyrannos*
- Act of Abjuration

ENLIGHTENMENT (1600–1800)
- Mayflower Compact
- Petition of Right
- *A Model of Charity*
- Hobbe's *Leviathan* Published
- Spinoza's *Theological-Political Treatise*
- Locke's *Two Treatises of Government*
- Edward's *Charity and Its Fruits*
- US Constitution Ratified
- War for Independence

Notes

Introduction

[1] Brooks, Arthur C., *Who Really Cares*, Basic Books, 2006.

[2] Corbett, Steve and Fikkert, Brian, *When Helping Hurts*, Moody Publishers, 2009.

[3] Schwartz, Glenn J., *When Charity Destroys Dignity*, World Mission Associates, 2007.

[4] Brooks, Arthur C., *Who Really Cares*, Basic Books, 2006. The figures within this section can be found on pages 34 – 52. The sources for this information are more fully described in the book's appendix, along with additional statistical information.

[5] Corbett, Steve and Fikkert, Brian, *When Helping Hurts*, p. 78, Moody Publishers, 2009.

[6] A further explanation of this assertion is provided in *Do You Want To Be Free?*, Chapter 11.

[7] Corbett, Steve and Fikkert, Brian, *When Helping Hurts*, p. 46, Moody Publishers, 2009.

[8] Ibid, p. 164.

[9] Ibid.

[10] From 1 John 3:17, "But whoever has the world's goods, and sees his brother in need and closes his heart against him, how does the love of God abide in him?" *Today's Parallel Bible*, Zondervan, New American Standard translation.

[11] From 1 Peter 2:10, "For you once were not a people, but now you are the people of God; you had not received mercy, but now you have received mercy." Ibid.

[12] Wolf, Dan, *Do You Want To Be Free? Faith, Freedom, and Governance*, p. 284, Telemachus Press, LLC, 2013.

[13] Corbett, Steve and Fikkert, Brian, *When Helping Hurts*, p. 172, Moody Publishers, 2009.

[14] Ibid, p. 173.

[15] Brooks, Arthur C., *Who Really Cares*, p. 28, Basic Books, 2006.

[16] Rev. Alexander Roberts and James Donaldson, *The Ante-Nicene Fathers, Fathers of the Second Century: Hermas, Tatian, Athenagora, Theophilus, and Clement of*

Alexandria (Entire), Vol. 2, p. 423, Wm. B. Eerdmans Publishing Co., 1989. Stromata, Book IV, Chapter XI.

Chapter 1: A Model of Charity

[1] Wolf, Dan, *Do You Want To Be Free? Faith, Freedom, and Governance*, Telemachus Press, LLC, 2013.

[2] de Tocqueville, Alexis, *Democracy in America*, Volumes I and II, pg. 100, Bantam Dell, 2000.

[3] Rev. Alexander Roberts and James Donaldson, *The Ante-Nicene Fathers, Fathers of the Second Century: Hermas, Tatian, Athenagora, Theophilus, and Clement of Alexandria (Entire)*, Vol. 2, p. 444, Wm. B Eerdmans Publishing Co., 1989. Strom, V, I.

[4] Ibid, p. 307, Stromata, I, VI.

[5] Wolf, Dan, *Do You Want To Be Free? Faith, Freedom, and Governance*, p. 111, Telemachus Press, LLC, 2013.

[6] Ibid.

[7] Evans, M. Stanton, *The Theme is Freedom: Religion, Politics, and the American Tradition*, p. 23, Regnery Publishing, 1994.

[8] Wolf, Dan, *Do You Want To Be Free? Faith, Freedom, and Governance*, p. 4, Telemachus Press, LLC, 2013.

[9] Edwards, Jonathan, *Charity and Its Fruits*, p. 2, from the Chapel Library, at http://www.hisonelife.com/uploads/4/9/8/6/4986072/edwards_-_charity_and_its_fruits.pdf.

[10] Rev. Alexander Roberts and James Donaldson, *The Ante-Nicene Fathers, Fathers of the Second Century: Hermas, Tatian, Athenagora, Theophilus, and Clement of Alexandria (Entire)*, Vol. 2, p. 502, Wm. B Eerdmans Publishing Co., 1989. Stromata, VI, IX.

[11] Schaff, Philip, *Nicene and Post-Nicene Fathers, Augustin: City of God, Christian Doctrine*, Vol. 2, Wm. B. Eerdmans Publishing Company, 1989.

[12] Aquinas, St. Thomas, *Summa Theologicæ,* Vol. 31, p. 119, McGraw-Hill Publishing Co., 1970. Part 2a2ae, Question 4, Article 1. Future references to this work will be followed by the Section, Question, and Article reference. The actual quote from Augustine being cited by Thomas is "But hope deals only with good things, and only with those which lie in the future, and which pertain to the man who cherishes the hope. Since this is so, faith must be distinguished from hope: they are different terms and likewise different concepts. Yet faith and hope have this in common: they

refer to what is not seen, whether this unseen is believed in or hoped for." Schaff, Philip, *Nicene and Post-Nicene Fathers, Vol. 2, Augustin: City of God, Christian Doctrine*, p. 385, Wm. B. Eerdmans Publishing Company, 1989. Chapter II, 41.

[13] Ibid, Vol. 31, p. 9, 2a2ae, 1, 1.

[14] Ibid, Vol. 31, p.9, 2a2ae, 1, 1.

[15] Ibid, Vol. 31, p.165, 2a2ae, 6, 1.

[16] Ibid, Vol. 33, p. 35, 2a2ae, 18, 2.

[17] Ibid, Vol. 31, p. 125, 2a2ae, 4, 3.

[18] Ibid, Vol. 34, p. 29, 2a2ae, 23, 7.

[19] Ibid, Vol. 34, p. 33, 2a2ae, 23, 8.

[20] Ibid, Vol. 34, p.121, 2a2ae, 26, 1.

[21] 1John 4:16, p. 2809, *Today's Parallel Bible, New International Version, New American Standard Bible, Updated Edition, King James Version, New Living Translation*, Zondervan, 2000. The cited quote is contained in all four translations.

[22] Aquinas, St. Thomas, *Summa Theologicæ*, Vol. 37, p. 3, McGraw-Hill Publishing Co., 1970. 2a2ae, 57, 1.

[23] Ibid.

[24] Ibid, Vol. 34, p. 41, 2a2ae, 58, 8.

[25] Ibid, Vol. 30, pp. 109-111, 1a2ae, 110, 1.

[26] Bonhoeffer, Dietrich, *The Cost of Discipleship*, pp. 44-45, Simon and Schuster, 1995.

[27] Ibid, p. 45.

Chapter 2: Charity's Development

[1] Both Plato's *Republic* and *The Laws*, as well as Aristotle's *Politics* discuss these points. A summary of some of the key points is contained in Wolf, Dan, *Do You Want To Be Free?*, pp. 26-28, Telemachus Press, 2013.

[2] Bishop, Mathew and Green, Michael, *Ancient Giving*, http://philanthrocapitalism.net/bonus-chapters/ancient-giving/.

[3] Stark, Rodney, *The Victory of Reason*, pp. 26-27, Random House, 2005

[4] Ibid, pp. 35-63.

Notes

[5] Brodman, James William, *Charity & Religion in Medieval Europe,* pp. 2-3, The Catholic University of America Press, 2009.

[6] Ibid, pp. 2-3.

[7] Ibid, p. 3.

[8] Gavitt, Philip, *Gender, Honor, and Charity in Late Renaissance Florence*, p. 71, Cambridge University Press, 2013.

[9] Ibid.

[10] Walsh, Gerald G. et al, *City of God,* pp. 148-149, Doubleday Publishing, 1958. Book VIII, Chapter 4.

[11] Schaff, Philip, *Nicene and Post-Nicene Fathers, Augustin: City of God, Christian Doctrine*, Vol. 2, p. 413, Wm. B. Eerdmans Publishing Company, 1989. XIX, 19.

[12] Brodman, James William, *Charity & Religion in Medieval Europe,* p. 45, The Catholic University of America Press, 2009.

[13] Ibid, p.44.

[14] Ibid, p. 12.

[15] Ibid, p. 15.

[16] Ibid, p. 18.

[17] Ibid, p. 19.

[18] Rev. Alexander Roberts and James Donaldson, *The Ante-Nicene Fathers, Fathers of the Second Century: Hermas, Tatian, Athenagora, Theophilus, and Clement of Alexandria (Entire)*, Vol. 2, p. 369, Wm. B Eerdmans Publishing Co., 1989. Stromata, II, XIX.

[19] Ibid, p. 420, Stromata, IV, VIII.

[20] Schaff, Philip, *Nicene and Post-Nicene Fathers, Vol. 2, Augustin: City of God, Christian Doctrine*, p. 273, Wm. B. Eerdmans Publishing Company, 1989. Book XIV, Ch. 13.

[21] Brodman, James William, *Charity & Religion in Medieval Europe,* p. 35, The Catholic University of America Press, 2009

[22] Gavitt, Philip, *Gender, Honor, and Charity in Late Renaissance Florence*, p. 36, Cambridge University Press, 2011.

[23] Ibid, p. 39.

[24] Ibid, p. 41.

[25] Schaff, Philip, *Nicene and Post-Nicene Fathers, Augustin: City of God, Christian Doctrine*, Vole. 2, p. 268 - 269, Wm. B. Eerdmans Publishing Company, 1989. VI, 4. "But if it is too much to prefer a part of the divine to all human things, that part is certainly worthy to be preferred to the Romans at least. For he (Varro) writes the books concerning human things, not with reference to the whole world, but only to Rome; which books he says he had properly placed, in the order of writing, before the books on divine things, like a painter before the painted tablet, or a mason before the building, most openly confessing that, as a picture or a structure, even these divine things were instituted by men."

[26] Matt. 22:15-22. "Then the Pharisees went and plotted together how they might trap Him in what He said. And they sent their disciples to Him, along with the Herodians, saying, 'Teacher, we know that You are truthful and teach the way of God in truth, and defer to no one; for You are not partial to any. Tell us then, what do You think? Is it lawful to give a poll-tax to Caesar, or not?' But Jesus perceived their malice, and said, 'Why are you testing Me, you hypocrites? Show Me the coin *used* for the poll-tax.' And they brought Him a denarius. And He said to them, 'Whose likeness and inscription is this?' They said to Him, 'Caesar's.' Then He said to them, 'Then render to Caesar the things that are Caesar's; and to God the things that are God's.' And hearing *this*, they were amazed, and leaving Him, they went away." *Today's Parallel Bible*, New American Standard Bible translation, Zondervan, 2000.

[27] Matt. 22:36-40. "Teacher, which is the great commandment in the Law? And He said to him, 'You shall love the Lord your God with all your heart, and with all your soul, and with all your mind.' This is the great and foremost commandment. The second is like it. 'You shall love your neighbor as yourself.' On these two commandments depend the whole Law and the Prophets." Ibid.

[28] Mark 10:42-44. "Jesus called them together and said, 'You know that those who are regarded as rulers of the Gentiles lord it over them, and their high officials exercise authority over them. Not so with you. Instead, whoever wants to become great among you must be your servant, and whoever wants to be first must be slave of all.'"

[29] Deut. 1:17. "You shall not show partiality in judgment; you shall hear the small and the great alike. You shall not fear man, for the judgment is God's. The case that is too hard for you, you shall bring to me, and I will hear it." See also Deut. 16 and 2 Chron. 19.

[30] Edwards, Jonathan, *The Works of Jonathan Edwards*, Vol.2, pp. 7-12, Hendrickson Publishers, 2006.

[31] Ibid, p.511.

[32] Ibid, p. 937.

[33] Ibid, p. 937. 'Indeed all men and all creatures are his, as well since as before the fall; whether they are elected or not, they are his.'

[34] Ibid, p. 937. As for those who choose not to obey, "But yet in a sense the wicked may be said not to belong to God. God doth not own them."

[35] Ibid, p. 939.

[36] Ibid, p. 246.

[37] Ibid.

[38] Ibid, p. 944. "The saints are all of the same native country. Heaven is the native country of the church."

[39] Ibid, p.945. "All Christians speak the same language. They all have the same fundamental doctrines."

[40] Ibid.

[41] Ibid.

[42] Ibid, p. 943.

[43] Ibid, p. 944.

[44] Ibid, p.936, "But ye are a chosen generation, a royal priesthood, an holy nation, a peculiar people; that ye should show forth the praises of him who hath called you out of darkness into his marvelous light."

[45] Ibid, p. 937.

[46] Ibid, p. 940.

[47] Ibid, p. 941.

[48] Ibid.

[49] Ibid, pp. 941 – 2.

[50] Ibid, p. 944.

[51] Ibid, p. 945.

[52] Ibid, p. 485.

[53] Ibid.

[54] Ibid.

[55] Ibid, p. 486.

[56] Ibid.

[57] Ibid, p. 36.

[58] Ibid, p. 37.

[59] Ibid.

[60] Ibid, p. 38.

[61] Ibid.

[62] Ibid., p. 487.

[63] The Jonathan Edwards Center, Vol. 17, Yale University, http://edwards.yale.edu/.

[64] Ibid. pp. 357-8.

[65] Ibid., Vol. 14.

[66] Ibid.

[67] Ibid.

[68] Ketchum, Ralph, James Madison, p 652, University of Virginia Press, 1990.

[69] Aquinas, St. Thomas, *Summa Theologicæ,* Vol. 37, p. 89-91, McGraw-Hill Publishing Co., 1970. Part 2a2ae, 61, 1.

Chapter 3: Purpose and Collectivism

[1] Spinoza, Benedict, *Theologico-Political Treatise*, p. 185, Barnes & Noble, 2009. "The power of nature is the power of God, which has sovereign right over all things." This idea is repeated several times within this work.

[2] Ibid, p. 33. "So whatever human nature can furnish itself with by its own efforts to preserve its existence, may be fitly called the inward aid of God, whereas whatever else accrues to man's profit from outward causes may be called the external aid of God." Also, p.30. "If I were to enumerate all the passages of Scripture addressed only to individuals, or to a particular man's understanding, and which cannot, without great danger to philosophy, be defended as Divine doctrines, I should go far beyond the brevity at which I aim."

[3] Ibid, p. 195. "We must, then, fully grant that the Divine law and right originated at the time when men by express covenant agreed to obey God in all things, and ceded as it were, their natural freedom, transferring their rights to God in the manner described in speaking of the formation of a state."

[4] Ibid, p. 35. "For the ends of every social organization and commonwealth are ... security and comfort."

[5] Ibid, p. 189. "For everyone would keep most religiously to their compact in their desire for the chief good, namely, the preservation of the state, and would cherish good faith above all things as the shield and buckler of the commonwealth."

[6] Ibid. p. 229. "When I said that the possessors of sovereign power have rights over everything, and that all rights are dependent on their decree, I did not merely mean temporal rights, be also spiritual."

[7] Ibid, p. 226. "We see how necessary it is, both in the interests of the state and in the interests of religion, to confer on the sovereign power the rights of deciding what is lawful or the reverse." Also, p. 229. "Religion acquires its force as law solely from the decrees of the sovereign."

[8] Ibid, p. 233. "It is certain that duties towards one's country are the highest that man can fulfil."

[9] Ibid, p. 230. "Inward worship of God, and piety in itself are within the sphere of everyone's private rights, and cannot be alienated."

[10] Ibid, p. 241. "That in a free state every man may think what he likes, and say what he likes."

[11] Ibid, p. 229-30. "God has no special kingdom among men except insofar as He reigns through temporal rulers. Moreover, the rites of religion and the outward observances of piety should be in accordance with the public peace and well-being."

[12] Ibid, p. 231. "Justice, therefore, and absolutely all the precepts of reason, including love towards one's neighbor, receive the force of laws and ordinances solely through the rights of dominion, that is ... solely on the decree of those who possess the right to rule."

[13] Leiterhas, Yechiel M., *The Hebraic Roots of John Locke's Doctrine of Charity*, Jerusalem Center for Public Affairs, 2008, http://jcpa.org/article/the-hebraic-roots-of-john-lockes-doctrine-of-charity/.

[14] Ibid.

[15] Locke, John, *Two Treatises of Government*, pp 135-263, Cambridge University Press, 1988. Further references to this work will include the chapter and passage reference to make it easier for the reader to locate within the original text.

[16] Ibid, pp. 265-428.

[17] Locke, John, *A Letter Concerning Toleration,* Prometheus Books, 1990.

[18] Ibid, p. 13.

[19] Ibid.

[20] Ibid.

[21] Ibid, p.14.

[22] Locke, John, *Two Treatises of Government*, p. 170, Cambridge University Press, 1988. I, 42.

[23] Locke, John, *A Letter Concerning Toleration,* p. 14, Prometheus Books, 1990.

[24] Ibid. "Now I appeal to the consciences of those that persecute, torment, destroy, and kill other men upon pretense of religion, whether they do it out of friendship and kindness towards them, or no . . . For if it be out of a principle of charity, as they pretend, and love to men's souls, that they deprive them of their estates, maim them with corporal punishments, starve and torment them in noisome prisons, and in the end even take away their lives; I say, if all this be done merely to make men Christians, and procure their salvation, why then do they suffer "whoredom, fraud, malice, and such like enormities."

[25] Ibid, p.16.

[26] Ibid, p.13.

[27] Locke, John, *Two Treatises of Government,* p. 358, XI, 135.

[28] Plato, *Dialogues, Symposium,* p. 1181, Word Press, http://www.cakravartin.com/wordpress/wp-content/uploads/2008/08/plato-complete-works.pdf.

[29] Locke, John, *Two Treatises of Government,* p. 271, II, 6.

[30] Locke, John, *A Letter Concerning Toleration,* p. 57, Prometheus Books, 1990.

[31] Robert, Rev. Alexander and Donaldson, James, *The Ante-Nicene Fathers, Fathers of the Second Century: Hermas, Tatian, Athenagora, Theophilus, and Clement of Alexandria (Entire),* Vol. 2, p. 437, Wm. B Eerdmans Publishing Co., 1989, Stromata, IV, XXIII.

[32] Locke, John, *A Letter Concerning Toleration,* p. 44, Prometheus Books, 1990.

[33] Jefferson, Thomas, *Notes on the State of Virginia,* p. 265, London, 1787. http://books.google.com/books/about/Notes_on_the_State_of_Virginia.html.

[34] Locke, John, *A Letter Concerning Toleration,* p. 61, Prometheus Books, 1990.

[35] NASB, I Peter, 2:9-10, "But you are a chosen race, a royal priesthood, a holy nation, a people for God's own possession, so that you may proclaim the excellencies of Him who has called you out of darkness into His marvelous light; for your once were not a people, but now you are the people of God; you had not received mercy, but now you have received mercy."

[36] Locke, John, *Two Treatises of Government,* p. 269, II, 4.

[37] Ibid.

[38] Ibid, p.271, II, 6.

[39] For a further discussion of this issue see, Aquinas, St. Thomas, *Summa Theologicæ,* Vol. 38, pp. 65-69, McGraw-Hill Publishing Co., 1970.

[40] Aquinas, St. Thomas, *Summa Theologicæ*, Vol. 38, pp. 67-69, McGraw-Hill Publishing Co., 1970. 2a2ae, 66, 2.

[41] Robert, Rev. Alexander and Donaldson, James, *The Ante-Nicene Fathers, Fathers of the Second Century: Hermas, Tatian, Athenagora, Theophilus, and Clement of Alexandria (Entire)*, Vol. 2, p. 320, Wm. B Eerdmans Publishing Co., 1989, Stromata, I, XVII.

Also see Walsh, Gerard G. et al, *City of God*, pp. 104-107, Doubleday Publishing, 1958. Book V, Chapter 9.

[42] Robert, Rev. Alexander and Donaldson, James, *The Ante-Nicene Fathers, Fathers of the Second Century: Hermas, Tatian, Athenagora, Theophilus, and Clement of Alexandria (Entire)*, Vol. 2, p. 271, Wm. B Eerdmans Publishing Co., 1989, Paedagogus, III, I.

[43] Ibid, p. 235, Paedagogus, I, XIII.

[44] Ibid, p. 338, Stromata, I, XXV.

[45] Robert, Rev. Alexander and Donaldson, James, *The Ante-Nicene Fathers, Fathers of the Second Century: Hermas, Tatian, Athenagora, Theophilus, and Clement of Alexandria (Entire)*, Vol. 2, p. 306, Wm. B Eerdmans Publishing Co., 1989, Stromata, I, V.

[46] Locke, John, *Two Treatises of Government*, p. 271, II, 6.

[47] Ibid, II, 7.

[48] Ibid, p. 272, II, 8.

[49] Ibid, p. 274, II, 11.

[50] NASB, Matthew 16:25.

[51] Robert, Rev. Alexander and Donaldson, James, *The Ante-Nicene Fathers, Fathers of the Second Century: Hermas, Tatian, Athenagora, Theophilus, and Clement of Alexandria (Entire)*, Vol. 2, p. 232, Wm. B Eerdmans Publishing Co., 1989, Stromata, I, IX.

[52] Schaff, Philip, *Nicene and Post-Nicene Fathers, Augustin: City of God, Christian Doctrine*, Vol. 2, p. 405, Wm. B. Eerdmans Publishing Company, 1989. XIX, 7.

[53] NASB, Deuteronomy 16: 18-20, "You shall appoint for yourself judges and officers in all your towns which the Lord your God is giving you, according to your tribes, and they shall judge the people with righteous judgment. You shall not distort justice; you shall not be partial, and you shall not take a bribe, for a bribe blinds the eyes of the wise and perverts the words of the righteous. Justice, *and only* justice, you shall pursue, that you may live and possess the land which the Lord your God is giving you."

[54] Robert, Rev. Alexander and Donaldson, James, *The Ante-Nicene Fathers, Fathers of the Second Century: Hermas, Tatian, Athenagora, Theophilus, and Clement of Alexandria (Entire),* Vol. 2, p. 423, Wm. B Eerdmans Publishing Co., 1989, Stromata, IV, XI.

[55] Ibid, p. 423, IV, XI.

[56] Aquinas, St. Thomas, *Summa Theologicæ,* Vol. 28, pp. 151, McGraw-Hill Publishing Co., 1970 Part 1a2ae, Question 97, Article 3. Further references to this work will include the Part, Question, and Article reference.

[57] Ibid, Vol. 29, p.43, 1a2ae, 99, 4.

[58] Ibid, Vol. 28, p.95, 1a2ae, 94, 5.

[59] Locke, John, *Two Treatises of Government,* p. 277, II, 14.

[60] Ibid, p. 308, VI, 61.

[61] Ibid, pp. 393-394, XVI, 190.

[62] Ibid, pp. 322-323, VII, 85.

[63] NASB, Matthew 5 43-44.

[64] Locke, John, *Two Treatises of Government,* p. 286, V, 25.

[65] Ibid, p. 288, V, 27.

[66] Ibid, p. 290, V, 31.

[67] Ibid, p. 302, V, 51.

[68] Robert, Rev. Alexander and Donaldson, James, *The Ante-Nicene Fathers, Fathers of the Second Century: Hermas, Tatian, Athenagora, Theophilus, and Clement of Alexandria (Entire),* Vol. 2, p. 190, Wm. B Eerdmans Publishing Co., 1989, Protrepticus., IV. "For if the heavenly bodies are not the works of men, they were certainly created for man. Let none of you worship the sum, but set his desires on the Maker of the sun; nor deify the universe, but seek after the Creator of the universe."

[69] Ibid, p. 440, Stromata, IV, XXVI. "For all things are of one God. And no one is a stranger to the world by nature, their essence being one, and God one. But the elect man dwells as a sojourner, knowing all things to be possessed and disposed of . . . having care of the things of the world . . . but leaving his dwelling place and property without excessive emotion . . . and blessing [God] for his departure, embracing the mansion that is in heaven."

[70] Locke, John, *Two Treatises of Government,* p. 304, VI, 54.

[71] Ibid, p. 305, VI, 57.

[72] Ibid, p. 309, VI, 61.

[73] Ibid, p. 306, VI, 57.

[74] Ibid, p. 305.

[75] Aquinas, St. Thomas, *Summa Theologicæ*, Vol. 28, pp. 109, McGraw-Hill Publishing Co., 1970. 1a2ae, 95, 3.

[76] Ibid, p. 131, 1a2ae, 96, 4.

[77] Ibid, p. 131.

[78] Ibid, p. 131-133.

[79] Ibid.

[80] Locke, John, *Two Treatises of Government*, p. 282, III, 21.

[81] Ibid, pp. 276-7, II, 14.

[82] Ibid, p. 278, III, 16.

[83] Ibid, p. 284, IV, 23.

[84] Ibid, p. 283, IV, 22.

[85] Ibid, p. 284.

[86] Ibid, p. 355, X, 133.

[87] Locke, John, *A Letter Concerning Toleration*, p. 18, Prometheus Books, 1990.

[88] Ibid.

[89] Ibid, p. 26.

[90] Locke, John, *Two Treatises of Government*, p. 383, XV, 173.

[91] Ibid, p. 331, VIII, 95.

[92] Ibid, p. 383, XV, 172.

[93] Ibid, p. 279, III, 17.

[94] Ibid, p. 330, VIII, 95.

[95] Ibid, p. 350-1, IX, 124-126.

[96] Ibid, p. 325, VII, 89.

[97] Locke, John, *A Letter Concerning Toleration*, pp. 49-50, Prometheus Books, 1990.

[98] Aquinas, St. Thomas, *Summa Theologicæ*, Vol. 16, pp. 55, McGraw-Hill Publishing Co., 1970. 1a2ae, 2, 8.

[99] Ibid, p. 117, 1a2ae, 5, 1.

[100] Locke, John, *A Letter Concerning Toleration*, p. 58, Prometheus Books, 1990.

Chapter 4: Power

[1] Locke, John, *A Letter Concerning Toleration*, p. 49, Prometheus Books, 1990.

[2] Ibid, p. 18.

[3] Ibid, p. 19.

[4] Ibid.

[5] Ibid.

[6] Ibid, p. 20.

[7] Ibid, p. 21.

[8] Ibid, p. 58.

[9] Ibid, p. 59.

[10] Ibid.

[11] Ibid, p. 60.

[12] Locke, John, *Two Treatises of Government*, p. 268, I, 3.

[13] Ibid, p. 352, IX, 128.

[14] Ibid.

[15] Ibid, p. 349, VIII, 120.

[16] Ibid, p. 427-8, XIX, 243.

[17] Ibid, p. 415, XIX, 226.

[18] Ibid, p. 419, XIX, 232.

[19] Ibid, p. 375, XIV, 159.

[20] Ibid, p. 395-6, XVI, 195.

[21] Aquinas, St. Thomas, *Summa Theologicæ*, Vol. 28, pp. 59, McGraw-Hill Publishing Co., 1970. 1a2ae, 93, 3.

[22] Locke, John, *Two Treatises of Government*, p. 379, XIV, 168.

[23] Edwards, Jonathan et al, *Sinners in the Hands of an Angry God and Other Puritan Sermons*, pp. 3-4, Dover Publications Inc., 2005. The specific work is *Limitation of Government* by John Cotton – not dated.

[24] Locke, John, *Two Treatises of Government,* p. 379, XIV, 168.

[25] Ibid, p. 357-361, XI, 135-138.

[26] Ibid, p. 366-7, XIII, 149.

[27] Ibid, p. 363, XI, 142.

[28] Ibid, p. 330, VII, 94.

[29] Ibid, p. 378, XIV, 166.

[30] Ibid, Locke discusses the limits of prerogative and how it changes on pages 376-8 in paragraphs 162-7.

[31] Ibid, p. 410-1, XIX, 218-9.

[32] Ibid, p. 400, XVIII, 202.

[33] Locke, John, *A Letter Concerning Toleration,* p. 25, Prometheus Books, 1990.

[34] Ibid, p.13.

[35] Locke, John, *The Reasonableness of Christianity,* C. Baldwin, London, 1824.

[36] Ibid, p. 16.

[37] Ibid, p. 105.

[38] Ibid, p. 8.

[39] Ibid, p. 12.

[40] Ibid, p. 13.

[41] Ibid, pp. 13-14.

[42] Locke, John, *A Letter Concerning Toleration,* p. 22, Prometheus Books, 1990.

[43] Ibid.

[44] Ibid, p.23.

[45] Ibid, p.26.

[46] Ibid, p.25.

[47] Ibid, p.65.

[48] Ibid, p.43.

[49] Ibid, p.25.

[50] Ibid, p.32.

[51] Ibid, p.28.

[52] Ibid, p.49.

[53] Ibid, p.31.

[54] Ibid, p.41.

[55] Ibid, p.55.

[56] Ibid.

[57] Ibid, p.52.

[58] Aquinas, St. Thomas, *Summa Theologicæ*, Vol. 29, p. 269, McGraw-Hill Publishing Co., 1970. 1a2ae, 105, 1.

[59] Locke, John, *A Letter Concerning Toleration,* p. 73, Prometheus Books, 1990.

[60] Ibid, p.61.

[61] Ibid, p.73.

[62] Ibid, p.56.

[63] Robert, Rev. Alexander and Donaldson, James, *The Ante-Nicene Fathers, Fathers of the Second Century: Hermas, Tatian, Athenagora, Theophilus, and Clement of Alexandria (Entire),* Vol. 2, p. 308, Wm. B Eerdmans Publishing Co., 1989, Stromata, I, VII.

[64] Genesis 1:27-8: "So God created mankind in his own image, in the image of God he created them; male and female he created them. God blessed them and said to them, 'Be fruitful and increase in number; fill the earth and subdue it. Rule over the fish in the sea and the birds in the sky and over every living creature that moves on the ground.'" *Today's Parallel Bible*, New American Standard Bible translation, Zondervan, 2000.

[65] Edwards, Johnathan, *The Works of Jonathan Edwards,* Vol. 2, p.944, Hendrickson Publishers, 2006.

[66] Aquinas, St. Thomas, *Summa Theologicæ*, Vol. 31, p. 133, McGraw-Hill Publishing Co., 1970. 2a2ae, 4, 5.

[67] Robert, Rev. Alexander and Donaldson, James, *The Ante-Nicene Fathers, Fathers of the Second Century: Hermas, Tatian, Athenagora, Theophilus, and Clement of Alexandria (Entire),* Vol. 2, p. 308, Wm. B Eerdmans Publishing Co., 1989, Stromata, I, VII.

[68] Ibid, p.323, Stromata, I, XX.

[69] Aquinas, St. Thomas, *Summa Theologicæ*, Vol. 41, p. 135, McGraw-Hill Publishing Co., 1970. 2a2ae, 109, 1.

[70] Ibid, p.502, Stromata, VI, XI.

[71] Aquinas, St. Thomas, *Summa Theologicæ*, Vol. 37, p. 21, McGraw-Hill Publishing Co., 1970. 2a2ae, 58, 1. "Aristotle teaches that the requirements of a virtuous act are that it is done, first, knowingly, second, from choice and for a fitting end, and third, unwaveringly."

[72] Robert, Rev. Alexander and Donaldson, James, *The Ante-Nicene Fathers, Fathers of the Second Century: Hermas, Tatian, Athenagora, Theophilus, and Clement of Alexandria (Entire)*, Vol. 2, p. 302, Wm. B Eerdmans Publishing Co., 1989, Stromata, I, I.

[73] Ibid, p.420, Stromata, IV, VII.

[74] Ibid, p.369, Stromata, II, XIX.

[75] Aquinas, St. Thomas, *Summa Theologicæ*, Vol. 16, pp. 131-133, McGraw-Hill Publishing Co., 1970. 1a2ae, 5, 5.

[76] Ibid, Vol. 26, pp. 81-83, 1a2ae, 85, 1. "An inclination towards of two contraries necessarily diminishes any inclination towards the other. Since sin is the contrary of virtue, that good of nature which is the inclination to virtue is lessened by the fact of a person's sinning."

[77] Schaff, Philip, *Nicene and Post-Nicene Fathers, Augustin: City of God, Christian Doctrine*, Vol. 2, p. 102, Wm. B. Eerdmans Publishing Company, 1989. V, 20.

[78] Walsh, Gerald G. et al, *City of God*, p. 235, Doubleday Publishing, 1958. XI, 25.

[79] Robert, Rev. Alexander and Donaldson, James, *The Ante-Nicene Fathers, Fathers of the Second Century: Hermas, Tatian, Athenagora, Theophilus, and Clement of Alexandria (Entire)*, Vol. 2, p. 350, Wm. B Eerdmans Publishing Co., 1989, Stromata, II, IV.

[80] Edwards, Jonathan, *The Works of Jonathan Edwards*, Vol. 1, p. 122, Hendrickson Publishers, 2006.

[81] Robert, Rev. Alexander and Donaldson, James, *The Ante-Nicene Fathers, Fathers of the Second Century: Hermas, Tatian, Athenagora, Theophilus, and Clement of Alexandria (Entire)*, Vol. 2, p. 190, Wm. B Eerdmans Publishing Co., 1989, Protrepticus, IV.

[82] Ibid, p. 440, Stromata, IV, XXVI.

[83] Ibid, p. 271, Paedagogus, III, I.

[84] Ibid, p. 496, Stromata, VI, IX.

[85] Aquinas, St. Thomas, *Summa Theologicæ*, Vol. 38, p. 65, McGraw-Hill Publishing Co., 1970. 2a2ae, 66, 1.

[86] Ibid, pp.67-69, 2a2ae, 66, 2.

[87] Ibid.

[88] Ibid, Vol. 37, pp.89-91, 2a2ae, 61, 1.

[89] Ibid, Vol. 38, p.81, 2a2ae, 66, 7.

[90] Ibid, Vol. 34, p. , 2a2ae, 32, 5.

[91] Ibid.

[92] Ibid.

[93] Ibid.

[94] Edwards, Jonathan, *The Works of Jonathan Edwards,* Vol. 1, p. 122, Hendrickson Publishers, 2006.

[95] Ibid, p. 137.

[96] Ibid, p. 138.

[97] Ibid, p. 142.

[98] Rasmussen Reports, *Right Direction or Wrong Track,* http://www.rasmussenreports.com/public_content/politics/mood_of_america/right_direction_or_wrong_track.

Chapter 5: The Need for Education

[1] Cooper, John M., Ed., *Plato: Complete Works,* p. 1473, Hackett Publishing Company, 1997. Republic, Book VII, 804.

[2] Walsh, Gerald G. et al, *City of God,* pp.468-9, XIX, 21.

[3] Hayek, F.A., *The Road to Serfdom,* p. 259, The University of Chicago Press, 2007.

[4] Jefferson, Thomas, *Notes on the State of Virginia,* p. 379, London, 1787. http://books.google.com/books/about/Notes_on_the_State_of_Virginia.html.

[5] Ibid, p. 265.

[6] Robert, Rev. Alexander and Donaldson, James, *The Ante-Nicene Fathers, Fathers of the Second Century: Hermas, Tatian, Athenagora, Theophilus, and Clement of Alexandria (Entire),* Vol. 2, p. 320, Wm. B Eerdmans Publishing Co., 1989, Stomata, I, XVII.

[7] Washington, George, *Washington's Farewell Address,* http://avalon.law.yale.edu/18th_century/washing.asp.

[8] Cooper, John M., Ed., *Plato: Complete Works,* p. 1137, Hackett Publishing Company, 1997. Republic, Book VII, 520.

[9] Ibid, p. 1489. Laws, Book VII, 823.

[10] Ibid, p. 1479. Laws, Book VII, 812.

[11] Barnes, Jonathan, Ed., *The Complete Works of Aristotle: The Revised Oxford Translation*, Vol. II, p. 2120, Princeton University Press, 1995. Politics, Book VII, Part XVII.

[12] Cooper, John M., Ed., *Plato: Complete Works*, p. 1481, Hackett Publishing Company, 1997. Laws, Book VII, 814.

[13] Ibid, p. 1087. Republic, Book V, 460.

[14] Barnes, Jonathan, Ed., *The Complete Works of Aristotle: The Revised Oxford Translation*, Vol. II, p. 2121, Princeton University Press, 1995. Politics, Book VIII, Part I.

[15] Ibid, p. 2028. Politics, Book III, V.

[16] Cooper, John M., Ed., *Plato: Complete Works*, p. 1050, Hackett Publishing Company, 1997. Republic, Book III, 415.

[17] Ketcham, Ralph, *James Madison: A Biography*, pp. 646-658, University of Virginia Press, 1990.

[18] Schaff, Philip, *Nicene and Post-Nicene Fathers, Augustine: City of God, Christian Doctrine*, Vol. 2, pp. 502-3, Wm. B. Eerdmans Publishing Company, 1989. XXII, 24.

[19] The Heritage Foundation, *How Escalating Education Spending is Killing Crucial Reforms*, http://www.heritage.org/research/reports/2012/10/how-escalating-education-spending-is-killing-crucial-reform.

[20] Ibid.

[21] Mercatus Center, George Mason University, *K-12 Spending per Student in the OECD*, http://mercatus.org/publication/k-12-spending-student-oecd.

[22] Profit of Education, *High School Graduation Rates-the Truth*, http://profitofeducation.org/?p=148.

[23] U.S. Department of Education, *Trends in Academic Progress*, http://nces.ed.gov/nationsreportcard/subject/publications/main2012/pdf/2013456.pdf.

[24] Ibid.

[25] U.S. Department of Education, *Program for International Student Assessment*, http://nces.ed.gov/surveys/pisa/pisa2012/index.asp.

[26] Luke 12:47-48, "And that slave who knew his master's will and did not get ready or act in accord with his will, will receive many lashes, but the one who did not know it, and committed deeds worthy of a flogging, will receive but few. From everyone

who has been given much, much will be required; and to whom they entrusted much, of him they will ask all the more." *Today's Parallel Bible*, New American Standard Bible translation, Zondervan, 2000.

[27] 2 Thes. 3:6-13. "Now we command you, brethren, in the name of our Lord Jesus Christ, that you keep away from every brother who leads an unruly life and not according to the tradition which you received from us. For you yourselves know how you ought to follow our example, because we did not act in an undisciplined manner among you, nor did we eat anyone's bread without paying for it, but with labor and hardship we *kept* working night and day so that we would not be a burden to any of you; not because we do not have the right *to this*, but in order to offer ourselves as a model for you, so that you would follow our example. For even when we were with you, we used to give you this order: if anyone is not willing to work, then he is not to eat, either. For we hear that some among you are leading an undisciplined life, doing no work at all, but acting like busybodies. Now such persons we command and exhort in the Lord Jesus Christ to work in quiet fashion and eat their own bread. But as for you, brethren, do not grow weary of doing good." Zondervan, 2000.

[28] Cooper, John M., Ed., *Plato: Complete Works*, p. 1050, Hackett Publishing Company, 1997. Republic, Book III, 414. "How, then, could we devise one of those useful falsehoods, we were talking about a while ago, one noble falsehood that would, in the best case, persuade even the rulers, but if that's not possible, then the others in the city?" Also see, Republic II, 382, where Plato discusses the differences between a true falsehood and one that is an imitation, "not a pure falsehood."

Chapter 6: The Utopian Dream

[1] Hastings, Adrian, Ed., *A World History of Christianity*, p. 253, William B. Eerdmans Publishing Company, 1999.

[2] Schama, Simon, *A History of Britain, At the Edge of the World 3000 BC – AD 1603*, p.130, Hyperion, 2000.

[3] Hastings, Adrian, Ed., *A World History of Christianity*, p. 123, William B. Eerdmans Publishing Company, 1999.

[4] Schama, Simon, *A History of Britain, At the Edge of the World 3000 BC – AD 1603*, p.130, Hyperion, 2000.

[5] Hastings, Adrian, Ed., *A World History of Christianity*, p. 124, William B. Eerdmans Publishing Company, 1999.

[6] Stark, Rodney, *The Victory of Reason,* p. 191, Random House, 2005.

[7] Ibid. p. 163.

[8] Ford, Paul Leicester, *The Writings of Thomas Jefferson, Vol. X, 1816-1826*, p. 343, G. P. Putnam's Sons, 1899. As accessed through the Internet Archive in January, 2016 at https://archive.org/details/writingsofthomas10jeffiala_djvu.text. The quote is "But with respect to our rights, and the acts of the British government contravening those rights, there was but one opinion on this side of the water. All American whigs thought alike on these subjects. When forced, therefore, to resort to arms for redress, an appeal to the tribunal of the world was deemed proper for our justification. This was the object of the Declaration of Independence. Not to find out new principles, or new arguments, never before thought of, not merely to say things which had never been said before; but to place before mankind the common sense of the subject, in terms so plain and firm as to command their assent, and to justify ourselves in the independent stand we are compelled to take. Neither aiming at originality of principle or sentiment, nor yet copied from any particular and previous writing, it was intended to be an expression of the American mind, and to give to that expression the proper tone and spirit called for by the occasion."

[9] Burke, Edmund, *Reflections of the Revolution in France*, pp. 232-233, Penguin Books, 1968.

[10] Encyclopedia Britannica, *French Revolution*, http://www.britannica.com/print/article/219315.

[11] Burke, Edmund, *Reflections of the Revolution in France*, p. 304, Penguin Books, 1968.

[12] Ibid, pp. 297-298.

[13] Evans, M. Stanton, *The Theme is Freedom*, p. 35, Regnery Publishing, 1994.

[14] Burke, Edmund, *Reflections of the Revolution in France*, p. 256, Penguin Books, 1968.

[15] Ibid, pp. 124-125.

[16] http://avalon.law.yale.edu/18th_century/nworder.asp. Accessed January, 2016.

[17] Ibid.

[18] http://memory.loc.gov/ammem/amlaw/lwjc.html. Accessed January, 2016.

[19] Quotes in this section from The American Presidency Project, http://www.presidency.ucsb.edu/ws/?pid=26787, accessed March, 2016.

[20] U.S. Census Bureau, *Dynamics of Economic Well-Being: Participation in Government Programs, 2009-2012: Who Gets Assistance?*, https://www.census.gov/content/dam/Census/library/publications/2015/demo/p70-141.pdf, accessed March, 2016.

[21] Population statistics from the US Census Bureau, https://www.census.gov/hhes/www/poverty/data/historical/people.html, Table 6, accessed March, 2016.

Government assistance figures from Rector, Robert and Sheffield, Rachel, *The War on Poverty After 50 Years*, The Heritage Foundation, September, 2014. Accessed January, 2016.

[22] Rector, Robert and Sheffield, Rachel, *The War on Poverty After 50 Years*, The Heritage Foundation, September, 2014. Accessed January, 2016.

[23] Ibid.

[24] Bureau of Labor Statistics, http://www.bls.gov/data/. Accessed December, 2015.

[25] Wolf. Dan, *Do You Want To Be Free?*, pp.310-314, Telemachus Press, 2013.

[26] **Total Population figures** from the Bureau of the Census, https://www.census.gov/hhes/www/poverty/data/historical/people.html.

CNP figures from the Bureau of Labor Statistics, http://www.bls.gov/web/empsit/cpseea01.htm.

Medicaid figures from the Social Security Administration, https://www.ssa.gov/policy/docs/statcomps/supplement/2014/8e.html.

SNAP figures from the USDA, http://www.fns.usda.gov/sites/default/files/pd/SNAPsummary.pdf.

SSI figures from the Social Security Administration, https://www.ssa.gov/policy/docs/statcomps/.

TANF figures from the Office of Family Assistance, http://www.acf.hhs.gov/programs/ofa/resource-library/search?area[2377]=2377&topic[2351]=2351&type[3084]=3084 and Social Security Administration,

https://www.ssa.gov/policy/docs/statcomps/supplement/2005/9g.html. All accessed March, 2016.

[27] US Census Bureau, *Dynamics of Economic Well-Being: Participation in Government Programs, 2009-2012: Who Gets Assistance?*, https://www.census.gov/content/dam/Census/library/publications/2015/demo/p70-141.pdf, accessed March, 2016.

[28] Ibid, p. 11.

[29] Ibid.

[30] Ibid, p. 5.

[31] Us Census Bureau, https://www.census.gov/hhes/families/data/families.html. Accessed March, 2016.

[32] US Census Bureau, https://www.census.gov/hhes/www/income/data/historical/families/. Accessed March, 2016.

[33] Edwards, James Rolph, p.4, *The Costs of Public Income Redistribution and Private Charity*, Journal of Libertarian Studies, Summer, 2007.

[34] US Census Bureau, https://www.census.gov/hhes/www/income/data/historical/families/. Accessed March, 2016.

[35] Tax Foundation, http://taxfoundation.org/article/state-individual-income-tax-rates-and-brackets-2016. Accessed March, 2016.

[36] Ibid, http://taxfoundation.org/article/state-and-local-sales-tax-rates-2015.

[37] Brodman, James William, *Charity & Religion in Medieval Europe*, p. 45, The Catholic University of America Press, 2009.

[38] Fidelity Investments, *When to Give: The Four Phases of Disaster Relief*, http://www.fidelitycharitable.org/giving-strategies/disaster-relief/disaster-relief.shtml. Accessed March, 2016.

[39] Ibid.

[40] Kane, Colleen, *Where Are Your Charity Dollars Going?*, CNBC, December, 2010. http://www.cnbc.com/id/ Accessed January, 2016.

[41] Edwards, James Rolph, *The Costs of Public Income Redistribution and Private Charity*, p.3, Journal of Libertarian Studies, Vol. 21, No. 2, Summer, 2007.

[42] Ibid, p. 4.

[43] One example is provided in, Wilcox, Clair, *Competition and Monopoly in American Industry*, Temporary National Economic Committee Monograph, No. 21, US Govt. Printing Office, 1941, as cited in Hayek, A.F., *The Road to Serfdom*, p. 81, The University of Chicago Press, 2007.

Made in the USA
Middletown, DE
26 September 2016